The Santa Fe IN TOPEKA

A Book of Nastalgic Recollections about Santa Fe Personalities and Events.

ISBN No. 08369161

JOHN W. RIPLEY, *Editor*

ROBERT W. RICHMOND, *Associate Editor*

We wish to express our gratitude to the Public Relations Department of the Santa Fe for permission to reprint certain material

We are again indebted to the courteous staff of the Kansas State Historical Society for numerous services far beyond the call of duty.

CREDITS: Front cover scenic postcards from the Annie M. P. Bundy Collection at the Topeka Public Library. Back cover, a truly *"Santa Fe in Topeka"* commemorative plate of pewter-like metal, ten and one-half inches in diameter, designed and produced in a limited edition by Bart Kelley, Topeka.

Unless otherwise indicated, all illustrations in this volume are from Kansas State Historical Society, Topeka.

SHAWNEE COUNTY HISTORICAL SOCIETY
P.O. Box 56, Topeka Kansas 66601

BULLETIN No. 56   December, 1979

Printed by H. M. Ives & Sons, Inc., Topeka, Kansas

CONTENTS

	Page
The Santa Fe—A Child of Topeka, *William E. Treadway*	1
Yes, Virginia, There Is a Holliday Park, *Kathy Richardson*	6
Fred Harvey and the Santa Fe, *Minnie Dubbs Millbrook*	8
Frank W. Thomas and His Apprentice Program, *George Mack, Jr.*	18
Visits to Papa's Office, *Catherine Hayes McDaniel*	25
Santa Fe Women's Club, *Elizabeth E. Bowers*	27
The Revitalized Reading Rooms, *John W. Ripley*	31
Topeka Talent for Reading Rooms, *Peggy Greene*	34
Santa Fe's First Woman Employee, *Nancy Lykins Sherbert*	43
Official Tries to Catch a News Butch	44
The Fast Newpaper Train, *Joseph W. Snell*	46
Charles S. Gleed and the Santa Fe Reorganization, *Terry Harmon*	49
The Santa Fe Junction, *Paul Cooper*	55
Santa Fe's Passenger Depots, *Patricia Michaelis*	57
The Santa Fe Flyer	65
Students Commute on the "Plug," *Vernon French*	69
The Train Built Here in 1889	71
The Old Santa Fe Depot, *Paul Cooper*	72
Carl Schmidt, Land Salesman, *Tom Muth*	73
A Look Back at the Law Department, *J. B. Reeves*	78
Teddy Roosevelt Dedicates the R.R.Y.M.C.A., *C. Robert Haywood*	82
A Friendly Fire at R.R.Y.M.C.A., *John W. Ripley*	86
Hero of the 1903 Flood—Edward Grafstrom, *Barbara Elder Weller*	93
A Press Bureau for the Santa Fe	95
The Santa Fe Roundhouses, *Jack W. Traylor*	96
The Business Cars, *Bobbie Pray*	99
The Shops Make Headlines, *Warren Taylor*	103
The General Offices, *Aileen Mallory*	113
The Stores Department in the 1930's, *James D. Wallace*	122
Fire at the G.O.B., *Mark Dinkel*	126
City Passenger Agents, *George F. Sherman, Jr.*	128
The Santa Fe and Four Generations, *Joseph D. Konrade*	131
Safety First Taught by Phonograph, *Vernon French*	134
The Santa Fe Sporting Scene, *Douglass Wallace*	136
Santa Fe's Time Service, *William O. Wagnon*	144
Thomas J. Anderson, Arch Booster, *Glenn D. Bradley*	150
Inspection Cars—Old and New, *Gomer Jones*	154
The Santa Fe Shops Today, *Gomer Jones*	158
Complete Roster of Santa Fe Employees in Topeka, 1897	183
Officers and Trustees, Shawnee County Historical Society	196

Foreword

The Atchison, Topeka and Santa Fe has been a vital part of Shawnee county history since the 1860's, a time when the expansion of a rail network was of incalculable value to the rapidly expanding United States. Because of those close ties it seemed to the editors that the time had come to examine the railroad's history, particularly as it related to the county and its residents, past and present.

This volume sheds light on facets of Santa Fe history which may be familiar to many readers but it also deals with some aspects of the road's development which are little known in 1979. Some of those things that happened were extremely interesting and at times dramatically innovative when compared to what other roads were doing. For example, Frank Thomas' apprentice system was a model for American industry and provided the Santa Fe with a reservoir of skilled labor that could not have been matched in any other way. The reading rooms and the athletic teams under the road's auspices were fringe benefits that relieved boredom and provided relaxation to people engaged in demanding work.

This history includes information on buildings, motive power, rolling stock and people—heroes, developers, dreamers and eccentrics. There are some personal views of Santa Fe history which embody both factual data and nostalgia.

The editors hope that this *Bulletin* makes clear the relationship between the Santa Fe and its original "home town."

ROBERT W. RICHMOND

CYRUS K. HOLLIDAY

...every property owner in Topeka owed him a debt of gratitude.

The Santa Fe— A Child of Topeka

BY WILLIAM E. TREADWAY

ON SEPTEMBER 26, 1868, Cyrus K. Holliday electrified Topeka by this message from New York: "The child is born and his name is 'Success.' Let the Capital City rejoice." And rejoice it did. Many times before, the expectations of the little Topeka community had been raised to exciting heights by the ebullient optimism of Holliday only to be dashed upon the rocks of disillusionment. The birth of the Santa Fe had experienced the travail of one man's faith that at last breathed freely after near extinction in doubts and derision. A local newspaper, in publishing the glad tidings, assured its readers that this time its editor was satisfied the unrelenting efforts of Colonel Holliday had met with genuine success and that every property owner in Topeka owed him a debt of gratitude. Without Cyrus K. Holliday and his overriding devotion to Topeka, the presently familiar history of the Santa Fe could hardly have been written.

Holliday was born near Meadville, Pennsylvania, on April 3, 1826. He graduated from Allegheny College with a degree in the liberal arts and sciences in 1852. Two years later, although just recently married, he responded to an emotional appeal to young men of the Northern and Eastern States to go West immediately to help make Kansas a free state following passage by Congress of the Kansas-Nebraska Act. While he subscribed to that worthy cause, he also saw a chance of a lifetime to make a fortune in a newly opened country.

In November of 1854 he headed a small party that selected a new town site on the south bank of the Kansas River, some 25 miles west of the prairie outpost of Lawrence, and he became president of an association organized to lay out and sell lots of a town christened with the Indian name "Topeka."

He became a member of the Council, the upper house, of the Territorial Legislature beginning in 1858 and in the closing days of the 1859 session he wrote, introduced and obtained enactment of a bill to incorporate the Atchison and Topeka Rail Road, which by subsequent charter amendment underwent a change in name to the Atchison, Topeka and Santa Fe Railroad Company. The Santa Fe was neither the first nor the last railroad to be incorporated by Holliday, as he became adept at being a legislator incorporator. In fact, at the time he seemed not to have considered perfection of the Santa Fe charter sufficiently important even to be mentioned in a contemporary letter to his wife, in which he informed her of his success in removing the Shawnee County seat from Tecumseh to Topeka and of the celebration which it occasioned in the latter place.

Cyrus K. Holliday had an obsession for developing "our town," as he called Topeka, into a future metropolis. This involved its becoming the capital of the future state. As an effective member of the territorial legislature he had sponsored a resolution calling for the constitutional convention, to meet in July of 1859, at Wyandotte. However, he adroitly avoided becoming a delegate to the convention in order that he could concentrate upon a one-to-one approach to the elected delegates in support of his single objective without risking involvement in multiple controversial issues on the floor. His strategy succeeded and Topeka received the coveted designation. Thereafter, he was three times elected mayor of Topeka.

A drought had plagued Kansas beginning in the middle of 1859 and it continued with increased severity through 1860. Settlers who remained in the territory were dependent for survival upon charitable relief organized and delivered by the sympathizing public of the northeastern states. Holliday saw arising from this adversity a new dimension to what had been his plea for a self-sufficient Kansas. By including the emerging need for gainful employment of those otherwise compelled by circumstances to accept a charitable handout, he reasoned that equivalent funds invested in building a Kansas railroad would restore a number of people to the dignity of earning their necessities and give a transfusion to the local economy. He superimposed this argument upon others going to the national interest in western railroad expansion and to the sound economy needed to accompany the admission of Kansas as a free state. His incorporated, but as yet unorganized, Atchison and Topeka Rail Road Company would be his vehicle for such a plea.

At Holliday's instance, a meeting of those incorporators of the company residing in Topeka was held early in September of 1860 in the newspaper office of Edmund G. Ross. It was there determined that organization of the company should be completed in spite of the chaos prevailing in the territory, and that in fact Eastern investor participation and public assistance should be invited as a palliative for the distressed situation. As a result of the preliminary unofficial meeting in Topeka, Holliday arranged for a formal organizational meeting of all interested incorporators in the office of Luther C. Challis, a private banker, at Atchison on September 15, 1860. At that meeting, Cyrus K. Holliday was elected a director and first president of the corporation. Holliday, as the unsalaried president, agreed to head a drive to obtain a congressional land grant, and efforts were started immediately to get petitions from throughout the settled portions of the Territory asking such government aid for the dual purposes he had outlined.

Holliday called a convention to be held in Topeka on October 17, 1860, for the purpose of agreeing upon a priority among projected railroads in their requests for congressional assistance. He had reasoned that if the various interests promoting different railroads were to descend upon Congress separately, their competitive and conflicting proposals could be self-defeating. The meeting resulted in a single petition to Congress for grants of land to four railroads in the Territory of which one, of course, was the Atchison and Topeka. Owing to the imminent change in the national administration and to the interlude of war, Holliday's quest for federal land grant assistance was destined to require his time and effort for several years to come.

Even before the end of the war, Holliday drafted a bill for a grant of public lands by the federal government to the state of Kansas to be sold in aid of constructing those railroads settled upon at the Topeka Railroad Convention, including by route description his Atchison and Topeka. This he forwarded to Samuel C. Pomeroy for introduction in the Senate. It passed Congress exactly as written and was signed into law by President Lincoln on March 3, 1863.

Holliday had no personal ambition to become an active executive officer of a functioning railroad company, and in fact at no time in his life did he ever hold an office other than that of director in a viable rail line. On January 13, 1864, he relinquished the presidency of the still inert Santa Fe to Samuel C. Pomeroy, who as president of the company and as United States senator should have been of great help in matters of Indian treaties and land grants. In retrospect, it appeared that Holliday's confidence in the senator was not justified.

With the return of peace between the states Holliday, as a stockholder and director and for the most part at his own expense, gave freely of his energy for the next three years in furthering an actual start on construction of the now renamed Atchison, To-

The Holliday residence, northeast corner of 6th & Monroe.

peka and Santa Fe. Much of this time he was in New York helping to reorganize the corporate management and to interest Eastern capital in investment. The balance of the time, he was in Washington lobbying for favorable Indian treaties and land grants. It was then from New York that he had wired Topeka of the birth of it's child, "Success."

Holliday's efforts towards the single objective of advancing his town had been divided between perfecting the Santa Fe as a railroad and accomplishing the selection of Topeka as the state capital. An active legislator in the Kansas senate after statehood, he served as chairman of several committees including those on the judiciary, public buildings and railroads. In a speech on the floor of the senate, Holliday as president of the Topeka Town Association, offered "to donate to the state, free of all costs, 20 acres of land for the Capitol Building." His offer was promptly accepted by a joint resolution. He later sponsored an appropriation from which construction of a first wing was to commence. However, he knew that a predominantly rural legislature would be unsympathetic to the costly edifice he comtemplated, and he carefully projected its construction upon an extended installment plan that assured an impressive exterior. He was confident that the interior, in time, would be suitably adorned.

From Holliday's knowledge of geology, he was convinced that veins of coal were present near the surface in paying quantity in

Osage county, and he incorporated the Osage Coal and Mining Company, the declared purpose of which was to produce coal for railroad and public use. Over the objection of Atchison interests he insisted that the first Santa Fe trackage be built from Topeka south to the coal fields to make fuel immediately available for motive power and to offer instant freight cargo to the public by rail connection at Topeka. He organized and became president of Excelsior Coke and Gas Company for manufacturing both coke for heating and artificial gas for residential and street lighting in Topeka. Kansas Avenue had night illumination by 1870. The first artificial gas produced from Osage county coal was of such high sulphur content that even the street lighting had an objectionable odor, but this distraction seems to have been overcome by a change in methods or source of supply.

As a recognition of his personal accomplishment, and unknown to him in advance, the management of the Santa Fe had named its first locomotive the "Cyrus K. Holliday," and he was returned to the mayor's chair in Topeka by an almost unanimous vote. The *Kansas State Record* of March 31, 1869, announced: "C. K. Holliday (we mean the engine, not the next mayor of Topeka) crossed the new railroad bridge yesterday drawing a construction train of six or eight cars."

Holliday had been a subscriber to a substantial number of shares in the Santa Fe Railroad. In addition, he organized and became president of the Topeka and Lawrence Railroad which he envisioned as a future connection with the Santa Fe towards the East from Topeka. He invested heavily from his own funds in the latter company, but was bitterly disappointed when a heavy negative vote from north of the Kansas river caused defeat of a Shawnee county bond issue sought for its assistance. The effort eventually succeeded and the line became an integral part of the Santa Fe route towards Chicago.

For several years the value of Holliday's Santa Fe shares on the market was well below par and no dividends were paid. However, his immediate interest was not in a return upon his investment but in the influence his shareholding gave him as a director. It would enable him to secure the general offices and machine shops of the company, with their ultimately substantial payrolls, as material community assets for Topeka.

After having served three terms in the office of mayor of Topeka, Holliday took the somewhat unusual step of making a formal announcement through the local newspapers that he would not be a candidate to succeed himself for that position. Almost simultaneously, a petition appeared in the Topeka *Commonwealth* in which Holliday was joined by more than a hun-

(Continued on p. 160)

YES, VIRGINIA,
There is a Holliday Park

KATHY THOMAS RICHARDSON

A<small>SK ALMOST</small> any Topekans to list things in their city christened in honor of Santa Fe Railway founder Cyrus K. Holliday and there'll be little hesitation.

Why, there's the shopping center, they'll likely respond, and the junior high school, the bus, a street, and of course, the well-known locomotive.

It's unlikely, however, that Topekans would include in their lists one of the Holliday family's most pleasant if not obscure legacies to the city—Holliday Park.

If you have trouble placing Holliday Park, it will be no consolation to know that it is bounded by two major streets leading to and from the downtown area.

Bordered by 12th on the north, Western on the west, Huntoon on the south and Taylor on the east, Holliday Park's distinctive triangular tract certainly is not tucked away from the city's mainstream.

Nonetheless, you will be encouraged by a local straw pollster, who said that among nearly 250 persons he asked about the park, only two could pinpoint its location. Included in the sampling was a number of retired Santa Fe employees.

In any case, it is not surprising that Holliday Park has existed for at least two generations in near anonymity. Considering the confusion and misinformation which has surrounded the park since it's turn-of-the-century origin, it's a wonder the park exists at all.

To measure the amount of confusion, try this yardstick: The city of Topeka is unable to produce a deed to Holliday Park. No record of the deed exists in the city clerk's office, nor does the park appear on any of the city engineering department's maps.

In order to explain the park's origin and how it has remained undeeded to the city, we first must examine a myth which was published about Holliday Park in two city reports and the minutes of a Holliday Park Association meeting.

One park department report credits Col. Holliday as the donor of the park in 1882, at the time or soon after he was to have donated another triangular tract at 12th and Topeka Ave.

This is refuted by a later Park Commissioner report, which

MARY K. HOLLIDAY
Title to the park is still in her name.

states so-called Huntoon Park was acquired by purchase.

Another park department report credits Col. Holliday's wife, Mary D. Holliday, as donor of the park through a quit claim deed in 1901. No record of this transaction could be found.

And finally, in the April 24, 1948, edition of The Topeka *State Journal* came what was believed to be the definitive story about Holliday Park's origin.

The story quoted the minutes of the Holliday Park Association, which described how Col. Holliday allowed the city in 1895 to condemn the property for use as a park. The minutes said residents whose homes faced the 1.46 acre tract subscribed funds to grade and landscape it, and to pay back taxes of approximately $700, which Col. Holliday said he had paid as representative of several owners in the East.

The association minutes did not contain the definitive story, however.

Records at Columbian National Title Insurance Co. of Topeka show Mrs. Holliday obtained the triangular piece of land through a quit claim from John D. Knox on July 20, 1880. At that time it was a favorite camping ground for itinerant tribes of gypsies.

Further, records show the property never has been transferred to the city or, for that matter, to anyone. It remains in Mrs. Holliday's name.

(Continued on p. 181)

He took his ideas to ... his own road ... but they ... advising him to try the Santa Fe for "They will try anything"

A CRACK COALITION
Fred Harvey and the Santa Fe

MINNIE DUBBS MILLBROOK

By THE centennial year of 1876, The Atchison, Topeka & Santa Fe Rail Road felt its accomplishments were worthy of celebration. After 13 years spent mostly as a stub line out of Topeka, building rather spasmodically to the south and west, it had acquired 786 miles of track with desirable connections on the east at Atchison and Kansas City as well as a western terminal at Pueblo, Colorado. Though perhaps it did not have the best, shortest and cheapest route from the Missouri river to the Rocky Mountains as it boasted, still it did have a bright future. And it did in 1876 acquire an asset that would in time make it unique among railroads. It acquired Fred Harvey.

Fred Harvey was a man with an idea that he had been working on for many years. English born, he had come to the United States in 1850, aged 15 years and with two pounds, English money, in his pocket. His first job was washing dishes in a hotel in New York for two dollars a week. He worked in many eating places in New York, New Orleans and St. Louis, where by 1859 he had a restaurant of his own. The Civil War intervening, he lost his business and went to work on a river packet and then as a mail clerk on a railroad. From there on he progressed, working in various capacities for the railroads proliferating west of the Mississippi. He became the general freight agent on the Chicago, Burlington & Quincy Railroad but he remained a restaurateur at heart.

Fred Harvey, 1835-1901

Traveling as he did in his work, Fred Harvey could not but have been acutely aware of the difficulty of getting a decent meal and a place to sleep in the new, poorly developed towns strung along the western railroads. If there was a lunchroom or eating house, the food was terrible. The usual meal offered was greasy fried steak or salty ham, beans, heavy biscuits called "sinkers" and coffee freshly made—once a week. A delicacy sometimes offered was dried apple pie, a heavy crusted abomination hated by all traveling men. There was little attempt at cleanliness or pleasant surroundings; there were no napkins, and oil cloth covered the tables. The train crew allowed but twenty minutes for lunch and started up sooner, forcing the unfortunate traveler to leave the dinner for which he had already paid. Surely if travel was to be encouraged on these new competing railroads, better accommodations would have to be provided. There was an opportunity here and Fred Harvey sought to take advantage of it. A hotel at Ellsworth, Kansas was his first attempt, a venture so short-lived that no details of it remain.

But Harvey kept on trying. He held on to his job with the Burlington but by 1875 with a partner, J. P. Rice, he was operating two eating houses on the Kansas Pacific, one at Wallace, Kansas, another at Hugo, Colorado. These projects were apparently successful but were soon terminated, it was said, because his partner did not agree with Harvey's strict standards of operation and excellence. At any rate he began to seek other fields. He took his ideas to the managers of his own road, the Burlington, but they were unresponsive, advising him to try the Santa Fe for "They will try anything."

In 1874 the Santa Fe had opened a lunchroom in Topeka primarily for the convenience of its own personnel since its complex of offices, shops and yards were located some distance from downtown Topeka where meals were more readily available. This lunchroom was located on the second floor of the station and was accessible by a stairway leading up from the freight depot. It was very small, accommodating only ten stools and a counter. Later it had been enlarged and relocated on the first floor. On January 1, 1876 the Topeka *Commonwealth* described the red frame Santa Fe station building: "In the lower story are the offices of the local station, public waiting rooms for ladies and gentlemen, the freight depot and the passenger dining room. At this dining room the passengers of five trains are fed daily." Though designated as a dining room the facility was still only a lunch room with a larger counter and room for more patrons. Peter P. Cline was in charge and the service provided was said variously to be passable, adequate or unexceptionable.

The need for dining facilities along the Santa Fe to the west was dramatically demonstrated about the same time. On February 26, 1876 the last rail had been laid completing the line to Pueblo and on the 28th the first train was put through. An excursion to Pueblo from Topeka was announced for March 5, arranged particularly for the Kansas legislators, who had been meeting in the Kansas capital. The train would leave Topeka at 1:20 P.M. on Sunday and arrive in Pueblo Tuesday morning. The train would stop at Newton for dinner Sunday afternoon and after that "the party must fall back on their lunch baskets, which should be well-filled." The fare, round-trip, was $10 and at that price a lot of other people besides the legislators decided to go along.

As might be inferred from the instructions about well-filled lunch baskets, there were few places to eat west of Newton. Though towns had sprung up all along the route, they were small and the country around was sparsely settled. Dodge City was an exception as it was at that time the headquarters of the cattle herds driven up from Texas to be shipped east. West of Dodge, towns were few and consisted of little more than pumping stations for the railroad.

In the end, 446 excursionists, including 83 ladies, bought tickets to Pueblo. Two full trains were put into service to carry them. The trip was a big adventure and several of the tourists wrote letters to the Topeka newspapers telling of their experiences. Shortly out of Hutchinson, heavy snow began to fall. One passenger wrote, "At Ellinwood stopped for a few moments and made an attempt to get some hot coffee and found snow eight inches deep." Another on the second train reported on Larned:

> The majority of them never having been west before, had started without taking the precaution of bringing a little grub along and the consequences were when they laid over at Larned, the hotel accommodations of the city were inadequate to the demand. An onslaught was then made on all the provision stores and butcher shops in the town, and by the time we arrived there were but two sacks of flour left. Crackers, cheese, jerked buffalo, cove oysters, sardines and canned goods had all disappeared down the hungry maws of the famished *excurts*, and Larned was high and dry so to speak.

At Dodge City apparently most of the travelers got fed one way or another. Two hundred of them were said to have had "an elegant dinner" at the Dodge House. But later near Pierceville the snow plow that had been clearing the track in front of the trains, ran into a cow, tearing up some of the rails and causing a long delay. One of the trains backed up to Pierceville, which consisted of a windmill, a water tank and a residence for the station agent and operator. Again the travelers sought refreshment. A few "of the more lucky ones obtained a species of slop or slum gullion at twenty-five cents a cup and drank it under the misnomer of coffee."

The two trains coupled together, "the engines blasting and whistling to wake the echoes," arrived at Pueblo Wednesday morning twenty-four hours late. At Centennial Hall "a sumptuous breakfast awaited the almost famished excursionists at the moderate price of 75 cents a meal." In order to cope with such a crowd, every home in town had been opened and "each visitor got a ticket telling him where to go for food, bed and entertainment."

While the Santa Fe in its earlier years had concentrated on freight revenue, it now turned more attention to the passenger service. Charles F. Morse, general superintendent at Topeka, liked good food and when Fred Harvey came to him with his story of quality materials and better cooking, he listened attentively. President Thomas Nickerson was also receptive to the idea that the Santa Fe should sponsor better eating along its lines and an agreement was made. It was an oral agreement and the details have not survived though they probably were the same ones that were later put into written contracts. The Santa Fe would provide the space for the lunch room or dining room and would haul free the foodstuffs and other materials that would be imported from other places. Fred Harvey would provide the equipment, operate the food service and receive the profit, if any. At last the little Englishman was going to demonstrate that

Western Foundry AND MACHINE WORKS.

R. L. COFRAN, Proprietor,
TOPEKA, KANSAS.

Mill Work and Repairing a Specialty.
Write for Circular and Prices.

THE EATING HOUSES

Along the line of the A. T. & S. F., between terminal points, are under the charge of Mr. Fred. Harvey, a caterer of long experience, and all the delicacies served at first-class hotels, are found at the dining stations at Topeka, Florence, Lakin, Las Vegas and Lamy. Neatness, cleanliness, and carefully-prepared dishes await the traveler who dines at the Santa Fé Eating Houses. Mr. Harvey knows what the traveling public wants, and he provides it.

Buried among advertisements on the back page of an 1881 Santa Fe time table, is probably the railroad's first public announcement of Fred Harvey's management.

Dinner

Blue Points on Shell

English Pea, au Gritton

Filet of Whitefish. Maderia Sauce.
Potato Francaise

Young Capon. Hollandaise Sauce.

Roast Sirloin of Beef, au Jus.   Pork, with Apple Sauce
Turkey. Stuffed. Cranberry Sauce

Mashed Potatoes.   Boiled Sweet Potatoes.   Elgin Sugar Corn
Marrowfat Peas.   Asparagus Cream Sauce.

Salmi of Duck. Queen Olives
Baked Veal Pie. English Style.
Charlotte of Peaches. Cognac Sauce.

Prairie Chicken. Currant Jelly

Sugar-Cured Ham.   Pickled Lamb's Tongue
Lobster Salad, au Mayonnaise

Celery.   Beets.   French Slaw

Apple Pie   Mince Pie
Cold Custard, a la Chantilly.

New York Ice Cream.   Assorted Cakes.   Bananas
Oranges.   Catawba Wine Jelly   Grapes

Edam and Roquefort Cheese.
Bent's Water Crackers.   French Coffee

Meals 75 Cents.

WEDNESDAY, NOVEMBER 14, 1888.

For the opulent traveler during the 1880's Fred Harvey's dining cars served a right good meal for 75¢.

good, fresh food, well cooked and offered at a reasonable price in clean, pleasant surroundings would be profitable and attract passengers for the Santa Fe.

Negotiations between Cline and Harvey were soon completed and early in 1876 Harvey took possession of the Topeka

Santa Fe dining room. He closed the place for two days, scrubbing it down thoroughly and furnishing it with new silverware and china. Guy Potter was said to have been brought in as manager. Harvey, himself, with a family to support, continued in his job with the Burlington.

In 1876 in Topeka a meal could be found in many places for a quarter but the better restaurants and hotels charged thirty-five cents. At Harvey's Santa Fe lunch room the price was thirty-five cents. A typical breakfast consisted of steak with eggs, hashed brown potatoes, a six-high stack of pan-sized wheat cakes with maple syrup, apple pie and coffee. The coffee was fresh and fragrant, the pie crust feather light and the apples newly peeled. There was no immediate comment in the newspapers but historians would later write that the news spread "far and wide, nowhere more swiftly than among the drummers or commercial travelers who formed a ponderable part of the railroad patronage in those days and who began planning their itineraries so as to be in Topeka at mealtime." Fred Harvey's lunch room was a success right there under the eyes of the Santa Fe top brass, who no doubt savored the fine food as much as did the traveling public.

In later years the Topeka lunch room would host many famous and unusual guests. The first ones to draw newspaper attention was the party of 96 Sioux Indians from the Red Cloud and Spotted Tail agencies. On November 5, 1876 they passed through on their way to look at possible locations for their tribesmen in Oklahoma. They too, it seems, appreciated good good and fresh fruit. The reporter from the Topeka *Commonwealth* looked upon the travelers with amazement and some disdain:

> Upon arriving at the depot a number of bucks with tin buckets made a break for the eating house where they got hot coffee and returned to their cars where they partook of their frugal meal, which consisted of boiled beef, without seasoning, and coffee. They gorge themselves when they eat. They all eat out of the same pan and drink coffee out of the same can. This is the reason they are not allowed to go into hotels to eat. They don't know how to behave themselves.... However a few of the "big injuns" were allowed the privilege of setting [sic] at the white man's table. Messrs. Spotted Tail, Red Dog and Fast Bear were taken to the railroad eating house, there they partook of double rations. They got away with everything set before them, in fact everything that was within reach.... Old Pap Bear gave the crowd away. After getting up from the table he reached over and grabbed up all the apples he could hold in his big hands, which were about four apiece....

Though historians agree that the Topeka lunch room was Fred Harvey's first collaboration with the Santa Fe, there is

Fred Harvey lunch counter at Topeka depot; below, dining room. Photos made about 1910.

Harvey House girls at an unidentified station, 1926. In the Harvey system, like the military, the status and rank of the women employees was indicated by the uniforms worn. The women who worked in the kitchen did not wear uniforms; the lunch room girls wore black dresses with white bib aprons; the dining room girls wore black dresses and white aprons without bibs. The head waitress wore an all white uniform while the manager wore a white blouse with a black skirt.

"WILL you have the table d'hote dining room meal at one dollar—or do you prefer the a la carte lunch room service?"

Your response to the trainman's inquiry—shortly before arrival at a dining station—is not a commitment, but simply a general guide; for, as Elbert Hubbard said years ago, "at Fred Harvey's you are always expected."

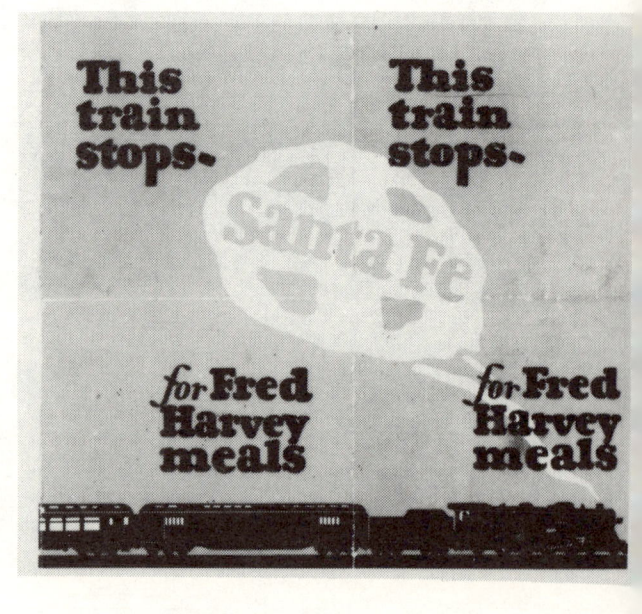

16

disagreement as to the second. Probably the second was the eating house at Lakin, Kansas, which may have come under his supervision as early as April, 1877. Guy Potter was the first manager at Lakin according to the old-timers there, opening the lunch room as early as April, 1875. However Matthew Fisher was the manager when Harvey took over. Other sources state that Guy Potter was Harvey's first manager of the Topeka lunch room, installed when Harvey took over in 1876.

The situation at Lakin was quite different from that at Topeka. With one exception all the buildings and people at Lakin were connected with the Santa Fe. The exception, John O'Loughlin, kept a trading post in a dugout where he sold everything—flour, bacon, buffalo meat, whiskey, rifles, ox bows, spurs and saddles. He catered to the hunters, trappers, cowpunchers, freighters, railroad men, and immigrants on the Santa Fe trail. His was the only store in southwestern Kansas, south and west of Dodge City. For a time the railroad men subsisted on provisions from O'Loughlin's but the Santa Fe soon built an eating house and dormitory for their use as well as for occasional passengers on the trains. As has been said Guy Potter was the first manager of this facility.

Through the recorded memories of several old-timers we know more about the Harvey operation at Lakin where but two trains a day were serviced—one going west, one going east—than we do about the Topeka lunch room which catered to the passengers of five daily trains. When Fred Harvey came to Topeka he was mentioned in the newspapers as a visitor but never connected with the Santa Fe lunch room. In Lakin everybody knew Fred Harvey. Mrs. Harvey and the children came out to spend several weeks in the summer time and Mrs. and Mrs. Fred Harvey led the grand march when an occasional ball was held in the dining room, the music imported from Pueblo. Harvey established a cattle ranch, the XY, six or seven miles east of Lakin, which for many years provided not only beef but more exotic meats, like buffalo tongues and antelope, for the Harvey Houses. In 1880 the Harvey House at Lakin was moved bodily by the Santa Fe to Sargent, a town about two miles east of the Colorado line and about a hundred miles west of Dodge City. A division point had been established there and the town's name changed to Coolidge in honor of T. Jefferson Coolidge, then president of the Santa Fe railroad. The Harvey House operation continued in this frontier town much as it had in Lakin.

No doubt the Harvey success in Topeka impelled C. F. Morse, Santa Fe general superintendent, to call Harvey into consultation late in 1877 when the railroad eating house at Florence, Kansas,

(Continued on p. 170)

Frank W. Thomas' Remarkable Apprentice System

FROM GEORGE MACK

FRANK W. THOMAS

UNLIKE today, when virtually every teen-age boy knows something about automobile mechanics and farm boys usually are expert with tools for repairing tractors and other farm machinery, few boys at the turn of the century even knew which end of a wrench was the handle.

In the industrial east it was slightly different, but where the Santa Fe Railway operated—through sparsely settled farm land and over mountains and deserts—the rail line serving this territory had great difficulty hiring men versed in the necessary mechanics of keeping the trains running.

Consequently, Santa Fe management in 1907 decided to develop a source of skilled mechanics. They established an industrial educational system which was so successful that eventually most of the system's mechanical force was made up by graduates. It was the first school of its kind and it had its inception in Topeka.

Fortunately, Santa Fe had a man who was ideally suited to

supervise this school system. He was Frank W. Thomas, a graduate of Virginia Polytechnic Institute with a degree in mechanical engineering. In addition to his education and experience as assistant engineer of tests for the system with headquarters in Topeka, he was a man whose personality was characterized by high ideals and friendliness. He set a high example for the boys he and the schools he established were training to become the type of employees the Santa Fe wanted. Starting with the program in the Topeka shops. which were the largest in the system, he eventually spread it to most points along the line where green lads could learn to become skilled mechanics.

During the years of Thomas' service, ending in 1936, more than 4,300 were graduated from Santa Fe apprentice courses under his direction.

In a talk Thomas delivered to the Western Railway Club in 1917, he related how the apprentice schooling was begun a decade earlier.

"There are two correlating and supplementary features," he explained. "We have a room, preferably in a separate building, right in the midst of our shops, fitted up with desks, tables, lockers, blackboards, drawing boards, instruments, models for drawing lessons, etc. This is called our Apprentice School Room and is established and dedicated to educational work. It is the educational communal center of the whole shop and mechanical organization. It is a place where the mechanics, the foremen, officers and clerks can and do obtain any information, help upon any mechanical device or questions. The apprentices assemble in classes at stated hours, in this room, where they are taught a number of subjects that will be of value to them in mastering their trades. We teach them mechanical and free hand drawing, sketching, etc., practical shop arithmetic, problems in mechanics, some descriptive geometry, algebra, etc. They study a treatise on their trade, something about the materials with which they work, a little railroad business letter writing, etc. Through the medium of charts, working models and reading matter, the different auxiliary devices are studied. . . . Each apprentice also familiarizes himself with the company rules and the federal rules pertaining to this trade."

This was only a portion of the training. Thomas went on: "In the shop we have a man known as the shop instructor, one for each department, or one for about every 25 boys. He is selected from the ranks, a man of character, skilled in his trade, patient in his teaching and capable of imparting his knowledge intelligently to the boys in this charge. He is responsible for the thorough instruction of the boy, and jointly responsible for the maximum effort of the boy. He sees that each boy gets a fair and equal opportunity, and he is particularly charged with responsibility for the careful training of the timid or backward boy."

Back in those early days children were not required to attend public schools for as many years as they now are. For this reason —and because many boys had to help with family finances, usually at a younger age than now, even if only by taking care of their own needs—many of the applicants for apprentice training were in their early teens. Indeed, quite a number of Topeka men who went through the apprentice system and spent their working lives as skilled workmen in various crafts, now are retired. Most proudly they tell of their Santa Fe experiences.

Thomas, in that speech, explained that how much education a boy had had or how many letters of recommendation he could obtain mattered little. (Thomas deplored the latter, saying that anyone could get someone to write something nice about him.) "We do, however, investigate each applicant, finding out as much about him from himself, as possible," he said. "Our inquiries range from who his grandfather was, to the names of the boys with whom he 'runs', or the girl whom he accompanies to the movies. We have a set of apprentice regulations of 20 articles, but only two prohibitions appear therein. We say he must work and apply himself diligently. We say he must NOT use cigarettes, must NOT use intoxicating liquors, the former being a depraved habit and the latter a crime, on the Santa Fe."

An apprentice board not only selected the boys to train, but kept in touch with their progress during the four-year schooling. Pay was not high and hours were long. In the early days the boys had to be on the job 10 hours a day.

In 1914, seven years after Thomas started the Topeka apprentice school, Zenas L. Potter of the Russell Sage Foundation, New York City, made an indepth study of industrial conditions in Topeka. He devoted considerable attention to the apprentice school and wrote that in October, 1913, 233 young men and boys were registered.

"From the start, apprentices perform useful work and, as is everywhere the custom, receive pay for it," Potter wrote. "Daily earnings range, according to trade, from $1.00 to $1.10 at the start, and increase by degrees during the four-year term until, during the last months, they reach from $1.95 to $2.10. Rates of pay for apprentices are slightly less than in other shops in the vicinity, but their total earnings, if the $150 bonus paid apprentices after graduation is included, are greater than in adjacent shops. Regular rates are paid for time in the class room as well as in the shop.... Though less skilled than journeymen, about one-third of them attain 66.7 per cent efficiency or more and earn bonuses. To encourage them to finish their four years' course and stay in the company's employ, they are given $75 upon graduation and another $75 if still in the company's services six months later."

Potter said since the school was started there had been 172 graduates, about two-thirds of whom had remained with the company, and 12 per cent had been promoted to supervisory positions in its shops.

"Apparently the opportunities offered in the apprentice school for boys to learn a trade, and the wages to be earned by those who complete their courses are sufficient to attract a supply

SUPERVISOR OF APPRENTICES AND STAFF—1911
Front row, left to right—William Stewart; W. B. Lyons; F. W. Thomas, supervisor of apprentices; John H. Linn, chief clerk. Center row—P. W. Riach, O. O. Hendickson, J. H. Lewis, Samuel Magill, Ward N. Rhodes. Rear row—G. C. Parker, Thomas Creary, W. L. Davis, C. O. Sage and R. O. Smith.

Topeka Apprentices, 1911, with prize-winning baseball team and uniformed band. (From Santa Fe Magazine, July 1911)

1924 Topeka Apprentice Baseball Team, Winner of the Fred C. Fox Trophy Cup.

of candidates large enough to meet the company's needs, for there is always a long waiting list at the Topeka shops," Potter added.

He said Santa Fe had never claimed the school was a money losing venture—"it is a business, not an educational venture." He said costs averaged $2.39 per apprentice per day during the last year. Figuring an apprentice is two-thirds as efficient as a journeyman whose wage was $3.80 per day, "the company thus gets $2.53 worth of service each day from each apprentice, at a cost of $2.39, clearing 14 cents per apprentice per day—over $32 per day on the total payroll."

"We have no rule or standard as to the number employed," Thomas said in 1917. "We use as many as we think can be properly trained. This is our source of supply for skilled mechanics."

For some the opportunity to earn college scholarships was open. However, Thomas and his staff thought little of college graduates who had not gone through their apprentice school.

"They are apparently unwilling to start at or near the bottom and work up," he said. "The young college men in railroad work will not look ahead, will not reason with the future. They must, however, in railroad work, acquire the practical knowledge. You can't afford to put anyone in mechanical authority who does not know the business. It seems that the great majority are unwilling to practically prepare themselves. We have now a few who are doing very well and give promise of becoming very useful men."

Apprentice classes were held in most division points along the Santa Fe, with enrollment ranging from a handful to several hundred, as was the case in the classes at Topeka.

Moreover, the apprentices' leisure time was considered almost as important as their hours on duty. All of the apprentice schools had athletic teams, which pitted their prowess against others along the line. Basketball was most popular because it required only five players on a team, sometimes a large share of the class taking part. Baseball, football and other sports also were played.

Moreover, trophies were awarded. Yearbooks, much like high school and college yearbooks, were issued. The Santa Fe's was dubbed "The Iron Horse." One issued in 1927, would stand up well against any published anywhere as to printing, illustrations and text. That year's book was dedicated to Thomas "in sincere appreciation and recognition for his work and the influence his life has exerted upon us; and in gratefulness for his fatherly interest which has so endeared him to us...."

Of the numerous full page illustrations was one captioned: "The dome of 'the Holy City.' State capitol at Topeka, Kansas."

As in other yearbooks, pictures of each student were printed, as well as his accomplishments.

Apprentice conventions were held annually. In 1927 it was at Wellington, with the three-day program consisting of speeches, dinners, a basketball tournament, and a carnival dance—with Wellington young people, especially young women, joining what was called "one of the most delightful of the midwinter season's social affairs."

Pictures were printed of apprentice convention officers, winning athletic teams, views along the Santa Fe system, locomotives, and other material of interest to the apprentices and their friends and families.

Following Thomas' retirement as supervisor of apprentices, the position was vacant for 10 years. Then W. D. "Bill" Major served from 1946 through May, 1963; Glenn E. "Pinky" Rogers from then through August, 1973, and L. C. "Louie" Pratt from September, 1973 to the present.

"Santa Fe Today," in its Nov. 3, 1946, edition said Major had 900 apprentices in the school at that time (in Topeka). The article said that in the 1920's there were 40 apprentice schools on the Santa Fe's lines, the largest being at Topeka, San Bernardino and Albuquerque.

"Other railways, staffed by Santa Fe's trained men, have profited from the Santa Fe apprentice system," the article stated. "Many Santa Fe mechanical supervisors are graduates of the school. More than 8,000 men, all qualified shopmen in their par-

(Continued on p. 169)

... "to see if the buildings are still there!"

Visits To Papa's Office

CATHERINE HAYES McDANIEL

CHILDHOOD memories most often are happy ones, and high among mine, as it must be for others, are the times I spent with my father at the then new Santa Fe general office building on Jackson Street.

My father, John M. Hayes, at that time was custodian of buildings. Papa's office was on the first floor of the new building, a large room housing his office on one side and on the other, a floor to ceiling wired cage for the general office's post office, manned by two employees who daily were locked in and out by Papa, a wonderment to a small child who secretly felt sorry for the men.

I was quite young when I started accompanying Papa from our home at 1255 Polk to the Santa Fe offices. Usually, it was on Sunday to make sure all was in order for the coming week, or as my mother often said "to see if the buildings are still there!" Sometimes we took the street car and later drove, abut usually walked from our home down the tree-lined streets of Topeka, past the Capitol to the Santa Fe offices.

The adventure started on entering the building thru the revolving doors, of course, with a couple of extra run arounds. Once inside we were greeted by one of Papa's staff asking me with a straight face for my building pass, required of all entering the buildings after working hours on week-ends, but with Papa vouching for me I was admitted.

While Papa attended to his business, I tagged along, but frequently I had "work to do," such as counting the number of people going up and down the elevators. This, of course, was a delight riding up and down while "working," but one time the elevators wouldn't go down to the basement floor as "something was wrong." I reported such to Papa who showed proper concern assuring me he would look into it. Years later I learned the reason was my Christmas present was hidden there.

Saturdays at the general offices were the days I liked most. More of Papa's staff were there than on Sundays and I enjoyed meeting them. One person stood out more than others—a kind, patient, black man who made a little girl feel very important. He

JOHN M. HAYES, *from Santa Fe messenger boy in 1876 to building superintendent, General Offices.*

was William D. Cooper and in my early years I couldn't say his name, and called him "Coopie." Nightly, he reported in to Papa at home, and thru those reports I learned to use the telephone, and am sure he was Santa Claus calling from the North Pole.

The highlights of Saturdays at the offices was Papa sending out for lunch to Green's grocery store near the present site of Walgreen's drug store. Always the same, the menu was a sandwich of Green's marvelous bread and a piece of their luscious lemon pie. After one o'clock, with the buildings emptied of employees for the week-end, we would stroll down Kansas Avenue stopping at Hayes Florist—no relation—for a rose for me, then the Santa Fe Watch Company for Papa to do building business and on to Rigby's for some candy, then home. Sometimes, we took in the Novelty Matinee of Vaudeville, but that wasn't one of Papa's greatest interests.

My trips to the Santa Fe general office building continued thru February of 1919 as in March of that year Papa retired following a stroke, and in February of 1921 he passed away.

Thirteen years passed before I made another trip, and then while visiting from California, my husband and I took our two-year old daughter to the second "new" general office building to see her paternal grandfather's office. Having my first real building pass, we also went to Papa's old office, and "Coopie" was there. He took our little daughter in his arms, pointed to the wall saying, "I used to hold your mother up to wind that clock. Would you like to wind it too?" As "Coopie" held our daughter winding that clock, I realized with a lump in my throat a full circle had been completed for me at Topeka's Santa Fe general office buildings.

26

Santa Fe Women's Club

ELISABETH E. BOWERS

IN FEBRUARY, 1934 the Santa Fe Women's Club was started by Miss Mary McGiffen, who was employed for 43 years in the Auditor's office—retiring in 1944. She was inspired by the Santa Fe slogan—"Friendliness is a tradition," and the Club was organized to promote acquaintance and friendship among the women employees of the Santa Fe Railway Company in Topeka, including women office employees, nurses, and women employees of A.T. & S.F. Hospital Association. There were 81 charter members, and 113 attended the first dinner meeting. There is an initiation fee of $1.50 and dues are $1.50 a year. Meetings are held the second Wednesday of each month—dinner meetings.

Santa Fe management thoroughly approved the organization from the start, and has always been most supportive. The first three presidents during the thirties were Mary McGiffen, Dorothy Galligher Harvey and Margaret Irwin Haucke (Mrs. Frank Haucke). Interest was great for a few years, and then interest lagged—perhaps because the Club seemed to have no definite purpose. Through the years it became more or less inactive.

Then in 1956 the new president, Mrs. Adrian Gamlowski, accepted the challenge to revitalize the organization, and under her guidance and enthusiasm, it became the dynamic organization which it is today. When Bessie Gamlowski took over, the membership numbered 68, and at the end of her term of office it had been increased to 135 members and 35 retired members, who are always urged to participate in the meetings.

In 1956 the organization began to be involved in community projects, some of their first efforts being the gift of a $150 scholarship for training a teacher for retarded children, the gift of a record player for the Family Service Nursery section, furnishing boxes to be placed in various places in town for State Hospital Christmas gifts, and the making of Christmas tray favors for Santa Fe Hospital patients. From this beginning the Santa Fe Women's Club has branched out to furnish aid in many community organizations.

At its monthly dinner meetings, the members of the club enjoy many interesting and varied programs, such as talks on law enforcement, hair styling, Southwest Indians, First Ladies of Kansas, Gay Nineties Review slide show, Civilian Defense rescue instruction, talent shows, fashion shows, and one talk by the manager of the Topeka Hawks Baseball Team. At each place

Newly elected officers of The Santa Fe Women's Club on its 22nd anniversary, February 11, 1956. Seated, from left: Miss Betty Brooke, 2nd Vice-president; Miss Jean Spicer, 3rd Vice-president; Mrs. Ivan Joy, co-1st Vice-president; Mrs. Adrian Gamlowski, President. Standing, from left: Miss Ruby Neis, co-1st Vice-president, and Past President; Miss Thelma Keyser, Secretary; and Mrs. Loretta Elwell, Treasurer.

at these dinners is a handmade program appropriately featuring the subject presented at the meeting.

Regular and outstanding events of the Club year are the annual Christmas party and the May Queen dinner dance. A few years ago the members of the Club made a trip to the Gallup Indian Ceremonial Festival, and distributed clothing gifts to the Zuni Indians. This was the first of many such interesting trips which the girls have taken through the years.

The Santa Fe Women's Club is one of the most important and active clubs in Topeka. The 1979-80 officers are: President, Mary Baker; 1st Vice-President, Linda Bozarth; 2nd Vice-President, Carol Naylor; 3rd Vice-President, Sharon Gilbert; Secretary, Jette Dorr; Treasurer, Jeanne Evers. The theme of one of the Club's Style Shows was "A Business Girl Can Possess Beauty and Glamour as Well as Ability," and this pretty well describes the members of the Santa Fe Women's Club.

SANTA FE GIRLS' REVIEW, TOPEKA, 1924

This musical and dramatic club is composed entirely of girl employees of the mechanical and stores departments in Topeka. Their playlet, "The Old Fashioned Garden," is a decided hit, the premiere performance having been given at the dedication of the new one and a half million dollar Masonic Temple in Topeka on November 12, last. It was repeated for the entertainment of Santa Fe supervisors and their families and friends on December 19, and again, on a larger scale, before the Shop Crafts' Association in the City Auditorium on January 14. Arrangements now are being made to have the club appear at the Santa Fe reading rooms outside of Topeka. Manager Grant Burdette would be glad to hear from any Santa Fe organization which contemplates dedicating new buildings, etc., with a view to putting on the play. The girls standing in the photograph, from left to right, are—Arlene Barnes, Ina Wood, Ethel Linder, Hattie Schmerr, Josephine Knierim, Isabel Howe, Edith Smith, Eva Kettering and Bessie Luke. Seated, left to right—Hazel Levett, Mildred Grice and Elsie Reed. Other members of the club who do not appear in the picture are Gertrude Schlegel, Francis Schoenfeldt and Viola Stephens. Theresa Watson is director.

THE 1924 TOPEKA-SANTA FE GLEE CLUB

SANTA FE GLEE CLUB OF TOPEKA, ca. 1940
Back row, from left, Basil Willis, narrator, Lawrence Thomas, Robert Shreffler, Dr. Fred R. Ford, Wyatt Kirk, Al Treesh, Clarence Heatherington, Mike Adams, William Lommanson, Robert Rice. Front row, from left, Harold Naill, William Rodgers, Walter Zimmerman, director, Morris Richardson, pianist, John Giffin, Harlan Steele, Dale McNamar. Photo from Harold Naill.

Santa Fe Fire Department. Photo made in 1907.

30

Rev. C. E. Busser   *John Player*   *Pres. E. P. Ripley*

From Busser to Player to Ripley,
a Letter that Sparked...

The Revitalized Reading Room System

JOHN W. RIPLEY

THE EXACT DATE is unimportant, but we know that it was during the month of October, 1898, when the Rev. Samuel Edwin Busser, 48-year old rector of St. Mathews Episcopal Church in Emporia, got the urge to write a letter to his friend in Topeka, John Player, superintendent of machinery at the Santa Fe Shops. In the letter Busser outlined an entirely new concept designed to revitalize the railroad's employee-welfare program. In writing that letter Rector Busser had unwittingly written himself right out of the clergy and into an eminently successful career with the Santa Fe.

John Player, London born in 1847, who had come up in the

ranks from machinist apprentice, was thoroughly intrigued by Busser's recommendations. Adding his unqualified endorsement, Player forwarded Busser's letter to the president of the Santa Fe, Edward Payson Ripley in Chicago. What followed was reported a quarter of a century later in the *Santa Fe Magazine*, November, 1926:

> This letter reached Mr. Ripley, to whose big heart the plan made an immediate appeal. As a consequence, Mr. Busser was called to Chicago for a conference which brought about his appointment as the first superintendent of Reading Rooms which Mr. Busser often described as "a parish of 40,000 souls."

Busser who had graduated in 1874 from the Yale Divinity School, had served as pastor of seven midwestern churches before 1890 when he was engaged as minister of the North (Topeka) Congregational Church. Two years later he resigned "to engage in a new endeavor at Dodge City," as itemed in the *North Topeka News*, without revealing the nature of the new endeavor. But within a few weeks word was received here that Busser, finding Dodge City without a single house of worship, had opened (or possibly re-opened) a Presbyterian church.

After a year or so in the role of a Presbyterian minister, successfully building the congregation, Busser seeking greener pastures, again switched denominations. He was ordained by the bishop of the Kansas Episcopal Diocese of Kansas, and in 1895 became rector of St. Mathews Episcopal Church in Emporia. He remained an Episcopalian the rest of his life.

When Topeka's nationally famous Congregational minister, Charles Monroe Sheldon, agreed to edit the *Topeka Daily Capital* as he thought Jesus would, for one week during March, 1900, Busser reasoned that his successful year-old Reading Room operation would make an ideal story for friend Sheldon's Christian daily. It is doubtful that Editor Sheldon ever set eyes on Busser's manuscript, what with the flood of appeals for "write-ups" of causes, moralistic and religious.

But Busser found a friend in L. L. Kiene, city editor of the opposition daily, the *Topeka State Journal*, who hailed the rejected story as a journalistic beat, and printed the entire manuscript.

Busser served as superintendent of Reading Rooms from the time of his appointment in 1898 until his death, Sept. 17, 1926 when he was succeeded by Gaillard M. Miller, a Topekan who before his appointment in 1916 as Busser's assistant, was in the Santa Fe's general superintendent's office, Topeka. Miller passed away in Topeka on July 12, 1937. He was a native of Lyndon, Kansas.

From the State Journal, *March 17, 1900, a portion of Busser's article quoting President E. P. Ripley, Santa Fe Railway, on the objectives of the Reading Room project.*

REJECTED MSS.

Excellent Article by a Minister Refused by Mr. Sheldon.

History of Work of Santa Fe Reading Rooms.

MR. BUSSER, AUTHOR.

He is an Episcopal Minister From Emporia.

Great Good Being Accomplished by the Railroad.

One of the articles rejected by Rev. Charles M. Sheldon was a well written report of the work of the Santa Fe reading rooms by Rev. S. E. Busser, an Episcopal minister. Mr. Busser was formerly a minister of Mr. Sheldon's own denomination, Congregational, and was for several years in charge of the North Topeka Congregational church.

His account of the good work being done is worthy of publication and is herewith reproduced:

"What is known as "The Santa Fe Method" or organizing and operating reading rooms, is the outgrowth of Mr. Ripley's broad and progressive policy in the treatment of his employes. This policy is expressed in his own words, which constitute the foundation stone on which the work is built, and breathe forth the sublime spirit by which it is conducted.

"Whether or not there is a world beyond the one we live in, is a disputed matter; but we may be perfectly sure that the man who walks with truthfulness, sobriety and morality; who is what the world calls 'straight' and who can look every body in the eye, will command the respect of his neighbors, and of himself, and will be infinitely happier in this world than the man who does not; and if there be another world he need not fear it, whatever may be his religious beliefs, or non-beliefs. The officers of this company expect, and propose, to deal justly and fairly with its employes and they believe the latter want also to be just and fair.

"We want them to see what is right as between themselves and the company, to the end that we may all pull together, and the more they read and study, the better it will be for us and for them. We make no pretense to unselfishness —we aim only to practice enlightened selfishness: we want better men, and we are willing to spend money to make them better, because they will do their work more intelligently, and more conscientiously, besides being much happier themselves. We concern ourselves with no man's religion or politics—we only ask in him the qualities that make him valuable to the company, which are also the qualities that will make him a good husband, good father, and good citizen."

These words are taken from Mr. Ripley's letter of instruction to the superintendent of reading rooms of the Santa Fe system, appointed by him to conduct the enterprise, and are made public now, contrary to the modest desires of the president, because the time has come when every wage-earner of this country and every employe of this company, ought to be acquainted with the broad and sublime spirit, simply but eloquently expressed, by which the affairs of a great corporation are guided. They should be printed on every time card, suspended in the cab of every engine, on the walls of every round house, office and shop, and most of all treasured in the heart of every one. They ring a bell of hope and good will in every department of the railroad service and reflected from every reading room and book, they have already dropped untold blessings on every home and family.

These words were born of a lofty motive. They have given inspiration to every move that has been made for the advancement of the men. They have lighted fires of good resolutions, genial friendships, and winsome considerateness for one another in every public gathering of the employes, and hence, if we study the origin of great reforms and the philosophy of history, they are worthy to constitute, and do constitute, our method of conducting reading rooms, as distinctively "The Santa Fe Method."

> *During June, 1952 our family was veiwing the Grand Canyon, standing in front of the fine old hotel on the south rim of the canyon, when my father Rollin W. Ayers, a member of the 1906 Washburn College Glee Club that toured the Reading Room circuit, told us, "I was standing right here when someone from the hotel came running and said that there had been a terrible earthquake in San Francisco, and that the auditorium where we were to perform had been demolished. When we returned to Topeka, Dr. Plass gave stereopticon lectures of the trip, illustrated by photos from three cameras in our group, including shots of the San Francisco earthquake."*
>
> *Jane Ayers McAleavey (Washburn, '34)*
> *Ft. Worth, Texas.*

Topeka Talent Furnished
Fun and Culture for the...

Santa Fe Reading Rooms

PEGGY GREENE

"GIVE man a bath, a book and entertainment that appeals to his mind and hopes and as he becomes more faithful to himself, he is more valuable to the company."

This motto for cleanliness, culture and personal worth set in motion a movement that may have no parallel in the history of business. In 1898 the Santa Fe railroad, inspired by a former Topeka clergyman the Rev. Samuel E. Busser, opened Reading Rooms of an unusual type, along its lines from Chicago to California. They were located at points where crews had long layovers and where the country was undeveloped, such as those west of Albuquerque, where saloons and gambling were about the only recreations offered. In the Reading Rooms "the temptation to drunkenness" was met with music and other entertainment.

Old buildings were secured and spruced up with paint. They were furnished with tub baths, several with "plunge baths," with books, current newspapers and magazines, pianos, pool and billiard tables, card rooms, "and the presence of ladies." Many provided sleeping rooms and a few had restaurants. They were clubhouses where employees could go and find recreation, companionship and entertainment.

Into these reading rooms, like a vaudeville circuit, came troops of entertainers, actors and actresses in costumes, singers in evening dress, the brightness and gaiety of the theater and concert stage. Well-known entertainers made the tours, such as dancer Ted Shawn and song writer, Carrie Jacobs Bond, actors and singers from Broadway, even entertainers from Europe and our big universities.

No money was expected in measurable return by management. The reward being the changed lives of 55,000 employees. President Edward P. Ripley of the Santa Fe referred to the reading rooms as a kind of enlightened self-interest, believing that a change in the lives of lonely employees would benefit the company. He refused all charitable help, insisting that all expenses come from the company. Busser, who was given to flowery speech, said, "The motive underneath this movement is one of the noblest and sweetest that can govern the human heart."

At first the employees were naturally suspicious. Nobody had ever done anything for them without expecting something in return. They suspected that money for the Reading Rooms was being taken from their hospital funds. But finally they began to realize that the Reading Rooms were something offered for

The Shawnee
Concert and Dramatic Company
OF THE STATE OF KANSAS

Personnel

Miss Nanon Herren, Reader and Director of Sketch
Miss Marie Witwer, Manager and Sketch Artist
Miss Bess Wharton, Pianist
Miss Ella Robbins Black, Soprano
Mr. J. W. Risteen, Sketch Artist
Mr. Max Krueger, Violinist and Sketch Artist
Mr. Dick Elmore, Sketch Artist
Mr. Waldo Heywood, Sketch Artist

The touring Modocs of 1916 with the accompanying Carlton Wood orchestra consisting of A. von McFarlane, first violin; George Chandler, second violin; Fred J. Jehlicke, viola; William W. Menninger, cello; Louis Kerle, double bass; P. Kraum, flute; Harry Samuels, cornet; Frank Crawford, clarinet; J. R. Cowdry, tympani; and Carlton Wood, first violin and director.

In February, 1916, the club toured Santa Fe Railroad reading rooms between Topeka and San Francisco as guests of the railroad. In the two weeks of the tour the club gave 13 concerts.

which they were not expected to pay.

At one place during the cattle rush the sleeping rooms were used three times in 24 hours at 25 cents a night. Needles, California, may have had the finest Reading Room—three bowling alleys, card rooms, a gymnasium, auditorium, "the best plunge bath and many bathtubs."

Santa Fe's investment in the Reading Rooms was $250,000, with $50,000 a year spent in maintenance. 17,500 books were bought, 40 per cent fiction. On any day the Reading Rooms were used by 7,000 people. By 1920 there were 35 Reading Rooms, with several tours of entertainers going at the same time. Each Reading Room had one concert a week or other entertainment and employees "were anticipating the fiddle a week before it comes and talking about it a week afterwards."

Though no fee was paid the entertainers, a free trip to California was pay enough—traveling in Pullman sleeping cars, eating in diners and at Harvey Houses, staying in the best hotels, being wildly cheered by audiences. Who would want more? Not many traveled early in the century and a train trip to California was a luxury.

Many talented people in Topeka were Reading Room entertainers. In April, 1906, a male quartette from Washburn

Arthur H. Platt

Earl H. Voorhis

Franklin Koons

Rollin W. Ayers

One of the first local groups to tour the Reading Room circuit was the Washburn College Y.M.C.A. Quartette in April, 1906. (Photo, Washburn KAW, 1906.)

College YMCA had a two weeks tour during which they performed in 11 places. Quartette members were Arthur H. Platt, Rollin W. Ayers, Earl S. Voorhis and Franklin S. Koons. They were accompanied by Washburn President Norman Plass (who lectured on "When Pay-Day Comes"), by his wife and his daughter, Helen M. Plass, accompanist. Among the songs were "My Old Kentucky Home," "Dried Apple Pie" and "Doan' Ye' Cry, Ma' Honey." Miss Plass and Mr. Voorhis gave mandolin and piano duets. Three cameras secured pictures all along the route.

In 1913 the Washburn Glee Club, 16 men, had a tour that rated a long story in the annual Kaw. "When the train pulled out," it said, "we were without a care on earth, riding in our private car toward the 'sunny and ample lands' where we could toss sea shells into the Pacific and pick oranges any time from the back platform of our car."

Their Glee Club Special was hooked to the end of a 46 car freight train and after a rough ride they came to Albuquerque. Each member of the Club bought a Navajo rug, "from the size of a pocket handkerchief up."

They were accompanied by Prof. Horace Whitehouse, dean of Fine Arts at Washburn, who gave readings. Their white-face minstrel was popular and Frank Ripley, vocal soloist, brought down the house with "At that Yiddisher Ball." Sherrill Smith, with his falsetto voice, was a hit as Juliet. They traveled 3,000 miles, gave 16 concerts, spent a week in California and had a memorable tour.

The Washburn Girls Quintet made the tour in 1924 offering a variety of entertainment—voice, flute, Spanish dance, piano and violin solos, flute, violin and piano trios and a vocal quartet. The members were Betty Schick (Mrs. Faye Bennett), Bernice Hemus (Mrs. Donald Farquarson), Eleanor Allen (Mrs. Olin Buck), Anna Louise Casler and Lucelia Harris (Mrs. Paul M. Powell).

Another Washburn men's quartette toured in 1926—Howard McCord, Milton Smith, Martin Baker and Albert Marlin, accompanied by their director, Frank S. Kenyon. Some thought this Quartette was the best in the history of the school.

In February 1916 the Modoc Club of Topeka gave 13 concerts in two weeks, accompanied by Carlton Wood's nine-piece orchestra. In a story on their return the *Daily Capital* said the Modocs were the oldest singing organization in continuous existence in the nation and cited M. C. Holman for his 32 years as director. According to another article they were organized in 1876 and disbanded in 1973.

Floy Ebert, left, and Ann Myers (now Mrs. L. L. Sargent), members of a Topeka troupe, are photographed in front of Fred Harvey's La Castaneda hotel, Las Vegas, N.M.

THE WASHBURN COLLEGE GLEE CLUB ON TOUR

Topeka State Journal, Feb. 1, 1913

The Washburn Singers Who Will Make a Tour of the Santa Fe Lines

The Washburn College Glee club has accepted an invitation from the Santa Fe Railroad company to take a two weeks' concert tour to California, furnishing entertainments at the Harvey House reading rooms. The trip will be from Topeka to Richmond, Cal., and return, and will last at least fifteen days. The club will leave Topeka February 3. The Washburn club is one of three large musical organizations which secured a similar trip this year. The other organizations are the Emporia College Glee club and the Santa Fe Apprentices' band. Dean Horace Whitehouse, president and director of the Glee club, will accompany the men to California. It is quite probable that Prof. Edward Schoenberger will also go, and furnish a short program of dramatic readings.

The program arranged by the club is in two parts. The first part will consist of the regulation classic songs. The second part will be in the way of a burlesque representation entitled, "A Scene in a Sorority House." The playlet is original, and was arranged by Pericles Miller and Sherrill Smith.

The officers and members of the Glee club are as follows, Dean Horace Whitehouse, president; Pericles Miller and Sherrill Smith, managers; Pericles Miller, Theodore Post, Willis Lusby, first tenors; David Neiswanger, Sherrill Smith, Willard Troxell and Earl Farrish, second tenors; Herbert Blinn, Milton Gugler, Edwin Seeley and Don Campbell, first basses; Carl Hathaway, Frank Ripley, Willis Garvey, Neil Rogers and W. J. Rosecrans, second basses.

Top, Miriam Franklin; center, left, Jean Root, Edna Bell; bottom, Lois Gish.

In the early 1920s the Marine Maids, four young Topeka women, toured the reading rooms, dressed in sailor suits and singing sea songs. They were Miriam Franklin, Edna ("Ted") Bell, who imitated Harry Lauder, Jean Root and Lois Gish. Miss Franklin gave readings, including "Ben Hur's Chariot Race" and "Scene in a Farmer's Kitchen," events some distance from the sea. They were advertised as "Bringing you all the fun of a sea voyage without the sea sickness."

The Sunflower Concert Company of Topeka, Kansas made a tour in 1919, advertised: "A noted singer who recently appeared in a Santa Fe Concert in Topeka; A violinist who has been trained under the Masters; A Pianist and Accompanist Famous for her Excellent Work; A reader who is not an Elocutionist but an Impersonator."

Otherwise they were known as Mrs. Ruth Rider Bomgardner, Lena Anderson, Lucile Bomgardner and Eleanor Adams. Mrs. Homer Ward Bomgardner was in charge of properties and management.

Probably one of the most ambitious groups was The Shawnee Concert and Dramatic Company of the State of Kansas. Members were Nanon Herren, reader and director, Marie Witwer, manager, Bess Wharton, pianist, Ella Robbins Black, soprano, J. W. Risteen, actor, Max Frueger, violinist, Dick Elmore, actor and Waldo Heywood, singer and actor. Miss Black and Heywood sang a duet. Heywood sang a tenor solo from Hiawatha's Wedding Feast, Miss Black sang a solo. Miss Herren gave a reading and directed a sketch, "The Man Who Married a Dumb Wife."

Another Topeka touring group was Jessie M. Tipton, voice teacher, Sargent Brownell, cellist, Floy Ebert, violinist, and Ann Myers, now Mrs. L. L. Sargent. The group played semi-classical music including several compositions by Fritz Kreisler.

"We loved every minute of the trip," they said. "We had lovely accommodations and wonderful meals. The towns were small and a little concert group was entertaining. We would get into evening clothes and do it really nice." At Needles no two A's on the piano were in tune.

In 1917 Georgia Neese Gray, Nanon Herren, Ruth and Lucile Bomgardner, Mrs. E. D. Clithero, Mrs. Monte Kistler, Arloa Bell McHugh, Betty Jane Graham 11 years old and her mother were on a tour, which was probably from the College of the Sisters of Bethany.

Mrs. McHugh remembers being impressed by things that Mrs. Gray said: "I always take an hour to get ready for a date." Also, "We should say dawghter, not dotter." And "I think your name would be all right as Loa."

Robert F. Steiner was one of a company of five Topekans who toured the Reading Rooms in 1923. He sang bass. The others were Ilomay Bailey, soprano; Harold Carr, tenor; and Mrs. Lucille Dotterweich, contralto. Prof. Henry Dotterweich, pia-

H 3217. SANTA FE READING ROOM, SLATON, TEXAS.

nist, from the Washburn Fine Arts department, was accompanist. The program ranged from the quartette from *Rigoletto* to "Thanks for the Buggy Ride" and "The Parlor is a Pleasant Place to Sit on Sunday Night."

They enjoyed Harvey House meals, Pullmans, hotels, two nights in Los Angeles and the round trip, all at Santa Fe expense. The trip, Steiner said, was like winning a big prize on TV.

Other Topekans who were on Reading Room tours were Mrs. W. J. Deacon and Mrs. J. P. Wahle, in 1914 and Vaida Beard Thompson, Grace Rickenbacker Peck and Mabel Spivey in 1916.

Lucile Elmore, who was acting in New York and on the road, made many tours of Reading Rooms and as "the petite star of Broadway" was much admired. She would complete a road tour or a Chautauqua season in the fall and then enjoy a tour to California. She organized her own companies, three to five singers and musicians, sometimes a quartette, all capable of good programs. She seems to have made eight consecutive tours beginning in 1927 and one was made in 1939, the last year for the Reading Rooms.

(Continued on p. 178)

As organizer and headliner of high class troupes of entertainers for at least five seasons, petite Lucille Elmore, ventriloquist, singer and dancer earned the sobriquet of "Queen of the Reading Rooms."

Reading Room Entertainment

Lucille Elmore & Company

PERSONNEL

CLAIR FOSTER . . . . Piano
JOSEF SERPICO . . . . Violin
RAYMOND STUMP . . . . . . Clarinet and Saxophone
LUCILLE ELMORE . . . . Impersonator
MRS. E. P. ELMORE . . . . . . Assistant and Manager

First Lady Employee of Santa Fe

Nancy Lykins Sherbert

CAROLINE E. CAMPBELL

THIS is to introduce Caroline E. Prentis, who opened the door of the Atchison, Topeka, and Santa Fe Railroad offices to women. She has the distinct honor of being the first woman employed by the company.

Caroline E. Campbell was born March 16, 1847, at Greenfield, Ohio, the daughter of Hugh and Elizabeth Johnson Campbell. The family, Mr. and Mrs. Campbell and their five children, moved to Kansas during the spring of 1859, to establish a home in Topeka. At the age of 17, Caroline left home and accepted a teaching position at Bazaar, in Chase county. Four years later she met and married Harmon Anderson. The Anderson family occupied an old concrete house on the southeast corner of 6th and Tyler streets. Harmon Anderson's health had been impaired by prison life during the Civil War, and he died of consumption in January, 1874, leaving his wife and a small daughter.

In order to support herself and her daughter, Mrs. Anderson entered the business world. She was employed by the Atchison, Topeka, and Santa Fe Railroad in 1874, in a clerical position, first at the depot at $30.00 a month, and later in the office of Edward Wilder, Treasurer, at $50.00 a month. Mrs. Anderson's first work in the general offices was one of the most important in the system, that of writing paychecks.

She remained in Wilder's office until October, 1881, when

James Smith, Secretary of State, appointed her commission clerk. Mrs. Anderson held this position until November 28, 1883, when she married Noble L. Prentis, a newspaper writer who became widely known, serving on the editorial staff of the Topeka *Commonwealth,* Atchison *Champion,* Newton *Republican* and the Kansas City *Star.* With Caroline's help, Noble Prentis wrote a history of Kansas, which was used in the public schools.

Few women have taken a more active part in club and state affairs. When the Woman's Suffrage Association was organized in 1884, she was a district vice-president and member of the executive committee, and she also served as president of the Kansas Social Science Club during 1888 and 1889. Mrs. Prentis attended many legislative sessions, and was an ardent champion of reforms: prohibition, suffrage, and especially measures wanted by women. She was quoted as telling her women associates in social work, "We live in a man's world and those of our generation always will. Conduct yourselves with gentleness and dignity. If our cause wins, let the men believe they have won for us; if it does not, we still should have them as our allies and not as our enemies in public life."

From Topeka Daily Capital, Aug. 27, 1897

Official Tries to "Catch" a Train Boy...

The Boy Sold Ugly Literature

The Official Thought Out a Scheme to Have Him Suppressed

THERE is a state law in Kansas against the sale of obscene literature. The typical train boy, however, pays little attention to the law, and continues to "fleece" unsuspecting passengers with "hot stuff."

This is a source of great trouble to railroad officials. A passenger, after "bucking up'" against a "news butcher," is usually green enough to hold the railroad responsible for the "skin" game. He will often, in the future, refuse to ride on the railroad and will do all the "knocking" possible.

This story has reference to a high-up Topeka railroad official's experience in an attempt to detect a train boy who was working one of his "flim" games. The official is big enough to draw one of those big salaries you hear about and ride in a special car.

One day the official left his private car in Topeka. He was only going a short distance, so he boarded a regular passenger train and took a seat in the smoker. Before the train had gone far the official noticed the "news butcher" engaged busily in a whispered conversation with an unsuspecting farmer-looking youth across the aisle. The official, surmising the "butcher's" game, decided to save the farmer his money.

Calling the train boy to him, the official whispered in his ear, and the boy replied, "Yes, something fine, rich and racy."

The official nodded his head and the boy made a rush to his box in the front end of the car. Digging down in the bottom he pulled out three books with yellow covers and highly colored pictures on the leaves. He took them to the official. "How much are they?" he inquired of the "butcher."

"Dollarunahalf a piece," was the reply.

The official tried to get them at a reduced price and after some parleying did get them for $1.25 each.

When the train reached the next station the official instructed the conductor to have the boy removed from the train. This was done.

A day later the official walked into the railroad's legal department in the general office building, with the three books he had purchased. Turning to one of the lawyers he recited the facts and said: "I want this boy punished to the full extent of the law. He ought to be sent up."

"All right," replied the attorney, "but if this boy goes up you will have to go too. The law says explicitly that any purchaser of such a book shall be liable to the same punishment as the seller."

"The h—l it does," the official yelled as he jumped up and kicked a chair across the room, "and that boy has my $3.75."

"The Kansas City Times' Fast Newspaper Train...."

A slightly condensed version of an article that was first printed in the Santa Fe Magazine, February, 1972. The author, Joseph W. Snell, is Executive Director of the Kansas State Historical Society, Topeka.

IN TOPEKA, KAN., A SMALL 4-4-0 locomotive eased its way out of the Santa Fe yards and rattled eastward toward Kansas City. Following behind its tender was a single mail car proudly labeled "Kansas City Times' Fast Newspaper Train."

It was January 11, 1876, and the stubby little special was making its initial journey between the two cities, carrying news of the Kansas legislature to the *Times*' editorial and composing rooms. On its return in the morning it would deliver the newspaper to subscribers in Lawrence and Topeka, almost beating the capital city's own newspapers to the streets. For 54 round trips the Kansas City Times' Fast Newspaper Train would make the journey, only ceasing its operations after the Kansas legislature adjourned.

The Fast Newspaper Train was the brain child of both the *Times* management and officials of the Atchison, Topeka and Santa Fe Railroad.

Just who conceived the idea for the Kansas City Times' Fast Newspaper Train is not known today but it is obvious that the newspaper was the leader in the negotiations which consumed six weeks before details of the venture were worked out. Representing the Santa Fe in the conferences were C. F. Morse, general superintendent, and Thomas J. Anderson, general passenger agent.

What the newspaper wanted was rapid transportation for its reporters who would bring news of the day's happenings in the Kansas legislature to the offices of the *Times* so that the next day's paper could carry the detailed story to its readers. The object, of course, was to increase subscription lists and to give the paper a decided advantage over its competitors through sheer audacity.

The railroad stood to gain from the free advertising which would of necessity result from the venture.

The Kansas City Times' Fast Newspaper Train and its crew proudly pose for a formal portrait in Topeka. The writing appears to be "H. V. Farin, general M.M." while the cab is lettered "T. J. Peter." The large building in the background was the Santa Fe's first depot as well as its first general office building. Photo courtesy The Kansas State Historical Society, Topeka.

In addition it was paid for its services in good hard cash.

The Santa Fe was to provide a locomotive and mail car for each day of the session. The engine chosen was No. 11, the "T. J. Peter," appropriately named after the first real builder of the railroad. It had been purchased in 1871 but was still bright and shining from the tip of its weirdly shaped stack to the end of its little coal bearing tender. The mail car was lettered with the special's name, not just once, but four times, twice on each side.

The crew of the train was William Parr, engineer; J. M. Taylor, fireman, and J. L. Rathborne, conductor.

The Topeka staff of the *Times*, J. G. Pangborn, chief; W. G. Souther, senate reporter, and Levi Hensel, house reporter, spent its time in the mail car and as the little locomotive puffed its way eastward in the dark of the winter's evenings, the reporters worked feverishly to prepare their stories from notes taken during the day. At Kansas City their copy was rushed to the Times building where local staff members would work all night to edit, make up and print the paper so that by five the next morning the "T. J .Peter" could steam out on its return to home base loaded with the latest edition. At Lawrence, papers would be thrown off for breakfasting readers to peruse before going to work. In Topeka, additional papers would be distributed while the sky was just turning pink in the east.

Day after day, the Kansas City Times' Fast Newspaper Train made its rounds, and each day the paper would tag its legislative columns with the line "By the Kansas City Times' Fast Newspaper Train."

As the Kansas legislators began to wind up their duties, the *Times* announced that a special excursion, courtesy of the paper, would be run for invited guests on February 25, 1876. Those invited would leave the Kansas City station at six a.m. and arrive in Topeka about three hours later. There they would be free to visit the city, the capitol and even attend a legislative banquet in the evening. Those who chose to attend the dinner, however, would have to find their own way back on regularly-scheduled trains at standard fares because the Fast Newspaper Train was scheduled to return at eight p.m.

For days the *Times* carried numerous articles about the coming excursion and pleaded with readers not to attempt to join the crowd as only 200 invited guests could attend. Those favored with invitations were urged not to miss the event since the Santa Fe Railroad was "the finest in the West; the scenery between this city and Topeka the most picturesque in the State, and the time to be made on this occasion will be the fastest yet attempted. . . ."

Finally the great day arrived and the Kansas City station became a beehive of activity. Guests—newspapermen, politicians, businessmen, community leaders and their ladies —from Missouri, Kansas and Arkansas poured through the gates and filled the cars. They were soon in a jovial mood and made the five coaches and mail car one grand portable party.

A late start prevented the excursionists from arriving in Topeka before 9:30 but the sky was cloudless and the weather pleasant. Many chose to walk from the depot into town and on to the capitol. Though no official city welcome was given, countless citizens greeted the excursionists as they ambled along the streets. The trip was a resounding success and the Kansas City *Times* devoted several front page columns describing minute details of the journey.

THIS PAPER
Is delivered in
Lawrence & Topeka
EVERY MORNING
At Early Breakfast Hour, by the
KANSAS CITY TIMES
FAST
NEWSPAPER TRAIN
Over the Atchison, Topeka and Santa Fe R R., leaving Kansas City at 5 a. m.

Readers of the Times *were not allowed to forget the unusual facilities that brought them news of the 1976 session of the Kansas legislature. This notice appeared on the front page of every issue.*

But the excursion came to an end and the Kansas legislature was fast approaching adjournment. The days of the little train were numbered. The *Times*, March 7, 1876, reported the demise of the train:

"Last Saturday morning the Kansas City Times' Fast Newspaper Train completed its fifty-fourth round trip between this city and Topeka, and with the adjournment of the legislature, having fulfilled its allotted course, and run its two score days and fourteen, on the morning in question it graciously delivered its package of the Times to Lawrence and Topeka subscribers, and then, about 8 o'clock, slowly and reluctantly withdrew to the yards of the company. . . ."

CHARLES GLEED AND THE...
Reorganization of the Santa Fe Railroad

TERRY HARMON

DURING the mid-1890s the Santa Fe and hundreds of other American railroads were forced into bankruptcy. In order to finance rapid expansion throughout the Southwest, often in spaarsely settled areas, the Santa Fe had borrowed large sums of money. The bonded indebtedness and annual fixed interest charges of the company increased much faster than its earnings, partly because general economic conditions were depressed throughout the Santa Fe's territory during the late-1880's, while severe competition offered by other railroads forced reductions in passenger and freight rates. The board of directors worsened the financial position of the company by paying unjustifiably high dividends. It became increasingly difficult for the firm to borrow additional money and refinance its old debts as repayment became due. The Santa Fe was unable to pay the interest on its bonds, and operation of the company was turned over to receivers appointed by a federal judge in December, 1893.

A prominent Topeka attorney, Charles S. Gleed, became involved in efforts to achieve a financial reorganization of the Santa Fe in 1894. A native of Vermont, Gleed had spent most of his youth in Lawrence, where he attended the University of Kansas and worked for several newspapers. Beginning in 1879 he was engaged in advertising work for several railroads, and he also served as a clerk in the law department of the Santa Fe. For a short time in 1884 he was editor of the Denver *Tribune*, before returning to Topeka and establishing a law partnership with his brother, James Willis Gleed. This partnership—which for many years was known as Gleed, Ware and Gleed after Eugene "Ironquill" Ware joined it in 1893—long was recognized as one of the leading law firms in the state.

B. P. Cheney, Jr., a young financier from Boston, hired Gleed to help protect his family's investments in a number of corporations which were experiencing serious financial difficulties during the depression of the 1890s. Gleed and Cheney began participating in the efforts to reorganize the Santa Fe early in

CHARLES S. GLEED

1894 by seeking support among the stockholders for a group of men known as the General Reorganization Committee, who wanted to cooperate with the old management of the company in formulating and implementing a reorganization plan as rapidly as possible.

When the General Reorganization Committee announced its plan, the response was far from enthusiastic. Many stockholders felt that they were being mistreated with a heavy cash assessment of $12 per share. At the same time, some critics of the plan complained that the interests of bondholders were being sacrificed for the benefit of stockholders.

A group of stockholders in New York formed the Protective Committee to block implementation of any reorganization plan until more information became available and until the earnings of the company improved.

Cheney, Gleed, and seven other men were elected Santa Fe directors "rather mysteriously and without any intimation to the generality of Atchison stockholders or to the public" at a meeting of the board of directors on September 13, 1894. Six of the directors associated with the old management of the company resigned, and there were three additional vacancies created by the deaths of two men and the resignation of the company president, J. W. Reinhart. It was an unusual proceeding in which the old directors resigned a few at a time during the meeting so there would be a quorum for the election of their successors, and it occurred less than two months before the stockholders were scheduled to conduct their annual vote on the composition of the board.

After their election the new directors chose a committee, which included B. P. Cheney, Jr., to solicit proxies for the stockholders' meeting on October 25, 1894. They were determined to secure their own re-election, and the Protective Committee was equally determined to obtain control of the board. The result was a well-publicized struggle between the two factions for the support of the stockholders. There were reports that the Protective Committee planned to "sweep the general office at Topeka clean," removing all of the old Santa Fe officials; but the real issue at stake was which faction of stockholders would control the reorganization of the company. The directors were apt to have considerable influence in the negotiations necessary for formulation and adoption of a successful reorganization plan, and both sides in the struggle wanted to obtain a majority of directors willing to support their position.

The Protective Committee attacked the old management of the Santa Fe, filling the newspapers in New York and New England with "literature tending to inflame the minds of shareholders against the late management." Supporters of the directors and the General Reorganization Committee responded that the Protective Committee was a group representing no major Santa Fe security owners which was "simply working a Wall Street speculation game." The Philadelphia *Record* reported on October 18 that this battle for control of the Santa Fe was "at fever heat," with both sides claiming victory. At a board meeting on the previous day the incumbent directors asserted that they had proxies for 596,742 shares of stock, out of the total of 1,020,000 shares issued. They also announced the resignation of a director and the selection of H. R. Duval, a representative of the Dutch stockholders, to be his replacement. This maneuver brought in proxies for about 80,000 Dutch shares and clinched victory for the directors.

Gleed was deeply involved in this struggle for the support of stockholders. He informed one of his law partners on October 6, 1894: "We are chasing proxies with neatness and dispatch.... I am working very hard—up late. And early." One of his friends claimed many years later that Gleed wrote about 4,000 letters during the effort to reorganize the Santa Fe and that some of these letters were instrumental in obtaining the cooperation of the

Dutch stockholders. He also was the author of a circular sent by the directors to the 12,000 Santa Fe stockholders which was widely reprinted in the press. It was not a very sensational document, but when he sent a copy to one of his law partners Gleed remarked that "it has taken like fire water." Throughout this struggle for the proxies of stockholders Gleed utilized his journalistic experience, frequently granting interviews to newspapermen and issuing statements to the press.

Although they failed to gain the support of a majority of the Santa Fe stockholders, members of the Protective Committee hoped to obtain representation on the board of directors because of the Kansas cumulative voting law, which enabled minority groups of stockholders to concentrate their voting strength on a few candidates. The incumbent directors, however, were in no mood to cooperate with their opponents after the wild accusations they had been making; and they insisted that the cumulative voting law was not applicable to the Santa Fe. The railroad operated under a charter granted by the territorial government of Kansas which supposedly constituted a contract that could not be altered by subsequent state legislation. This position ultimately was upheld by a federal court, and the incumbent directors were re-elected.

Before the matter was settled, however, there was a dramatic confrontation at a stockholders' meeting in Topeka on October 25, 1894. Gleed served as the spokesman for the incumbent directors and engaged in "sharp sparring" with Newman Erb, the New York attorney who represented the Protective Committee. Efforts by the Protective Committee to influence the election of a chairman for the meeting, to obtain representation on the credentials committee, and to introduce a resolution calling for another investigation of the company's financial records were thwarted by Gleed's rapid parliamentary maneuvering and the favorable rulings he obtained from the chairman. Members of the Protective Committee complained bitterly that they had been treated unfairly, but they did not have enough proxies to achieve their objectives.

About nine months later, the New York *Financier* bestowed elaborate praise on Cheney and his attorney in an article about this episode:

> Young Cheney, now representing this large block of stock, succeeded in saving the property from confiscation and probably further wreck at the hands of a Wall Street syndicate calling themselves "the protective committee!"
>
> With the assistance of Director Gleed, of Kansas, a man whom he holds in very high esteem, he accomplished results that are almost

marvelous. Young Cheney is really responsible for the retirement of the old board of Atchison directors. It was his arguments, his letters and his demands that really brought about the change and opened the way to a clean and new "deal."

....

This movement for the control of the Atchison property for the real stockholders had been met with bitter opposition at every step, but, despite this fact, Mr. Cheney succeeded in getting the support of over 600,000 out of the 1,000,000 shares of the stock, something that has never been done before in the history of this or any other corporation, and something that was especially remarkable in view of the existing differences of opinion among the various interests.

It may be that the *Financier* exaggerated the importance of their victory, and the degree to which it was unprecedented. Nevertheless, it was not an easy task to unite thousands of widely scattered stockholders behind any particular position, and the adverse publicity about Santa Fe affairs resulting from a report by Stephen Little, a railroad analyst, made it especially difficult. Moreover, it should be remembered that Cheney was only twenty-six years old, while Gleed was still under forty years of age and had little experience in high finance before he, Cheney, and their associates won this victory over the Protective Committee in 1894.

Before the reorganization plan could be implemented it was necessary to obtain the consent of a majority of the security owners. They had to deposit their stock and bonds with the Union Trust Company of New York City and pay their cash assessments in order to receive the new securities. During 1895 Cheney and Gleed spent much of their time seeking to persuade the owners of Santa Fe stock and bonds that they should participate in the reorganization and thereby make the plan successful and retain their investments in the railroad. They made a long journey from Chicago to San Francisco in June and July in order to publicize the reorganization plan, to meet with security holders who had not yet given their consent, and inspect the property of the Santa Fe. In several of the major cities they visited Gleed was interviewed by reporters about the progress of the reorganization effort, and after completion of the journey, the New York *Times* contained an interview with Gleed about the 4,000-mile inspection of the Santa Fe system he had made with Cheney. His optimistic remarks were reprinted by a number of publications throughout the country. Supposedly in response to a request from its editor, he also wrote a comprehensive article about the Santa Fe reorganization for the *Bond Record*, a financial journal published in New York.

Gleed's familiarity with Kansas politics proved valuable in at least one instance in 1895 during the efforts to reorganize the

Topeka Capital, December 11, 1895

IT IS SOLD.

The Great Santa Fe Railroad Auctioned Off

To the Highest Bidder for Cash, For $60,000,000.

A MATTER OF FORM,

The Amount Offered Being a Nominal Sum

To Fulfill the Requirements of the Law.

The greatest auction sale in the world took place this afternoon in Topeka, and Captain J. B. Johnson, of Topeka, was the auctioneer. The Santa Fe railroad, worth $350,000,000, was bid off to the highest bidders, who were Edward King, E. C. Beamer, and Victor Morawetz, for $60,000,000.

Nothing was reserved of the 2,000 locomotives, 10,000 miles of track, and other property worth more than any man's private fortune in the United States.

Shortly before 2 o'clock the great men of the Santa Fe railroad began to gather at the little red brick depot at the foot of Fifth street. There were many people there from around town who were present largely through curiosity. It isn't every day that one can see a $350,000,000 auction.

Santa Fe. Some of the men who helped prepare the reorganization plan wanted to incorporate the new company in Illinois and move the Topeka offices to Chicago. Gleed helped prevent such a change by drawing up a bill permitting the issue of preferred stock by Kansas corporations and by successfully lobbying for its passage by the legislature. The exchange of preferred stock for certain bonds was an essential part of the reorganization plan, and Kansas law previously had prohibited such securities. The Topeka *State Journal* observed that in preparing the legislation Gleed had "made it so simple that no one could fail to comprehend it fully at a glance."

The efforts of Gleed and his associates to persuade security holders to participate in the reorganization were quite successful. By June enough support had been obtained for the Joint Executive Reorganization Committee to declare its plan effective, and by September 21 "practically all" the stockholders and bond owners had deposited their old securities and had paid their assessments. The reorganization was completed with a foreclosure sale on December 10, which was described by one historian as "the greatest auction sale in history." Representatives of the reorganization committee purchased the property of the Atchison, Topeka and Santa Fe *Railroad* company for

(Continued on p. 176)

The Santa Fe Junction
(North Topeka)

PAUL COOPER

A SMALL frame building at the junction of the Santa Fe line to St. Joseph, Union Pacific and Rock Island (Chicago, Rock Island & Pacific) tracks crossed the Santa Fe tracks here. The building was located on East Laurent, several blocks from the north end of the Santa Fe bridge spanning the Kaw River. A room for freight faced the switch tracks on the west. A small waiting room (for passengers) was at the south end which served as a ticket office, telegraph service and freight records.

Charles Gertisen, an old time telegrapher, was in charge. Wet batteries on the floor supplied electricity to the keys. Mail was carried from St. Joseph and other towns along the line.

Charlie Armstrong, a retired blacksmith and horse shoer, pushed a cart delivering mail to the North Topeka postoffice and the Union Pacific depot. R. W. Ferguson and Harry Grant were assistants to Gertisen.

The old junction depot was abandoned and a brick depot building was built on East Gordon. Martin Nystrom was in charge there. Charles Gertisen, who had spent a lifetime as a railroader, after his retirement was killed as he crossed the tracks at the old Union Pacific depot (east of Kansas Avenue).

The Central Sash & Door Company, located west of Kansas Avenue (801 N. Jackson), unloaded cars of material at the old junction. A team of mules pulled the company wagon from the junction to the planing mill. About once a month the mules would run away, going west on Laurent.

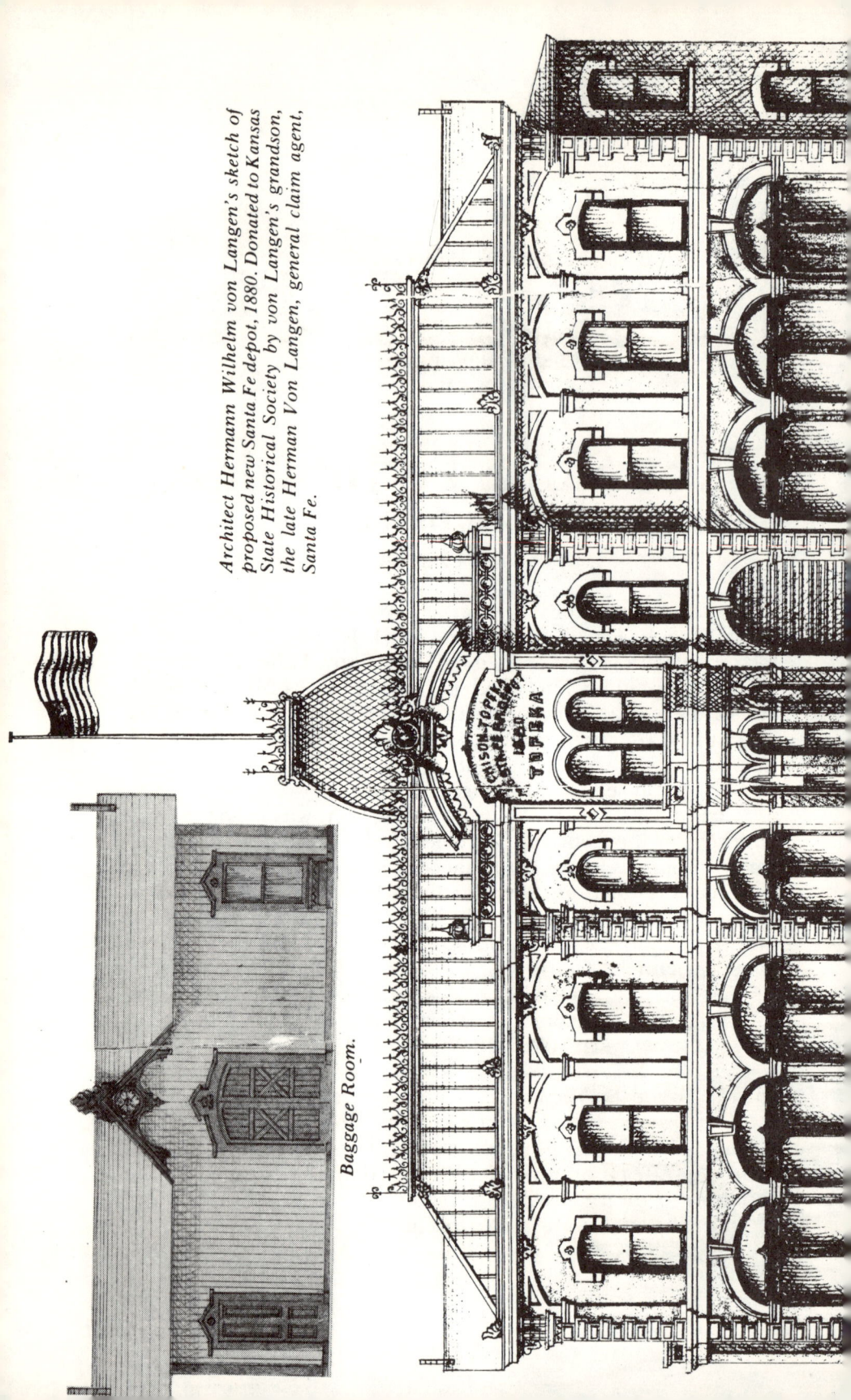

Architect Hermann Wilhelm von Langen's sketch of proposed new Santa Fe depot, 1880. Donated to Kansas State Historical Society by von Langen's grandson, the late Herman Von Langen, general claim agent, Santa Fe.

Baggage Room.

GONE AND ALMOST FORGOTTEN
Santa Fe's Passenger Depots

PATRICIA MICHAELIS

As THE frequency of traveling by train decreases, younger generations of Shawnee countians will not experience the excitement of arriving at the railroad depot to purchase tickets and board the train for a trip to some other part of the country. This experience is, however, familiar to many and any memory of a train trip includes memories of the railroad depot.

The first depot built by the Atchison, Topeka, and Santa Fe in Topeka was located on the west side of the main line on Washington Street between Fourth and Fifth streets. It was constructed in 1869 and was a two-story wooden structure approximately 30 feet by 70 feet. The building served as both a passenger and a freight depot and was enlarged several times. The second floor was the site of the second general offices during the 1870s. The first lunch stand in this building was operated by Peter Cline who sold out to Fred Harvey in the spring of 1876. The building was used as a passenger depot until 1881 and as a freight depot until 1904, when it was moved to the company's lumber yard to serve as a warehouse.

Construction of the brick depot located between Fourth & Fifth on Holliday, began in 1880 and the building was opened in 1881. The building was designed by Hermann von Langren, an architect from Marion Centre, Kansas, and was 37 feet by 108 feet. It was a two-story-structure approximately 33 feet high. Wooden platforms were constructed on the south and west sides of the depot as well as a platform north of the baggage room, which was 18 feet by 48 feet and located just north of the main building. A covered wooden platform was built on the east side of the depot and ran for 450 feet. The cost of construction totaled $35,000.00 for the main building, the baggage room, and the platforms, with J. A. Boyle of Topeka serving as the contractor.

The first floor had separate waiting rooms for both "ladies" and "gentlemen" as well as the office of the ticket agent that opened onto the covered platform. The restaurant was originally located on the second floor. The permit to construct the two additional wings on the north and south ends of the building was issued on October 2, 1902. The additions were brick and stone with metal roofs and the cost was estimated at $20,780.00. When the additions were completed, the restaurant was moved to the south wing of the lower floor.

Paul Cooper, former Santa Fe employee, described the depot as he remembered it as a child. "Two waiting rooms were provided, one at the south end where no smoking was allowed where both men and women were seated. At the north end was the men's waiting room; smoking allowed. Between the waiting rooms, on the east side, was the glass-enclosed office displaying Indian pottery and blankets, connected with the ticket office.

"Next to the ticket office was the Fred Harvey news stand where candies, cigars, cigarettes were displayed, together with local and out-of-town newspapers, magazines and books. Fred Harvey dining room was at the far south end of the building, with a lunch counter between the dining room and waiting room. The lunch counter had an entrance from the waiting room. On the north end of the building was the baggage room."

During the 1880s, for example, the depot was a busy place. Depending on the direction the passenger was going, he could purchase tickets for the Colorado Express, the New York Express, the Kansas City and Atchison Express, the Atlantic Express, or the Pacific Express. Passengers could also make connections to Kansas City on the Kansas City and Topeka Accommodation. East and west bound Emigrant trains also passed through Topeka, as well as a number of freight trains that accepted a limited number of passengers.

The brick depot was used until 1949 when a new station was built. In addition to serving the needs of passengers, it had housed the division superintendent's staff, had served as a dormitory for Harvey House workers, and was used as a USO canteen during World War II.

The new depot was dedicated on April 3, 1949, the date chosen being the birthday anniversary of Cyrus K. Holliday. The building was designed by C. O. Coverly and J. A. Lippitt, Santa Fe architects. It was constructed by J. A. Lundgren and Son of Topeka. The new depot was 274 feet by 36 feet. It was a one-story building constructed of reinforced concrete faced with Indiana limestone. The July, 1949, issue of *Kansas Construction Magazine* described the interior. It had a "modernistic color scheme" with blue, green, and brown upholstered chairs and plastic covered wall benches. It had a snack bar and newstand on the east side that were finished in blonde oak. The April 3 dedication ceremonies were used to pay tribute to Cyrus K. Holliday, one of the founders of the railroad. A bronze plaque, noting Holliday's contributions to the Santa Fe and Topeka, had been installed in the new depot and was unveiled during dedication ceremonies. Gov. Frank Carlson, Santa Fe and Topeka officials, and several leading industrialists attended the festivities. The last Santa Fe operated passenger train passed through the Topeka depot on May 3, 1971.

...anta Fe's first depot, a red frame all-purpose structure, passenger, freight, general offices. Located ...t southwest corner 4th & Washington. Built in 1869.

Rowley's drug store, 600 Kansas, served as Santa Fe's uptown ticket agency.

ROWLEY BROS.,

DRUGGISTS

Southeast Corner Sixth and Kansas Aves.,
Topeka, Kansas.

Prescriptions Accurately Prepared.

The Oldest Established Drug Store in the City.

TELEPHONE NO. 82.

ROWLEY BROS.,
GENERAL
RAILROAD AGENTS,
AND
CITY TICKET AGENTS
FOR THE
A. T. & S. F. R. R.

Also Steamship Agents for all Foreign Countries.

West side of the old brick station, 5th & Holliday. Below, same view after wing added on south to give Fred Harvey first floor space for his food service.

East side of depot, with hack stand in foreground. Below, Fred Harvey newsstand under canopy on east side of depot. Photo dated, 1913.

Waiting room, Topeka depot, 1930. Below, Baggaage room cre[w] about 1910, Topeka depot. Pho[to] E. W. Tomlinson—Kansas St[ate] Historical Society.

Undated photo of depot and passenger car yards. Small building at left is the Wells-Fargo Express Agency. Below, Mrs. William Jacobs and daughter, Wilma were given a going-away party prior to their taking the Limited to California. Photo made in 1920 at Santa Fe depot. Photo from Mrs. Wilma Buchanan, Topeka.

A California train, in the age of steam, at Topeka depot. Photo by Vernon French. Below, fruit and vegetable hucksters await crates of supplies being unloaded at Wells Fargo agency.

Santa Fe Flyer
New California Train Passes Through Topeka with 75 Passengers Aboard

Topeka State Journal, Nov. 3, 1898

A WALDORF-ASTORIA on wheels passed through this city this morning on its way to California. It was the first of the California Limited trains on the Santa Fe, and it re-inaugurates the limited train service between Chicago and the Pacific coast.

The Santa Fe limited trains of the past have been veritable traveling hotels of a thoroughly up-to-date character, but the initial train proves that this year the limited service on the Santa Fe will excell that of any former year. To the advantage of a well appointed hotel is this year coupled some of the comforts of a splendidly furnished home.

Seventy-five people took passage on the train out of Chicago last night, and were aboard when it passed through Topeka this morning, and at La Junta and Albuquerque this number will be increased. In this connection the Santa Fe management has the satisfaction of knowing that every passenger rides on only a first class ticket, as no free transportation is honored on this limited train.

The train consisted of six cars, a composite car for baggage, library, smoking room and barber shop; a dining car, three Pullman sleepers—the Daertes, the Eumenis and the Orient —and a Pullman observation car—the Tryphosa. A portion of the observation car is furnished with tables and easy chairs, and is especially designed for ladies and children on the train. Here they can be as comfortable as in their homes.

Every car on the train is lighted with electricity, the sleepers being fitted with small incandescent globes arranged in arches at intervals along the ceiling. Electricity is generated from the cars' axles, and an electrician will accompany the train to look after this feature.

One new and particular feature of the limited train service is the electric lighting of the berths. Each berth is furnished with a small incandescent globe, frosted so as to do away with the glare and produce a light especially adapted for reading.

... heaved up his shovelful and that was the real beginning of the Santa Fe.

Passenger Trains Serving Topeka

GEORGE F. SHERMAN, JR.

SHORTLY before noon on October 30, 1868, Col. Cyrus K. Holliday, Sen. Edmund G. Ross, the man who cast the vote that saved President Andrew Johnson from conviction, and a friend of Holliday, and a few townspeople, overcoated against the blustery wind, met between Fourth and Fifth on Washington street in Topeka. After a few short speeches the Senator took a shovel, bore down on it with one foot, heaved up a chunk of brown earth and handed the tool to Holliday. The Colonel heaved up a shovelful of dirt and handed the shovel to Joe Blush, the contractor. He heaved up his shovelful and that was the real beginning of the Santa Fe.

On April 26, 1869, seven miles had been laid southwest from Topeka with 50-pound iron rail. A secondhand locomotive was purchased from the Ohio and Mississippi Railroad and some other used equipment was acquired elsewhere and the Wakarusa Picnic Special consisting of the "new" secondhand locomotive and two coaches (one borrowed) steamed out of Topeka with almost a hundred passengers. The end of the line was reached at the hell-bent speed of fifteen miles per hour over a roadbed that was pronounced the best in the prairie country.

The bridge across the Kansas river was completed March 30, 1869.

A railroad ordinarily is built before timetables are issued. The Santa Fe was an exception. Timetable effective May 1, 1869, was issued covering runs as far as Burlingame, the line was complete less than halfway.

Read Down					Read Up	
No. 3	No. 1				No. 2	No. 4
P.M.	A.M.				P.M.	A.M.
3:00	7:30	Lv.	North Topeka	Ar.	1:25	8:35
3:05	7:35		Topeka		1:20	8:30
3:45	8:15		Pauline		12:40	7:50
4:10	8:40		Wakarusa		12:15	7:25
4:45	9:15		Carbondale		11:40	6:50
5:09	9:35		Scranton		11:20	6:30
5:35	10:05		Burlingame		10:50	6:00
P.M.	A.M.				A.M.	P.M.

Trains ran daily, except Sunday, connected at North Topeka with Kansas Pacific and at Burlingame with Barlow, Sanderson & Co.'s Overland Stage. Patrons could purchase tickets for travel over as much of the line as was finished. All trains were mixed and carried only one passenger coach. The coach was open vestibule at each end with steps down almost to rail level. The final gap to the ground was bridged by a portable stepping stool, placed in position during the stops by a trainman. Heating was by stove at the end of the car using wood or coal. Windows generally were narrow and could be opened upwards, to admit (in summer) a cooling draught—and dust and cinders.

Through service to Burlingame was inaugurated September 18, 1869.

The line was completed to Emporia in November, 1870; Newton, July, 1871; Kansas-Colorado border, December, 1872; Las Animas, September, 1875; La Junta and Pueblo, February, 1876. An entrance to Kansas City was secured by the leasing of the Kansas City, Topeka and Western in late 1875. The line between Topeka and Atchison was completed in May, 1872.

———Timetable effective November 26, 1876:———

	Read Down No. 1	Fare		Fare	Read Up No. 2	
D	11:30 am 2:20 pm	$ 2.85	Atchison Topeka	$35.00	3:25 pm 1:00 pm	
D	11:30 am 2:40 pm	2.85	Kansas City Topeka	35.00	4:20 pm 1:10 pm	
S	3:00 pm 8:12 pm 8:32 pm 9:53 pm	8.95 10.60	Topeka Florence Florence Newton	32.40 26.30	12:40 pm 7:20 am 7:00 am 5:30 am	D B
	10:25 pm 11:45 pm	12:10	Newton Wichita	26.30	5:00 am 3:40 am	
B D	10:10 pm 9:05 am 9:25 am 2:26 pm 6:20 pm	24.20 30.50 35.00	Newton Lakin Lakin West Las Animas Pueblo	24.20 11.10 4.60	5:10 am 5:45 pm 5:25 pm 12:37 pm 8:40 am	S D

Trains run daily, are equipped with the Westinghouse Air Brake, Miller Coupler and Platforms and all the modern improvements.

The most popular train for Topeka was the Santa Fe "Plug" inaugurated between Topeka and Kansas City, June 1, 1884, leaving Topeka daily, 7:30 a.m., arriving Kansas City, 9:30 a.m. Returning, it left Kansas City 4:30 p.m. and arrived Topeka 6:30 p.m. Train consisted of baggage and express cars, smoker and coaches. It stopped at any station for passengers to entrain or detrain. The train made 17 stops over the short piece of single track which was 67 miles long. There were many trains to meet and pass, block signals were numerous and many other things required an engineer's attention. James E. Thomas, Santa Fe engineer and former Mayor of Topeka, when interviewed on August 1, 1915, stated he could not remember who first ran the Plug but he did remember when John Higgins began his railroad career with the Santa Fe on August 12, 1874, in the roundhouse as a helper. John Higgins worked his way up to an engineer. He ran on the Plug for 22 years. His long career on the Plug unsteadied his nerves and general physical condition and he retired July 4, 1910.

Fred Harvey provided a news agent who passed back and forth through the cars selling daily newspapers, magazines, candy, chewing gum, fruit, ice-cold pop and novelties. In August, 1887, the run was extended west to Osage City and the evening train stopped at Topeka 20 minutes for supper. In December, 1912, the run was again extended west to Emporia. The schedule was arranged so students attending Kansas University at Lawrence could leave Topeka in the morning arriving in Lawrence in time for classes and return home that same evening. The same was true for patrons who wished to have a day in Kansas City. The Plug was the first train that ran after the disastrous 1903 flood. The train was discontinued November 28, 1931, after 47 years of service.

When the "Plug" was discontinued comparable service was provided as shown below.

Read Down Emporia Express		Read Up The Hopi	
5:00 pm	Kansas City	10:10 am	
S 6:55 pm	Topeka	8:25 am	
7:15 pm	Topeka	8:00 am	B
9:00 pm	Emporia	6:25 am	

S—Supper, B—Breakfast. Fred Harvey Eating House.

The Emporia Express was the same as the "Plug." The Hopi was a through train from Los Angeles which previously operated over the Ottawa cutoff. It stopped only at Osage City, Burlingame and Lawrence and made no flag stops.

(Continued on p. 167)

Kansas University students at Topeka Santa Fe depot waiting to board the "Plug," during 1930's. Front row, from left, Leland Thompson, Martha Heaton, Esther Chubb, Margaret Fouch, Mildred Irwin, Mary Irwin, Richard Thomas. Rear, Eugene Brandt and Freeman French. (Photo by Vernon French)

Excerpt from University of Kansas Daily Kansas, Jan. 10, 1934

Twenty-eight Students Commute via Santa Fe "Plug"

VERNON FRENCH, c '36

WHEN SOMEONE mentions "commuters" to the average student, his first thought is of crowded trains from New York suburbs where jammed-up mobs read newspapers and play cards as they rush toward Gotham to work in an environment of riveters, honking motor cars and stock market crashes, but to certain K.U. students the name brings up a friendly, brotherly feeling which is sympathetic and understanding. These students are the "Kansas Kommuters" who constitute a unique group at the University of Kansas.

The greatest number of students who commute come from Topeka, some by train and others by automobile. To 17 fleet-footed enthusiasts, the "wasa" (very nasal) horn of the good old Santa Fe Plug,* means "Make it snappy or you'll miss that train."

---

*In July, 1932, a gas-electric locomotive with its "wasa" horn replaced the steam locomotive that had pulled the "Plug."

It even has something of the alarm clock qualities for Betty Parkinson, c '36, for living close to the Santa Fe depot at Topeka. She has bribed the engineer to toot extra long for her when the train approaches Topeka, so that she will start schoolward on time.

Besides Betty, the following Topeka students commute to and from K.U. on the Plug. Glenn Anderson, c '37; Eugene Brandt, c '37; Esther Chubb, c '35; Jane Clark, c '37; Freeman French, c '37; Orrin French, c '34; Vernon French, c '36; Ralph Grindoll, c '37; Martha Heaton, gr; Mary Irwin, c '36; Mildred Irwin, ed '34; Morris C. Richardson, c '36; Vincent Robinson, c '36; Reese Spurrier, c '37; Richard Thomas, fa '37; and Leland Thompson, c '37.

Now, some 45 years later, Vernon French, retired educator at Washburn University, has added 11 more names to the list of Santa Fe commuters to Kansas University, via the Plug: L. Theron French who commuted during the 1920's; Carlton French; Sam Foster; Mary Edith Challacombe Foster; George Challacombe; Sam Bruner; Francis Spurrier; Betty Parkinson; Margaret Fouch; Leonard Short; R. Stanley Alexander.

Keep Pluggin' for VICTORY
travel by train — save rubber, oil and gas for war work!

Santa Fe "PLUG"

provides daily — EXCEPT SUNDAY service for short trips between EMPORIA — TOPEKA — LAWRENCE and KANSAS CITY

SCHEDULE	
Read Down	Read Up
6:05 am Lv. Emporia	Ar. 10:15 pm
6:28 am Lv. Reading	Lv. 9:48 pm
6:45 am Lv. Osage City	Lv. 9:30 pm
6:58 am Lv. Burlingame	Lv. 9:15 pm
7:07 am Lv. Scranton	Lv. 9:06 pm
7:13 am Lv. Carbondale	Lv. 8:59 pm
7:50 am Lv. Topeka	Lv. 8:27 pm
8:25 am Lv. Lawrence	Lv. 7:42 pm
8:38 am Lv. Eudora	Lv. 7:29 pm
8:52 am Lv. DeSoto	Lv. 7:17 pm
9:26 am Ar. K.C., Kans. Lv. 6:41 pm (Argentine Station)	
9:40 am Ar. K.C., Mo. Lv. 6:30 pm (Motor Train Service)	

World War II time card for the "Plug."

Topeka Capital
March 13, 1932

IN 1882, TRAIN BUILT AT HOME WAS A NOVELTY

Santa Fe Shops Turned Out Such a Creation and Everybody Went to the Station to See It.

ENGINE NAMED 'WM. B. STRONG'

Compared With Monster Locomotives of Today It Was a Mere Pygmy, But It Puffed Along.

BY MILTON TABOR

Nearly all Topeka citizens were at the Santa Fe station. They were admiring the creation of a new train, all of which had been constructed in Topeka, by Topeka mechanics. It was the first passenger train manufactured west of the Mississippi river. From the "snout" of the cow-catcher to the signal lamp on the rear platform of the "sleeper," this train had been made right here at the home of the Santa Fe railroad.

This occurred 50 years ago. The Santa Fe shops had not long been in existence. Indeed, the railroad itself was not so old, but it already was reaching its iron tracks toward the Golden Gate and the setting sun.

Full Trains in Short Order.

Today the modern shops of the Santa Fe, or at many other points, can turn out full trains in short order. But back in 1882 a "home made" train was enough of a novelty to bring out the people all along the line where it was advertised.

The engine of this new train was christened "Wm. B. Strong," after the president of the road. It was the first built in Topeka. It was one of the biggest locomotives known at that time, tho a mere pygmy in comparison with some of the big "hog-backs" now in use on some divisions of the Santa Fe.

69-Inch Drivers.

The cylinders were 18x28 inches, with 69-inch drivers. The new creation was a wonder in climbing the stiff grades between Topeka and the western edge of the state—grades that long since have been planed down for speed. The cost of the engine was $8,587, while the regular price f. o. b. Kansas City, had been $13,500. The present Santa Fe officials laugh at that sort of a quotation on passenger locomotives.

The baggage cars, of which 24 had been built in the local shops, cost $3,574, including the "paper wheels," a composition wheel that was largely mythical, rather than practical.

Nine postal cars had been built at a cost of $3,714 each, a considerable saving over the "boughten" variety. The appointments in the coaches were said to be equal to any included in those purchased in the East.

From Santa Fe Employees Magazine, April, 1915

A fine new mail motor car has been purchased by the Santa Fe, displacing the old horse-drawn wagon which has been the means of conveying mail since 1884.

J. M. Hayes, custodian, general offices, Topeka, is very proud of the new auto mail car. About 2,000 pounds of mail is carried daily between the station, the general offices and the shops.

★ ★ ★

I REMEMBER

The Old Santa Fe Depot

PAUL COOPER

IN 1908 I purchased my first long pants suit, a blue serge, as required to work in Fred Harvey's News Stand in the old Santa Fe depot. Shell brass buttons were furnished to slip over the regular buttons of the coat. A uniform cap informed the public that I was a news agent or "butcher." Miss Clara Fry was manager of the news stand. My duties were making sales, checking baggage, scrubbing the floor and washing the glass cigar case. I also paraded on the platform when trains arrived, selling newspapers. Special trains arrived with Shriners or Elks on way to conventions. Probably six trains going east, and six west during the day. The California Limited, No.3, going westward, and No.4 to the east were the deluxe ones at that time. The "Plug" between Kansas City and Emporia departed, east bound from Topeka at about 7 A.M., returning about 6 P.M. A fellow newsie on the Plug named Smith, dubbed Smitty, had a job as a printer in Kansas City. A Mr. Griffith was the conductor. I sometimes substituted for Smitty on the Sunday trip to Kansas City.

Round trip excursions to Kansas City for one dollar were popular during the summer. All trains carried mail with traveling mail clerks.

Truck loads of cream cans arrived here for Continental Creamerie,* occupying much of space in the baggage cars.

Bill Butler was stationmaster. He had only one arm. Tom King was ticket agent. Bob Robinson was his assistant, later becoming assistant paymaster under Clyde Fink. Tom King was later city passenger agent.

Several shop officials ate lunch at the Harvey House, among them John Purcell, Frank W. Thomas, and H. E. Wray, the storekeeper. Purcell would buy a ten-cent cigar and give a dime to his church. Thomas was a Picayune cigarette smoker. Purcell would look over a newspaper while at the news stand but never bought one.

Other characters I remember were Mr. James F. Lytle, Wells Fargo Express district supervisor, a Capt. R. M. Spivey, a one-armed gentleman employed in some capacity by Fred Harvey. He traveled extensively. Another one was P.H. Coney, a bewhiskered attorney who was prominent in G.A.R. circles. Last but not least was Luther, a small hunchback who had a shoeshine stand in the men's waiting room. He was a foreigner, wore bushy red whiskers, and was not very sociable until you knew him.

*Later merged with Beatrice Foods.

LAND SALESMAN EXTRAORDINARY...
Carl Bernard Schmidt
TOM MUTH

BY THE mid-1850's, the federal government was the largest land owner in the United States. Millions of acres of land were lying undeveloped in the West and the South. While acreage was available to settlers at very low costs there were few buyers since these lands were often too far from markets and transportation.

It was during this period, through the efforts of statesmen such as Stephen A. Douglas, that the government adopted the policy of granting public lands to assist development of the railroads. These grants were based on alternate sections of land on either side of the tracks, along the railway.

By this manner of subsidy, the Atchison, Topeka and Santa Fe Railroad,* which was founded in 1859, acquired over 3,000,000 acres of land in Kansas when its line from the Missouri River to the Colorado border was completed in 1872.

With this completion began an agressive sales program to dispose of the land grants. Under the direction of A. E. Touzalin, in charge of the Santa Fe Land Department, branch offices were established in many European cities to attract new settlers. Besides offering land at reasonable prices to promote sales, Santa Fe agents gave lectures about the State and distributed literature extolling the virtues of Kansas.

One such agent was Carl Bernard Schmidt, who was hired in 1873 by Mr. Touzalin as Santa Fe's General Foreign Agent. Due to his untiring efforts, Germans, Swedes and Mennonites came by the thousands. In time, C. B. Schmidt came to be known as the "Moses of the Mennonites."

The Mennonite movement, organized in Switzerland, began in the 1520's. The group's name is derived from Menno Simons, a Catholic priest who left the Church and was active in the Anabaptist movement. With strong beliefs based on the New Testament, they dressed and lived simply. While loyal to civil government, they neither bore arms nor took oaths. Over the years, the Mennonites had divided into a variety of groups.

Forced from their original homes, the victims of countless persecutions, these professional farmers roamed Europe seeking a new home. The Mennonites found refuge in Prussia for a few hundred years but toward the latter part of the 1700's their stay became less comfortable.

---
*Until its reorganization in 1895 the corporation was the A.T.& S.F. *Railroad;* upon reorganization it was *Railway.*

CARL B. SCHMIDT

During this time, Catherine the Great of Russia made unoccupied areas of her country available to the Mennonites. Granted lands and exempted from military inscription, thousands of Mennonites resettled. Establishing villages, churches and schools in Russia, while maintaining the German language, the Mennonites prospered. By the 1870's, however, the political scene was changing in Russia. Land acquisitions, exemption from military service and the right to use German in schools was of questionable status. The time was right for a change and many Mennonites felt the lure of land and opportunities in the United States and Canada difficult to resist.

Carl Bernard Schmidt was highly successful in attracting the Mennonites to Kansas. He traveled to Russia many times to promote immigration to Kansas. A man of unusual skills, linguistic abilities and charm, he persuaded several Mennonite delegations to visit the State. By 1873, the Santa Fe lands had been inspected as potential farmland by the Mennonites.

The Foreign Immigrant Department of the Santa Fe Railway transported more than 7,000 Russo-German Mennonites from Southern Russia to Kansas over a period of several years. The Santa Fe Railroad assisted the Mennonites in every way possible. In addition to providing temporary barracks to shelter the immigrants until permanent housing was available, household effects and implements were brought to the U.S. on chartered ships. Cargo landing in Philadelphia was shipped by rail to Kansas at the expense of Santa Fe. Additionally, free transportation of building material from West of the Mississippi River was

Mennonite immigrants recruited by Santa Fe, in temporary quarters in Kansas.

given for one year. Other benefits granted were reduced coal rates, moratoriums on land payments when necessary and guarantees of help in event of disaster.

By September, 1874, Mennonite families were arriving in Topeka, a stop on their way to new homes along the Santa Fe lines. The Mennonites were officially welcomed by Gov. Osborn and some 2,000 toured the Capital building and attended a reception. Their guide for the event was Jakob Schmidt (actually, Jake Smith, a local resident). Local businessmen quickly discovered that despite their seemingly quaint clothing and manners, the Mennonites proved to be valuable customers. As a group, they had about $2 million to spend on supplies for their venture.

Topeka newspapers recorded these accounts of the Mennonite arrivals:

> September 17, 1874 (*The Commonwealth*):
> "Large crowds of visitors flocked to the King Bridge shops yesterday, to see the six hundred Mennonites who arrived in our city and took quarters there on Tuesday.... They were dressed in their primitive homespum garments which were usually of coarse wool.... Our crack tailors would have been puzzled at the droll appearance of these ancient dresses. The women and children ... had funny old handkerchiefs tied round their heads, and certainly no Broadway milliner ever supplied one of the quaint bonnets which the fair Mennonite beauties wore."
>
> "Their leaders said that 1,000 more were expected.... Some of the Mennonites bring a good deal of money, many as much as $1,000 or $2,000, but a great many are poor."

September 24, 1874 (*The North Topeka Times*):
"The King Bridge buildings are crowded with Mennonites. A fresh arrival of 1,000 came in on Wednesday, making almost 2,000 that have reached Kansas in the past two or three weeks...."

September 30, 1874 (*The State Record*):
"To the Editor: Would it not be well and polite for the citizens of Topeka to show some attention and little acts of courtesy and civility to these interesting strangers (the Mennonites), now in our midst? They will shortly leave us for their future home in the southern part of the State, which they will soon transform from its present wilderness condition into cultivated and improved farms.... It is well known that they are a thrifty, hard-working body of people.... They have chosen our young and growing state as the place in which to make their future homes, and it would be the dictate of wisdom and sound policy in our merchants and business men to conciliate their kind feelings toward Topeka and induce them to look upon our city as a place for them to trade in the future.... The Atchison, Topeka and Santa Fe Rail Road has assisted these people very much and the officers of that road, especially Mr. Schmidt... entitled to a great credit for inducing them to come to Kansas."

Carl Bernard Schmidt was indeed a promoter in the settlement of the Mennonites in Kansas. His birth and background had seemingly not indicated that his name would always be remembered in conjunction with the Kansas Mennonite immigration.

Mr. Schmidt was born September 7, 1843 in Saxony. His father was architect to the king of Saxony. Carl was educated in the public schools and at Queen Anna's College at Dresden. After a two-year session at the Dresden Commercial College, he went to Hamburg in 1863. Here, he held for eight months, a position as foreign correspondent.

He sailed for New York and arrived in September, 1864, on his twenty-first birthday. Moving west, he settled in St. Louis where he taught music and worked in a mercantile house. In 1866, he married Martha Fraim of Kentucky.

In 1880, Mr. Schmidt established the London office of the Atchison, Topeka and Santa Fe Railway and held charge there for three years.

In 1885, C. B. Schmidt settled in Omaha, Nebraska, becoming manager of the Equitable Trust Company. His work for Santa Fe, Equitable Trust and other concerns necessitated more than thirty-seven trips to Europe in development interests for the West.

The World Columbian Exhibition in 1893 found C. B. Schmidt as the head of their German Ethnographic Exhibition. In 1895 he and his family moved to Pueblo, Colorado where he managed the Suburban Land and Investment Company and was director of the Bessemer Canal.

Some of his other duties included: Director of the Concordia Loan and Trust Company, Kansas City, Missouri; director of the Pueblo Men's Association and Vice-President of the Pueblo Melon Growers Association. In 1898, he was appointed one of the Colorado Commissioners to the Omaha Exposition. He was for a time commissioner of Immigration for the Rock Island Railroad and for a time he was an agent of the Wyoming Development Company (1914-1916) attempting to entice groups of Mennonites to migrate to Wyoming. Mr. Schmidt died in the early 1920's.

Many interesting chapters of Kansas history have connections with its railroads. None are more important than that of Carl Bernard Schmidt and the Mennonite immigration. The Mennonites prospered in Kansas by utilizing their knowledge on the lands sold to them. They bred livestock, practiced crop rotation, and most importantly, introduced their winter wheat.

Hard winter wheat came in slowly with the immigrants until arrangements were made to acquire larger quantities from the Ukraine for shipment to the United States. This wheat and its improved strains revolutionized wheat growing in Kansas and the surrounding areas.

Due to the combined efforts of the Santa Fe Railway, Carl Bernard Schmidt and the Mennonite immigrants, Kansas did, indeed, become the breadbasket of the nation.

Kansas and the Santa Fe—A Winning Team

Cyrus K. Holliday, in a letter dated Oct. 3, 1874, written to a son Charles, then studying in Germany, wrote:

"For the past two or three weeks the mammoth buildings of the Bridge Shop Co. in this city have been filled with emigrants from Russia seeking homes in this—to them—very far-off land. They are what are called 'Menonites,' a peculiar religious society in Russia, and who have been expelled from Russia because they won't be soldiers. There are some 1,200 to 1,500 here now, and about 2,500 more on the ocean coming across. There has been a great contest among the Western States and Western Railroads who should get them, and Kansas as the state and the A.T. & S.F.R.R. as the road, have come ahead. The Santa Fe Company has succeeding in selling to all of them lands along the line of their road, and each day there are several loads of them going down to occupy their new homes. As there are quite a number of thousands of these people coming, securing them to Kansas and to our road will prove a great acquisition to both."

A LOOK BACK AT THE...
Law Department at Topeka

J. B. REEVES

THE ORIGINAL outline for this *Bulletin* entitled this Section "Law Department—Passes to Legislators." I am sure that the drafter of this outline was certain that any review of the records of the Santa Fe Law Department at Topeka would disclose the methods by which the Santa Fe—in the years preceding and immediately following the turn of the century—"owned" the Legislature by the simple expedient of issuing railroad passes.

Although there is a story to be told about railroad passes issued through the Law Department at Topeka—it has to do with litigation—not with legislation. I recognize that there will be those who have done me the courtesy of reading this far who will express everything from disappointment to outrage at this departure from the taught-tradition about the activities of Santa Fe lawyers in this period.

However, the story of this era is documented by the meticulous records of George N. Holmes who was the Docket Clerk at Topeka from September 1, 1882, until his retirement shortly before his death on October 23, 1932.

The Santa Fe Law Department at Topeka has its beginnings with the appointment of A. A. Hurd as Solicitor for Kansas in 1881, a position he held until succeeded by Judge William R. Smith who left the Kansas Supreme court in 1905 to be Solicitor for Kansas until his retirement in 1933. Others in the office at the same time were O. J. Wood, January 1, 1887—November 1, 1930; Alfred A. Scott, August 1, 1890—1933; and Alfred G. Armstrong, 1925—1930.

During the entire era of A. A. Hurd and of Judge Smith, local attorneys in the various Kansas counties handled far more litigation than they have since. The position of local attorney for the Santa Fe was highly prized, not only for the prestige of representing the company, and the fees attached thereto, but also for that all important railroad pass.

Although much of the routine litigation in that era dealt with land titles, collection of freight charges, sales of Santa Fe land

SANTA FE GENERAL ATTORNEYS FOR KANSAS
With Dates of Service

A. A. HURD
1881-1905

WILLIAM SMITH
1905-1933

and damages for injury to cattle, the very first entry in the oldest docket book extant deals with a type of case that is still with us. The docket reads: Atchison County, February 21st, 1880: "Suit brot [sic] by Ptff as next of Kin to Thos. Brown for $10,000.00 damages for running over and killing said Brown."

The dockets of this era indicate that Messrs. Hurd, Wood, Scott and Smith handled few cases at the trial level, leaving that to the local attorneys. They did, however, handle all cases on appeal, all cases of controversy with other railroads from the beginning, and on several occasions appeared as special attorneys aiding the prosecution of those accused of train robbery or malicious damage to railroad property. They also represented the Santa Fe before the legislature—thus giving rise to the stories about the "Legislative Passes."

Holmes' records show that in 1888 the Santa Fe Law Department at Topeka had issued 40 local attorney's passes, and by the turn of the century the list had grown to 103—hardly excessive for a railroad that was subject to suit in some 90 counties in Kansas, with more than one local attorney in the more litigation prone counties.

Whether or not any of the local attorneys were or had been members of the Kansas legislature was of no importance to Holmes, who makes no mention of that fact. Quite possibly, if not probably, many of them at some time in their careers had served in the legislature. Then, as now, such service was deemed a proper part of the background of any attorney. But if service in the legislature was a condition of appointment as local attorney,

SANTA FE GENERAL ATTORNEYS FOR KANSAS
With Dates of Service

BRUCE HURD
1933-1943

C. J. PUTT
1943-1968

one should find that the appointment ended with the cessation of legislative service. However, the records show that attorneys once appointed, served in that capacity for the balance of their professional lives. Correspondence with these attorneys deals with litigation, not legislation. I leave it to those who wish to draw conclusions from statistics to compare the list of Santa Fe local attorneys for the period 1888-1907 with the legislative rolls and draw such conclusions as they wish. This writer relies upon the records of George Holmes that shows that these local attorneys were leaders of their local bars.

The year 1907 is the breaking point, for that is the year that the Kansas Legislature restricted a railroad to the issuance of a pass good between points in Kansas to only one local attorney in any one county. This gave rise to the reference to the "good" pass, i.e., the one that could be used for a trip between points in Kansas. In counties where there was substantial litigation and the Santa Fe had a firm appointed as local attorneys, only one member of the firm could have the "good" pass. The others had passes good for interstate travel only.

This writer first met Judge William Easton Hutchinson of Garden City in 1949. Upon retiring from the Supreme Court, Judge Hutchinson joined a firm in Garden City that represented the Santa Fe. Being junior in terms of Santa Fe representation, his pass carried the restriction "good for interstate travel only." He had come to Topeka from Garden City by going to Kansas City, Mo., waiting for two hours, and then catching a train back to Topeka—all this in spite of the fact that the train from Garden

City had passed through Topeka hours earlier.

Such patience was not a common virtue among many of the local attorneys. Holmes' records show that upon the death of William Brownell in 1915, no less than six attorneys in Douglas county applied for the position of local attorney in Lawrence, all requesting the "good" pass. A classic letter in the file is from an attorney at Eureka, who advises in the first paragraph of the death of his partner, and then spends three long paragraphs stating why he should have the pass his deceased partner had that was not "restricted between stations in Kansas."

The Law Department in Topeka did obtain passes for some Kansas state officials but these were mandated by law. The legislative session of 1905 required the issuance of "free transportation" over all trains operated in Kansas to the State Board of Railroad Commissioners (later the State Corporation Commission), its attorneys, secretary, stenographers, accountants, experts or other agents. The laws of 1929 creating the State Tax Commission contained similar provisions.

And so, for 66 years in the case of the Corporation Commission, and for 42 years in the case of the Tax Commission, annual passes were issued that were superior to those held by Santa Fe employees of long years service—because the employees' passes were restricted to a few trains, whereas the legislatively mandated passes were good on all trains operated in Kansas. The advent of Amtrak in 1971 brought an end to these passes. In that year, 35 were issued to the Corporation Commission and its staff, and 24 such passes were issued to the Commissioners and staff of the State Tax Commission.

I suggest that the long years during which every Kansas railroad issued these legislatively mandated passes, is the basis for the allegations that have been made over the years on this subject. But I find no hint, no suspicion of the improper issuance of railroad passes.

As the *avant-garde* expression goes—George Holmes recorded the operations of the Law Department "warts and all." I find substantial merit to the stories about Judge Smith and his "deep shaft" bourbon supplied by a series of bootleggers. Until the passage of the Eighteenth Amendment, I find legal opinions duly recorded stoutly defending the rights of Kansas residents to receive alcoholic beverages moving in interstate commerce, leaving to the local authorities the issue of "possession."

Much of what George Holmes recorded is of interest only to attorneys—and then only to those members of the bar with a historical bent—for it deals with the mundane happenings of routine litigation. Then, as now, very little litigation involving

(Continued on p. 182)

THE BEST SHOW IN TOWN

Teddy Roosevelt and the Railroad YMCA

C. ROBERT HAYWOOD

IN EARLY December, 1902, Topekans learned that President Theodore Roosevelt had accepted an invitation to attend the Eleventh International Conference of the Railroad Department of the Young Men's Christian Association to be held in their city. Further, he was to speak and to assist in laying the cornerstone for the new YMCA building located at Fourth and Washington Streets. For the national and local leaders of the Railroad Department it was a programming coup of major significance, guaranteeing the success of the convention and the center of national press interest, at least, for one day. They were not to be disappointed.

When the Presidential Special train, pulled by a Santa Fe locomotive arrived at 6:49 P.M., registration at the conference had reached an all-time peak. A huge, demonstrative crowd was on hand to welcome the President and party with parades, bands, noise-makers and undisguised adulation. Teddy, in turn, looked upon the multitude, flashed his celebrated grin, reaffirmed his faith in the future of the country, and pronounced railroadmen, Kansans and Kansas good. Everyone thought it was bully.

It had not always been so. The visit and the acceptance of the Railroad Department's invitation had not come solely from a generous heart, filled with a compulsion to praise the work of the YMCA. It was, in fact, part of a greater strategy designed to thwart the machinations of "evil forces" and "big monied men" intent on keeping Roosevelt out of the White House in 1904. Topeka, the Santa Fe Railroad and the YMCA were to hold specific roles in Roosevelt's orchestration of this campaign strategy.

He had not relished being an "accidental president," courtesy of William McKinley's assassination. I'd rather be e-lect-ed to [the presidency] than have anything tangible of which I know," he had confided with rising staccato emphasis in his voice. So his plans were to be thorough, specific and exacting. History records his campaign fervor as a classic case of political over-kill, but in 1902 Roosevelt had no idea of how solid his support was to be. In political parlance, he ran scared. No one—no special interest was too insignificant to be ignored. "I have been told that there is a little lukewarmness among the Methodists...," Roosevelt informed a friend. "Cannot they be got at?... The Rev. Ezra Tipple, General Secretary of the Methodist Conference... is a great friend of ours. I think if you sent for him it would be a mighty good thing to do." All stops were out and the band wagon was to be driven at top speed, but always with careful purpose.

The usual "swing around the circle," which traditionally took the President briefly into New England and only as far west as Ohio, was expanded into "The Western Tour" of some 14,000 miles. Beginning on April 1, it lasted to June 3, 1903, with new adventures and new headlines at every turn. Topeka and the other midwestern capitals were particularly important since Roosevelt had cast Mark Hanna, long-time kingmaker and chairman of the National Republican Committee, as the main threat. It made little difference that Hanna did not accept the challenge, neither confirming nor denying his opposition. It was clear, however, that the strength of Hanna's organization, and, consequently, his opposition, if there was any, lay in the Midwest. "The Western Tour" was designed by the President to be a direct confrontation with the Hanna forces on their own homeground. Topeka, as the center of the Midwest, was to experience the full treatment.

The tour by rail was also more than a mere matter of transportation convenience. The Elkins Act, a much publicized weapon in Roosevelt's "trust busting" arsenal, was considered by many to be a railroad management bill, more sound than substance. Still the sound, i.e., the exposure, was important. Two days before the train arrived in Kansas, the Elkins Act made the headlines in the local press when the courts, for the second time, upheld an injunction against discriminating rebate practices. Few would miss the symbolism of Roosevelt speaking from the rear platform of one of the cars of the defeated railroad companies.

The train, itself, was a thing of beauty and power. The equipment, furnished by the Pennsylvania Railroad, consisted of a number of named cars such as the "St. James Diner," and the Pullman car "Elysium," six Pullmans, some with observation and parlor compartments, and various baggage and sleeping units for the entourage of guests, reporters, security force and retainers. The large, noisy crowds which pressed about the rear platform at each of the early stops, failed to lessen Roosevelt's anxiety or convince him that he had little to fear at the polls. "They came to see the President much as they have come to see a circus," he told John Hay. Certainly, that was part of the attraction.

Kansas University's Prof. W. W. Davis reported that as Teddy

This photo of the Presidential Special Train at Santa Fe depot, was made sometime following the dedication of the R.R.Y.M.C.A. Then the train was stopped at the East 4th street crossing.

"clacked" through his homilies on virtue, the glories of the strenuous life and the dangers of vested interests, i.e., non-Roosevelt supporters, his audiences grew more and more responsive. When the cheering reached a crescendo, it was time for the speech to end and the train to pull out. The President would step down from the car, seize the conductor's lantern and give the engineer the traditional looping high-signs to move out. As the train began to slowly move the President would trot along side until it gained momentum, then he would swing aboard, waving to the now wildly appreciative crowd. This was Teddy at his best, verifying the early press reports of how he "ran the train" from the engineer's cab, even taking a turn shoveling coal. If not a circus, it was, at least, the best show in town.

And now it was Topeka's turn.

Ostensibly Roosevelt came to speak to the young working men of the railroad and to lay a cornerstone. Topeka, not unexpectedly, had one of the largest memberships in the Railroad

Department of the YMCA with nearly 1000 members. The Santa Fe Railroad had contributed $20,000.00, about half of the total cost of the new building and lot. The laying of the cornerstone was to coincide with the meeting of the Eleventh International Conference.

The various railroads made special efforts to encourage delegates to attend. Most lines gave free passes and the Pullman Company charged only half-fare. Delegates did come from abroad (France, Denmark, Germany and Mexico), but the largest contingent arrived on a special Santa Fe train made up in Chicago consisting of seven Pullmans and four chair cars. The Topeka hotels lowered their rates and a number of civic organizations made contributions. Citizens were urged to display the flag wherever possible and to make all who attended welcome.

The result of the intensive preparations was a banner turn-out of 2000 enthusiastic delegates. The speech making began on April 30 with a welcome by Edward Wilder, Secretary-Treasurer of the Santa Fe. That was followed by other spell-binders on such topics as "Locomotive Religion," and "The Religious Life of a Railroad Man." Topeka's own Rev. Dr. Charles M. Sheldon spoke and one brave soul, even in the face of the announced appearance of the master of the subject, attempted to define "the strenuous life." In the words of the Topeka *Daily Capital*, it was "wholesome, man-to-man talk dealing with everyday responsibilities of living."

For the rest of the city, it was the President's visit which attracted interest. For them the excitement began with the arrival of the President's train at the Santa Fe depot. There a crowd of 15,000 gathered hours before the train arrived, standing in a chilling wind waiting to catch a glimpse of the great man. "The roof of every building, every tree, and every telegraph pole within three hundred yards of the building was black with humanity," the *Daily Capital* noted. Battery B began firing a twenty-one gun salute as the flag-decked train pulled to a stop. Roosevelt was on the rear platform flashing his "peculiar and inimitable smile a hundred times." The noise, naturally "tumultuous," eventually died down and the President spoke. His voice, a reporter explained, "is pitched in the tenor clef. Words rained down from him like hail beating on a tin roof. Every syllable is accented and the tag end of every word is tied to a cracker that pops and sings through the atmosphere."

From the depot the procession of thirteen carriages and much of the crowd moved to the cornerstone laying where the President spoke again, manfully handled the shovelsful of mortar and joked with the crowd. It was a brisk affair and then on to the

(Continued on p. 164)

FEATURES OF THE NEW BUILDING
A large gymnasium that doubles as an auditorium seating 350. Large reading room and three class rooms. Thirty-six bedrooms on third floor. A plunge-bath in basement, 3,400 gallons capacity; shower and tub baths including a family shower bath room. Two bowling lanes.

*The Fire That Routed
Saturday Night Bathers Was...*

A Blessing in Disguise for R.R.Y.M.C.A.

JOHN W. RIPLEY

Born in 1884 in a side-tracked baggage car, raised in an antiquated frame railroad warehouse, left homeless by a disastrous warehouse fire—those were a few of the growing pains experienced by the Topeka Railroad Young Men's Christian Association which was destined to become one of the nation's largest and most successful Railroad Y associations. The warehouse fire proved to be a blessing in disguise. From its ashes emerged a vision of a new, modern structure. That vision became a reality with the opening of the three-story headquarters on New Year's Day, 1904.

When organized in April, 1892, the association was housed temporarily in a Santa Fe combination baggage and chair car where its services were limited to Bible study classes. Later a room was provided in a dwelling on railroad property at the corner of Fourth and Washington where ten years later the "new" R.R.Y.M.C.A. headquarters would be built.

In 1885 Santa Fe's General Manager, A. A. Robinson, placed at the disposal of the association an old frame warehouse on the corner of Fourth and Adams, one block north of the present passenger depot, presently the location of the Santa Fe freight depot, presently the location of the Santa Fe freight depot. It was here at 6:30 P.M. on Saturday evening, April 26, 1902, when the building was crowded with railroad men taking their weekly baths, that a fierce roof fire put a stop to the ablutions as well as all other activities of the association at that location.

THOMAS E. PROUT, *executive secretary of the Topeka R.R.Y.M.C.A. for 25 years, was held in high regard by both rank-and-file members and Santa Fe officials. His dedication to a career of bettering the lives of railroad men earned the endorsement and financial support of Topeka's business and professional leaders.*

Born in England, Prout came to the United States when he was 20. His entire adult life was spent in Railroad Y work. He took over management of the Topeka association on August 1, 1900, after holding a similar position in Argentine, Kansas.

Ill health forced Prout to retire from the local R.R. Y.M.C.A. in August, 1925, when he moved to San Diego, Cal., where his three sons lived. He died there August 27, 1943.

At the time of the fire, the association had 820 members, according to Thomas Prout, general secretary, who two years earlier had joined the RRY staff, intent on building the membership and, hopefully, obtaining new, larger quarters. Following the fire, Prout managed to provide limited services for members in cramped quarters of the building's annex, next door.

In discussing events following the fire, Prout had nothing but high praise for Santa Fe's top brass. "President E. P. Ripley aware of our dilemma, agreed that the Santa Fe would give $20,000 toward the construction of a new building provided an equal amount would be raised in Topeka," said Prout, adding, "altogether, we raised $18,000 in Topeka, and President Ripley again came to our assistance with an additional $2,000 for furnishings." The total value of the building and land was approximately $48,000.

The location of the "new" building has repeatedly been reported erroneously in directories and in the press as at Fourth and *Adams,* and also as Fourth and *Holliday,* both on the west side of the tracks. The correct address was 705 East Fourth, *east*

(Continued on p. 92)

Born in a side-tracked baggage car in 1892—

The Santa Fe provided an old frame warehouse at 4th & Adams which served until a fire practically destroyed the structure in 1892.

Through contributions from the Santa Fe and local business and professional men, the new building was built, and occupied on Jan. 1, 1904.

(Photos on this and three following pages from Santa Fe Magazine.)

88

One of the services rendered by the R.R.Y.M.C.A. was cashing pay checks. On one day, Jan. 10, 1910, 710 checks were cashed here.

A large gymnasium served double duty as a meeting place for entertainments.

Good hearty meals at reasonable prices were served at the Y cafeteria at noon.

At noon hour, once each week during winter months, shopmen gather for socio-religious meetings under auspices of the R.R.Y.M.C.A.

90

Weekly Bible study sessions were held for Swedish employes in their own language.

Below, the association building was headquarters for talks about scientific and electrical equipment in general used by the railroad.

(Continued from p. 87)

of the Santa Fe crossing. The site is now a parking lot for customers of Whelan's, Inc. When the building was constructed by L. D. Eversole & Son (grandfather and father of Louis H. Eversole), the *Daily Capital* described it as "a model club house—one of the greatest institutions of its kind in the United States."

> **CHARLES S. GLEED,** representing directors of Santa Fe R.R., in presenting the building to the YMCA trustees. "... This is the proudest moment of my life.... I have wondered for years how it would seem to be a Rockefeller or a Carnegie and give away libraries, colleges, schools and Y.M.C.A. buildings just as an ordinary man gives away cigars. And here I am, doing it."
>
> **GOVERNOR OF KANSAS W. J. BAILEY**
> "... The Santa Fe railroad never made a better investment to the course of its existence than it did when it gave $20,000 to help erect this fine building...."

The first two floors of the building were designed for general services such as reading rooms, offices and meeting rooms. The third or top floor was devoted entirely to 36 bedrooms.

The big attraction of the lower floor, (actually the basement), according to the *Capital*, was the plunge bath. "This is made of concrete and holds 3,400 gallons which may be kept at any temperature by pipes coming from the furnace room."

By the end of the first decade the local R.R.Y.M.C.A.'s membership had reached 1,622 of whom, Secretary Prout reported, "about 400 are Roman Catholics; 400 members of some evangelical church and over 800 having no church preference."

Aside from the recreational facilities provided by the association—bowling alleys, swimming pool, billiard tables, etc., an excellent cafeteria was heavily patronized by shopmen and trainmen. Classes were conducted in rate-making, penmanship, spelling, mechanical drawing and arithmetic. In support of these educational courses and other activities, the Santa Fe contributed annually approximately $2,500.

On November 2, 1927, nearly 25 years after the opening of the association's headquarters at 704 East Fourth, it was announced, not unexpectedly, that the building was to be closed immediately. A membership drive, held the previous year, had flopped. Membership rolls had dwindled ever since the end of World War I. The closing was attributed to several causes—changing life styles, changing population in the community and, importantly, the Santa Fe's announced plans to build a spacious community center at nearby Ripley Park.

For several years after the closing the building remained vacant. During the depression years of the 1930's the National Youth Administration leased the place as a dormitory and training school for youths of this area. The structure was razed in 1940.

EDWARD GRAFSTROM
Hero of the 1903 Flood

BARBARA ELDER WELLER

ALTHOUGH it was not Topeka's last, the spring flood of 1903 may have been the worst in the city's history. Among the many lives lost during that incredible event was that of Edward Grafstrom, Chief Mechanical Engineer for the A.T. & S.F. in Topeka. In that capacity, he was principally responsible for saving the Santa Fe bridge from the flood waters.

Edward Grafstrom

He did so by anchoring the bridge with ten locomotives and several cars loaded with steel rails. Since the Santa Fe was one of only two bridges still standing when the waters abated, saving the bridge was no mean feat. However, it was the hundreds of lives he saved that earned Grafstrom the title "Hero of the 1903 Flood."

The waters of the Kaw river and Soldier creek began to rise appreciably on May 28. By May 30 both streams had overflowed their banks and joined forces in North Topeka. People began working around the clock to rescue as many of the stranded North Topekans as possible. To advance this cause, Edward Grafstrom

Prior to its last tragic trip, Grafstrom's boat unloaded refugees in South Topeka.

designed and built a side-wheel steam launch. Grafstrom and a crew of volunteers, all local Santa Fe men, rescued an estimated 200 North Topeka residents, trapped by the flood.

During the launch's last trip of the day, on June 2, 1903, it struck a floating tree, capsized and sank. Those on board were G. W. Bonney, William Havens, Frank Ecclesdon, Clarence Heer, Harry Hobson, chief signal engineer, Frank W. Thomas, who was later to become supervisor of the Santa Fe's apprentice system, and Grafstrom, the only casualty. One survivor reported seeing Grafstrom swimming behind the others, then suddenly disappear. Known to be an excellent swimmer, Grafstrom may have been struck by floating debris.

Three years later to the day, June 2, 1906, a bronze tablet honoring Grafstom was presented to the State Historical Society, then located in the State Capitol building. The plaque measuring three by five feet, was provided by "a group of Chicago railroad men and railroad mechanical engineers of the United States." An ornamental wrought iron pedestal to support the plaque was designed by the state architect, John Stanton, and made in the Santa Fe shops under the personal supervision of John Purcell, then shop superintendent and a close friend of Grafstom. In addition to detailing his heroic deed, the inscription read:

"In memory of Edward Grafstrom, son of Col. and Mrs. Cecilia Grafstom. Born in Motola, Sweden, December 19, 1862. He was educated at Orebro University and Boros Istiture of Technology, where at the age of nineteen, he received the degree of mechanical engineer."

The tablet concluded, "His noble personality endeared him to all. This tablet is erected in grateful admiration of his heroic sacrifice in giving his life to save others."

J. R. Koontz

Frank Jarrell

*Topeka Capital,
August 10, 1910*

A PRESS BUREAU FOR THE SANTA FE

New Department Will Be Established Under Supervision of J. R. Koontz, With Frank Jarrell Active Head.

KEEP PUBLIC INFORMED

Will See That Railroad Is Not Misrepresented and Try to Give People Clearer Understanding.

In order that the people may be given the news from the view of the railroads, President E. P. Ripley of the Santa Fe has established a press bureau which will have charge of the public side of the doings of the Santa Fe from now on. This work will be done under the direction of J. R. Koontz, general freight agent of this city. He will have as his assistant and head of the bureau, Frank Jarrell, a former Topeka newspaper man.

The new work will not remove any duties from Mr. Koontz as the new department is added to his present duties. Mr. Ripley has done this believing that as the freight department is the one most effected by public opinion, it should fall to the manager of that department to make friends for the system through the newspapers.

"The first thing the department will do," said Mr. Koontz last night, "is to make friends among the newspaper men. We are anxious to come to a full understanding with the public with regard to matters concerning the road and believe that the newspapers are the means of our doing so. Our first interests will be to find out if there are any points misunderstood by the newspapers or by us and to set both them and ourselves right.

"This move is an attempt on the part of the Santa Fe to get into a better condition of friendship with the public at large. While the Santa Fe has not been at variance with the public, other roads have and we wish to avoid such a condition of affairs. There is nothing political in this move. We do not intend to make it such. We will watch the newspapers closely and if we think a matter relative to the railroads is not being presented to the public with all the fairness of an open discussion we will be ready to issue statements of our side of the question. Besides this we will give out from time to time any information we think will be of use or interest to the public."

Mr. Jarrell, who will begin his new duties next Monday, was for years a political reporter on the Topeka Capital and the Topeka Herald. He was at one time city editor of the Capital. Three years ago he purchased the Holton Reporter which he sold recently. Mr. Jarrell has many friends in this city who will be glad to hear of his promotion.

Topeka's Santa Fe Roundhouses

JACK W. TRAYLOR

To the railroaders who operate and service the motive power of their company, the roundhouse traditionally has been the headquarters of their work. This is less true today when diesel locomotives often pull freight trains hundreds of miles without a service stop and pause just briefly on the main line at a division point about every 130 miles or so for a quick crew change. But during the age of the steam engine, and even into the post-World War II diesel era to some extent, every town of any great significance on a railroad had its own roundhouse where locomotives came for servicing. Topeka was no exception as the city actually had two Santa Fe roundhouses.

Why were locomotive service buildings constructed in a circular configuration rather than square or rectangular? It was a matter of space and time efficiency. The area approaching a rectangular building, particularly a large one, would require a mass of tracks and switches fanning out to each stall. But with a roundhouse, the hostler (the employee who operates locomotives in the vicinity of the roundhouse) could simply run an engine onto the turntable, wait for the table operator to point it to the correct stall, and then run it into the roundhouse.

The first Santa Fe roundhouse in Topeka was constructed in 1868. Located to the east of the present passenger station, across the tracks, it was in line with Fifth Street and its opening faced to the west. Originally it contained only six stalls. Three additional stalls were added in the early 1880s and six more were constructed in the mid-eighties[1].

As locomotive size increased, Santa Fe officials decided to build a larger roundhouse closer to the main shops, northeast of First and Adams streets. Perhaps they envisioned the need for two roundhouses as they built the newer structure in 1882, while the original one was still standing. Nevertheless, sometime late in the nineteenth century they decided that the new roundhouse would fill their requirements for locomotive servicing, so they relegated the older one to storage duties. But for a time, the company conduted an interesting experiment with its first Topeka roundhouse.

Sometime during the late nineteenth century, before more

advanced methods were adopted for controlling the temperature in railway refrigerator cars, company officials tested the effect of placing cars, loaded with fresh fruit enroute from the western states to points in the East, in the old roundhouse for a few hours. These tests were conducted during the winter months. The roundhouse had a fine steam heating system and the hope was that warming the fruit during a Topeka stopover would help preserve its freshness. Unfortunately the opposite occurred. The fruit withstood the continuous cold of the outside winter weather better than it did the drastic fluctuation in temperature of a Topeka warmup followed by the sudden chilling when the car was thrust back out into the cold. This spelled the end of the first roundhouse's usefulness, other than for storage, but the building was not razed until about 1910[2].

The newer of the two roundhouses entered service in 1882 and was the main Santa Fe locomotive servicing building in Topeka until the end of the steam engine era in the mid-1950s. It was positioned so that its open end was on the south, and in the center there was a 75 ft., 1000-ton turntable. Originally it contained 36 stalls, each with a pit between the rails so a worker could service the underside of a locomotive. In 1937 the east 18 stalls were converted to storage space, and the west 18 were reroofed and a foreman's office and locker room were installed in part of that section[3].

In 1941 the east 18 stalls were dismantled. Five of the tracks leading into these stalls were kept for storage for steam engines then being converted from coal-burning to oil-burning in the Topeka shops.

In 1942 an ominous event occurred—an inspection pit at the roundhouse had to be enlarged to accommodate a diesel switch engine then being used in the Topeka yards[4]. If the local railroaders could have looked into the future, they would have seen that the diesels would take over the Santa Fe in Topeka within a decade and a half, and the roundhouse would be gone in a little more than two decades.

This author, the son of a retired Santa Fe fuel foreman, W.B. Traylor of Emporia, who worked more than 30 years servicing both steam and diesel locomotives at the Emporia and Topeka roundhouses, has a personal interest in this story. During most of his years with the company, my father served as a "relief man," filling in at various points around the division for employees on their days off and vacations. For many years he worked two days each week at the Topeka roundhouse, normally commuting by train from his home in Emporia. His duties included unloading the heavy, black residual oil which the steam engines burned, and

Upper right, the central portion of the first roundhouse built in 1868. Lower left, Topeka roundhouse from photo made about 1920.

later unloading diesel fuel for the diesel locomotives. He also filled the engines with fuel and sand. Sand is used by all locomotives for traction where steel wheels pull against steel rails. In a recent interview, he described some of the activities connected with the Topeka roundhouse during the last twenty years of its existence—the post-World War II era[5].

Topeka was never a busy division point like Emporia, Newton, or Wellington, where fast transcontinental freights paused for engine servicing. Hence, the Topeka roundhouse rarely received visits from the biggest, fastest, and most modern motive power on the line. But it was home to several switch engines that worked in the Topeka yards and to one or two light-duty engines that pulled branch line locals out of the city. Most prominent of the latter category was steam engine #1079, which for many years pulled a local train on a daily round trip between Topeka and Alma by way of Burlingame, Harveyville, and Eskridge.

The late 1940s and early 1950s were a time of transformation from steam to diesel on the Santa Fe and other railroads. This was one of the greatest technological revolutions in the history of American industry, and during this period the Topeka yards and roundhouse were host to a mixture of steam and diesel locomotives. At the end of World War II, steam was still dominant in Topeka. Steam switch engines, which worked out of the local

(Continued on p. 166)

*Santa Fe's Ultra Limited
Passenger Service*

The Business Cars

BOBBIE PRAY

"'Business car!' What pictures those words probably excite in the mind's eye.... Extreme opulence. Lavish parties. Trips about the country in care-free manner while occupants view the 'common man' from their vantage point in the splendor of the observation room."*

The business car is still alive today, but the image of grandeur has been replaced by one of a more practical nature. The term "private car" once interchangeable with "business car," is no longer deemed an appropriate title by the Santa Fe railroad. The business car is what its name states—strictly business, and that functional name is reflected in their decor. Practical, compact, and more comfortable than their lavish predecessors, they reflect the attitude of the Santa Fe executive.

Until recently the business cars were based in Chicago, but are now managed and maintained in Topeka. There are 30 such cars; five business cars, six sleeper cars, and the remaining are dining and lounge cars. Todays business cars are self-contained and run on two motors which alternate to provide electricity. They can be hauled by freight or passenger trains anywhere in the Santa Fe system.

The business cars are designed for business, complete with an office area with a desk for the executive's secretary. Dials on the desk reveal the train speed, the outside temperature and other information. Telephones have also been installed. In the living quarters, furnishings are not plush but have been designed for comfort. Beds fold out Pullman style from the walls, and drawers and closets have been fitted in a neat compact style. There is a bedroom for the secretary and a larger executive bedroom with an adjoining room. The dining room seats eight comfortably, and the kitchen consists of a serving counter connecting to a small galley. The floors are covered with short shag carpeting, and bathrooms are either compact foldaway facilities or are separated from the bedroom areas. A small room with two bunk beds is provided for the crew.

Today a crew of 12 supervised by Leo LaRue, operates the business cars of the Santa Fe line. They often work a 10 to 12 hour day, and then are off for 10 days to two weeks. Crew members

---
*Frank M. Ellington & Joseph W. Stine *(Passenger Train Equipment of the A.T. & S.F. Ry.)*

Topeka Capital-Journa[l]

David Beard, left, retired business car attendant, and Leo La Rue, supervisor of business car attendants.

SANTA FE BUSINESS CAR ATTENDANTS & CHEFS, 1950

Standing, from left, Warren Nobles, T. B. Blunt, John Everett Sr., Albertus Pogue, Anthony Philips, Wallace Blackburn, Leo LaRue (supervisor), Bernir Cox, Edward Bryant, Abel Hayes, A. R. McDaniel, David H. Beard, Jr., who furnished this photo. Seated, from left, Claude Mothell, William E. Allen, George M. Lee, William A. (Doc) Gilbert, Orlanda Atkinson.

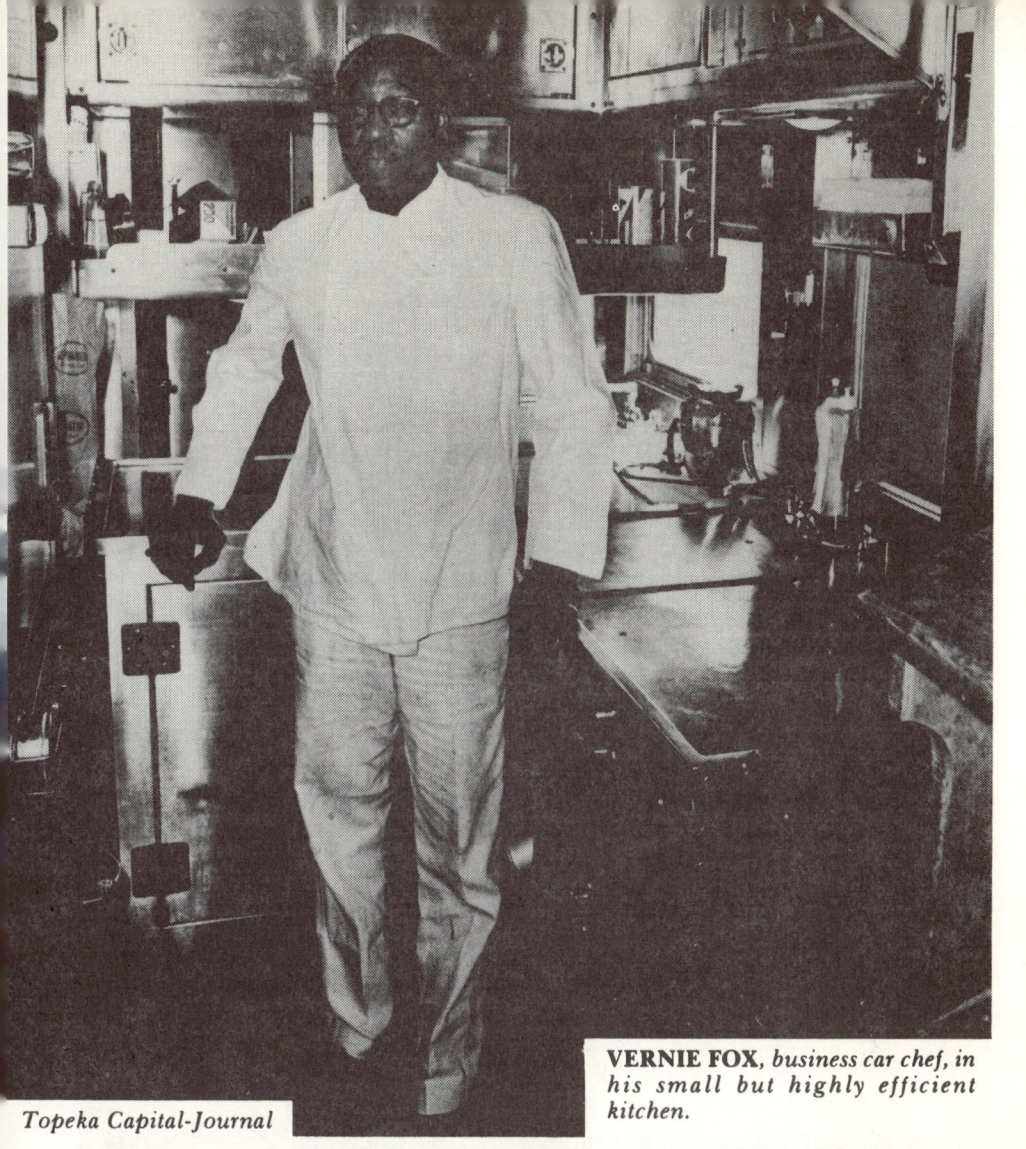

VERNIE FOX, *business car chef, in his small but highly efficient kitchen.*

Topeka Capital-Journal

can easily name many prominent figures who have been special passengers in the business cars over the years. Presidents, dignitaries, and famous entertainers have been among those who have taken advantage of the comfort and special services of these railway cars.

While it is true that across the country company planes have become a more popular means of travel for the American executive, the business railroad car has not fallen into obsolescense. Its forerunner, the plush "private car" that carried executives from one end of the country to the other in an elegant style, is however gone forever. Rich wood paneling, shining brass beds, and sparkling chandeliers have become mere items of the past.

Photo, Ray Hilner

FROM DINING CAR TO BUSINESS CAR TO BUNK CAR

In 1890 when Barney & Smith, car builders, delivered an elegant dining car to the Santa Fe, it was designated as Dining Car No. 7, but later it was re-named No. 1404. After nearly 20 years service as a Fred Harvey diner, it was converted in 1909 at the Topeka shops to become an equally elegant Business Car No. 18 which for years was assigned to the General Manager. After a half century the Santa Fe, in 1961, again sent No. 18 to the Topeka shops, not to be salvaged but for rebuilding into a Bunk car, a home away from home for Santa Fe mechanics.

Photo Frank M. Ellington

GREAT BOOM FOR THE NEW SANTA FE SHOPS.

The Shops Make Headlines

WARREN TAYLOR

Somewhere in the myriad columns of the *Commonwealth* newspaper for July 31, 1878, appeared this announcement: "At last the Atchison, Topeka & Santa Fe Railroad Company has purchased of J. R. Mulvane and Theo. Terry, the King Bridge Shops, that have so long laid idle. The railroad company pay [sic] $19,600 cash for them, and have bought of Mr. Mulvane two thousand dollars worth of lots near the buildings. They will go to work at once and repair the shops and occupy them. This is a big thing for Topeka."

Here, in hardly more than twelve lines, was an announcement of the beginning, a genesis if you will, of the huge Santa Fe complex that was to play such a powerful role in the development of that industry; the shops. Greater news of the railroad would come as years passed, but never again would its effect be so important or less heralded.

The Santa Fe shops, being the backbone of the industry, would always produce good news stories. Generally the reporter's accolades in the early days, were piled high and descriptive phrases ran rampant. In September of 1881 a *Commonwealth* writer told of a proposed "great increase" in the Santa Fe shops. He describes the size of the extension and tells us the cost will be

103

Main building of the defunct King Bridge Co., which was acquired by the Santa Fe as its first shops. (From a stereograph.)

about $200,000; however, the crowning glory of his brief article rests in these lines: "It is a great thing for the city and the State ... these new shops are worth more to the city than the government building, the capitol, insane asylum and reform school. Topekans will feel good this morning." Indeed, they must have.

On March 13, 1882 there appeared in the Topeka *Daily Capital* a small one column article captioned "A Topeka Train." The story tells of the construction in the shops of a complete passenger train, "... from the 'snout' of the cowcatcher to the signal lamp on the rear platform of the sleeper ... " This, we are told, is "... the first passenger train manufactured west of the Mississippi," and was "... made in Topeka, by Topeka mechanics ... " The author continues by describing the engine, named "William B. Strong."* He tells us the cylinders were 18 x 26 inches and 69 inch drivers; these sizes were reportedly unheard of in passenger engines. Could one blame the writer if a note of pride seemed to flow from his pen?

---
*President of AT & SF Railroad 1881-89.

By 1897, when Santa Fe was celebrating its 25th anniversary, Topeka *State Journal* headlines called out, "Finest Locomotive in the West, Planned and Built in Topeka." We are told of engine No. 50, "... built for mountain work ... It's weight, ready for business, ... 122½ tons," the story continues, "John Player, master mechanic of the Santa Fe road said, 'We can build just as good engines at the shops as can be built anywhere ... There isn't a more competent set of mechanics in any shop [than] we have right here ... " Player also states later in the article that if he had his way all engines used by the line would be constructed in Topeka.

A short two years later, in 1899, Player was again a featured news item along with his new tandem compound passenger locomotive. An article, headlined: "Santa Fe Tandem Compound Engine Being Tested," and "Locomotive Designed by Superintendent John Player," opens with these lines, "The new tandem compound passenger locomotive, No. 697, designed by Superintendent of Machinery John Player, has been completed at the Santa Fe shops ... as soon as it is in good running

MECHANICAL OFFICIALS AND OFFICE FORCE, TOPEKA, IN 1885
Clem Hackney, who then was assistant superintendent of machinery, is seated in the comfortable swivel chair. Standing, from left to right—J. J. Wehe, Ernest Mueller, Ed Knight, Charles A. Coons, Harry Ammon, C. E. Cain (chief clerk), John Scott, Ed Conklin and W. H. Bisslan. Mr. Cain afterward became quite well known in the railroad world, and at one time was general manager of the Rock Island. Mr. Wehe is at present in the plumbing business in Topeka, and Mr. Coons when last heard of was in the supply business in Chicago.

Chief Mechanical Officers of the A., T. & S. F. Ry. Company from its Inception to December 31, 1941

From Santa Fe Today, *No. 4, Nov. 30, 1946*

Harry V. Faries
Master Mechanic
July 1, 1870—Nov. 30, 1878

George Hackney
Superintendent of Machinery
Nov. 1, 1878—July 1, 1889

Harvey Middleton
Superintendent of Machinery
July 1, 1889—May 31, 1890

W. F. Buck
Superintendent Motive Power
Jan. 1, 1908—Jan. 31, 1912

John Purcell
Assistant to Vice-President
May 1, 1912—Dec. 31, 1941

John Player
Superintendent of Machinery
June 1, 1890—Jan. 1, 1902

George R. Henderson
Superintendent Motive Power
Jan. 1, 1902—July 31, 1903

Alfred Lovell
Superintendent Motive Power
July 31, 1903—Dec. 1, 1907

SANTA FE SUPERVISORS IN MOTIVE POWER AND SHOPS, 1921
First row, from left, Geo. G. Elloitt, Wm. Kienenger, J. H. Frizell, W. L. Jury, Geo. B. Fraser, J. H. Armstrong, Jos. Aigner. Second row, C. Goulding, Jos. Mullin, H. Goodrich, C. Marin, Jas. Gibbons, J. Lowrie, Geo. H. Gallety. Third row, A. G. Bender, F. C. Oberer, W. P. Davies, R. D. Humphries, J. McGinnis, Wm. Norton. Fifth row, A. Snyder, C. Havens, F. Skidmore, A. Domme, F. Martin, Wm. Herer, Geo. Real. Photo from John Holm.

A huge Mallet tandem locomotive assembled in Topeka Santa Fe shops dwarfs an early model engine.

order, it will be placed on some of the fast passenger runs where speed and strength are necessary requisites." Obviously Player's wish of a few years before was becoming reality.

The turn of the century saw the Santa Fe expanding more and more. By May, 1900, headlines in the *Capital* called out, "Great Boom for the Santa Fe Shops." At this time the railroad was asking the citizens of Topeka to back "a bond proposition to secure funds to purchase the site for the new Santa Fe shops." The shops, when completed, were to cost from $350,000 to $400,000. At this point the city was asked to raise about $70,000 to help complete the deal for the land. Of course progress meant more employment and it was estimated that from 1,000 to 2,000 new jobs would be created as a result of this plan. The citizens were agreeable and the proposition passed.

"The Santa Fe Has Built, in the Topeka Shops, the Largest Locomotive in the World." 1911 was a good year for the Santa Fe Railway. Headlines, like the one above, gave loud testimony to the giant strides being taken by this industry. In the Topeka shops gargantuan Mallet Articulated Locomotives were being constructed. Prior to building their own, the A.T. & S.F. had purchased its Mallets from the Baldwin Locomotive Works. But, always interested in reducing operational cost, a decision was made to build its own. The author of an article in the April, 1911,

Assembly line in the locomotive department Topeka, about 1911.

Santa Fe Employes' Magazine gives the best description of the Mallet evolution, "In the Santa Fe shops at Topeka two Prairie-type freight engines recently were combined into a Mallet for experimental purposes:... The rebuilt Mallet... is the largest locomotive in the world:... The locomotive... is 122 feet long. Oil will be used for fuel, the only effective way in which to maintain the required steam pressure of 225 pounds:... The locomotive rests on ten pairs of driving wheels, two leading under the pilot and two trailers under the cab, making twenty-four wheels under the locomotive itself, and twelve under the tender. The weight of the locomotive alone is estimated at 750,000 pounds—easily the largest and most powerful locomotive ever built." An accompanying photograph bears out the written description of this behemoth.

April 30, 1904 found the Santa Fe machinists, a union group in the open shop, dissatisfied and threatening strike. The *Capital* headline for that day, however, quiets the storm by declaring, "No Strike in Topeka." For a day or so all seemed well, until on May 2nd when all Santa Fe employees reporting for work found themselves locked out. Anticipating a call for a general strike, the railroad was one step ahead and locked the gates. "Santa Fe Shops Closed," read the headline.

Next day the *Journal* announced, "Shops Are Reopened." The striking machinists were still out but all others were reporting as usual. The headlines continued to report a stalemate, "Still Hold Out;" "Machinists Will Try to Compromise;" "Santa Fe Serves Notice on Machinists;" "Men Hired for Work;" until by May 19, when the *Capital* reported, "Affairs Are Quiet." In this article a third vice-president is quoted, "We will have no dealings whatever with the strikers in the future. So far as we are concerned the affair is ended." And so the great strike of '04 slipped quietly into oblivion.

1911 seemed to be a banner year for good Santa Fe shop stories. The July issue of the *Santa Fe Employes' Magazine* devoted 38 pages of story, pictures and maps to "The Santa Fe In Topeka." Author Tom MacRae prefaced his article in part with the following: "Among the largest and most completely equipped railroad shop plants in the United States is that owned by the Santa Fe and located in Topeka. Few people, even in the service of the road, realize the magnitude of these works or the organization necessary for their proper operation. In this article an attempt is made to give some idea of their extent and their value to the system:..." And indeed an idea, a multitude of ideas, is given. This article is recommended reading for shop buffs before and to 1911.

Not to be outdone by the company magazine the *Capital* sent one of its reporters to do an article entitled "A Glimpse of the Santa Fe Shops." A second, or under headline reads, "Some of the Things of Interest to Be Seen in an Afternoon's Hurried Visit to Topeka's Largest Institution." Although not 38 pages in length the author managed to paint an interesting picture of the shops and their workings. Perhaps he stated best the feeling of pride felt by most Topekans: "Other cities are known for their industries of which they are proud... but here in the shops of the Santa Fe in the city of Topeka, with 50,000 inhabitants, are built the largest locomotives in the world, modern passenger and freight cars, motor cars which make the world sit up and take notice...." If anyone could not conceive of the size of the shop area the author gave a verbal diagram: "The shops and yards of the road begin properly at Sixth street and extend to the Kaw river, then from Adams street, they extend two miles east to the old starch factory...."

As World War I drew to a close the employees of the Santa Fe were deciding it was time for total unionization. The *Capital* told the story well in February of 1918. "Organization of Union

An army of predominently black men who found work at the Topeka shops following the 1922 strike. Photo from Clovis N. Scott.

Shops Well Under Way," called the headline, followed by, "Santa Fe Employes, 1,5000 Strong, Take Preliminary Steps in Enthusiastic Meeting at City Auditorium." The article described in detail the meeting held the night before and the excitement of the participants. As all railroads were then under government control it was the best time for the A.F.L. to present it's package. The non-union shop was doomed at the A.T. & S. F.

Hard times crept into the yards of the railroad in 1921. "Slack business on the road is the reason... for the reduction.... There isn't enough repair work to keep the present force busy." This was the explantation given by W. D. Deveney, superintendent of the shops, when headlines read, "435 Shop Men Here Let Out by Santa Fe." The order, handed down in early March, was to affect 15% of the workers in the Topeka shops. The gloomy article continued: "A similar reduction of 15 per cent at the beginning of next month is under consideration." Bad times; hard times; yes, the war was over we had returned to normalcy.

April, 1921, brought more news. for those employees lucky enough to have missed being layed off the month before, the railroad announced a wage reduction. "Operating expenses, rentals and taxes" were the reasons given. Employees were still working for war scale salary and the railroad said, simply, it could not afford it.

"Railroad Shopmen Walk Out as the Clock Strikes 10," called the headline. On July 1, 1922, 1,000 workers from all areas of the shop laid down their tools and walked off the job. The headlines continued, "Men Quit Work in Orderly Manner Amid Cheers of Sympathizers—Numerous Meeting[s] Held During Day."

(Continued on p. 179)

SANTA FE'S GENERAL OFFICES TODAY

EAST SIDE, WEST SIDE . . .

All Around the Town— Santa Fe General Offices

AILEEN MALLORY

FROM a couple of rooms above a butcher shop, to a magnificent 10-story building—that's the story of the Santa Fe general offices.

Early in 1868 the Atchison, Topeka & Santa Fe rented its first office space above Costa & Hanley's meat market, 503 Kansas Avenue, present site of the New England Building. The first office force consisted of but two men, M. L. Sargent, secretary and paymaster, and a clerk, James Knox.

As the railroad extended westward other towns along the line became rivals for the location of the Santa Fe's headquarters —its offices and shops. According to Topeka's first banker and postmaster, Fry W. Giles, writing in his authoritative history, MY 30 YEARS IN TOPEKA, 1854-1884, "When Emporia reportedly offered $200,000 for the offices and shops, considerable apprehension was entertained that Topeka might lose these important advantages." But if the officials of the railroad ever considered the offer, a penalty clause in Topeka's bonds issued to assist the new railroad, proved a deterrent. (See p. 5)

In 1872 the general offices were moved from 503 Kansas Avenue to the second floor of the newly completed combination freight and passenger depot at the southwest corner of Fourth Street and Washington Avenue,* on the west side of the railroad tracks. Sharing the second floor of the 32 x 63 ft. frame structure was a lunch counter which in 1876 was taken over by Fred Harvey as the first unit of what was to become the celebrated Harvey System of restaurants and hotels along the Santa Fe main line. (See p. 8)

After about six years the overcrowded general offices were relocated (in 1878) to the imposing three-story building on the northwest corner of Sixth and Kansas, taking over the second floor. Soon, when additional space was needed for the thriving Santa Fe Railroad, an annex was established immediately across West Sixth Street in the Spencer building (later known as the Bates building), on the southwest corner of the intersection.

How a Santa Fe office boy "used his head to save his heels," was described a half-century later by former office boy, Clarence

---
*Washington Avenue, a north-south street, one block east of Adams, was vacated by the city "for railroad purposes."

The first general office, 503 Kansas Ave., upstairs over a meat market.

S. Bowman, an official of the Federal Securities Co., Topeka, in the *State Journal,* April 24, 1929.

"I stretched a heavy cord across Sixth Street to a window ledge of our offices on the second floor. The cord was passed over a grooved pulley and returned to our building where it passed over another pulley and returned to our building."

It was no different than an endless backyard clothes line. Letters or memos clipped to the cord were transferred without effort, between the main office and the annex.

Patrick Walsh, general baggage agent for more than 50 years, is credited with designing an overhead trolley wire, basket and pulleys for interoffice mail at the general offices.

THE RED BRICK BUILDING

Naturally, as the railroad grew, so did the office force. By 1884, the system was comprised of almost 2,800 miles in six states and Sonora, Mexico. There were 325 employees and a monthly payroll of $25,000.

Topekans watched the 4-story red brick building go up at 9th

General Offices and Land Department were located in this building on the northwest corner of 6th & Kansas Ave. Convenient to the horse-car line.

The general office annex was located directly south, across Sixth, on the southwest corner.

and Jackson in 1883-84. The price tag was $187,000. James McGoulgal of Leavenworth was the contractor.

Described as "the costliest office block in Topeka," the "massive building was elegantly furnished throughout." It was considered to be the most solidly built building in the capitol city. Giles described it as "a most substantial and commodious edifice indeed."

Five years later, the building was extensively damaged by fire. During restoration a fifth floor was added. A wing, extending from the south end to the east, was added 17 years later, in 1910.

Paul Cooper, Topeka artist, reminisces about the old red brick building. As a boy, he frequently went with his father, a clerk in the freight auditor's office, on Sunday visits to the offices.

Here's how Cooper remembers it:

"After mounting the many stone steps to the entrance, we would pass through the large heavy doors. The elevator *cage* was located near the heavy doors. Ernie, the friendly old black operator, would take us up to the 5th floor. It had small windows, high up on the wall, for ventilation. There were no desks, just high bookkeepers' counters with stools. A single light bulb with a shade hung above the tables.

"The *boss man*, freight auditor (probably C. S. Sutton) was separated by a glassed enclosure. He was allowed to puff

The red brick building before the fire. Steam dummy trains passed along Jackson street.

on cigars but the clerks were not allowed to smoke. Each man was provided with a cuspidor, and they were in general use.

"I would while away the time using soft pencils on scratch pads, and trying out all the rubber stamps."

Eventually the red brick building became outgrown, too. By 1910, the number of general office employees had increased to 979, their total monthly payroll to $72,000. The system's mileage had reached 9,961 miles.

THE NEW WHITE BRICK BUILDING

A new 10-story structure, of white glazed brick, was built south of the red brick building in 1910. Crossing the "bridges" from one building to another probably gave employees a "breath of fresh air."

Fifteen years later, in 1925, this structure became the south section of a new building. Employees of the "red brick" were given temporary quarters nearby in the Masonic Temple on 10th Street between Jackson and Van Buren.

One of the construction workers, an 18-year-old who was glad to get a temporary job, tells about his experience.

"I especially remember the view from up there," he says, "and the American flag flying high above the building as we worked. I'd climb all over the place, even above the top floor, without giving it a second thought, then. Now, you could never get me up that high for a minute," the 72-year-old admits.

He tells about several accidents, none fatal, fortunately. One time when the cement chute broke, an iron worker was hurt but was back to work in a few weeks.

Another time a man fell down the elevator shaft! Luckily he hung onto the four-by-four he had taken out of the forms. The board got caught in the shaft crosswise and held the worker from plunging to the bottom.

"Although he was bruised a little and pretty sore for a few days, the guy didn't miss work," the elderly gentleman recalls.

At last the impressive 10-story building was finished. It was heralded as "the largest structure in the U. S. devoted strictly to general offices of a single railroad company."

The May, 1925 issue of the *Santa Fe Magazine*, Chicago, devoted 22 pages to the new Topeka general office building. There were photographs of personnel, floor plans and detailed descriptions.

On April 18, 1925, people thronged to the formal opening. There were tours and refreshments. The assembly room was festive with floral tributes and paintings of the Southwest. (Remember the Santa Fe calendars through the years?)

An advertisement from Santa Fe Magazine, February, 1912

Dear Santa Fe Boys:—Starting west over the line, I made my first stop at Topeka. After shaking hands with the boys around the Shops, I called at the

SANTA FE GENERAL OFFICES

to pay our respects to the General Manager and his executive force. You notice I said "our respects." Representing all the boys on the line, I have always tried to encourage that spirit of good brotherhood, not only between ourselves, but between us and the splendid Officers above us. Perhaps not many of you boys ever get over to Topeka, you are too busy holding down a job out on the line—by the way that reminds me again that I don't like that expression. I think a man worth while will "hold the job up."

Railroad King Overalls and Jackets

are greatly in favor over here. I was thinking how nice it would look to have this whole General Office force wear them — suppose, of course, we'd have to get up a special style for the girls. Our General Office building is the tallest and handsomest in Topeka—and Topeka is the Capital and best town in Kansas. Our Pay Roll in Topeka is about five times any other in the town and one of the largest in the state. Everybody is very busy here. The boys at the Shops are getting in overtime and happy. All well. I'm going on West tomorrow. Will drop a line. In haste,

R. R. King

Chief of Uniforms

Genuine Railroad King Overalls have RED SEAL in the suspender crossing, the guarantee mark of the makers—R. L. McDonald Mfg. Co. St. Joseph, Mo. If you do not find the goods at your dealers, drop us a line—it will prove worth your while

Railroad King
1180
McDonald Make
HIGH-BACK
OVERALLS

The General Office building in 1910

and after the completion of the Kansas State Memorial Building in May, 1914.

Thus, in 1925, the stately white building became a landmark on Topeka's skyline.

In 1978 the annual payroll was $53,760,036 for the Topeka office and shop, with a total of 3,078 employees. (The shops and offices are about evenly divided in number of employees.)

Santa Fe employees have seen the seasons come and go on the statehouse grounds, a pastoral view for a downtown location.

Any company is more than an office building, of course. It's the people inside.

"The Santa Fe has touched the lives of so many Topekans that it staggers the mind," reminds Gertrude Lewis Wharton, retired special representative, Public Relations Department.

"The Santa Fe has contributed to the lifestyle of many families, from building maintenance crews, business car crews, middle management to top level executives—the list is endless."

Here is how Frank MacLennan, former *Topeka State Journal*, publisher, expressed it, in a 1925 tribute:

"Topeka lives through the Santa Fe. Practically half her people are directly sustained by the Santa Fe Company and the other half indirectly.

"The Santa Fe, through its prominent men, has always been a vital factor in the business, social and welfare life of Topeka."

TOPEKA'S "MILLION DOLLAR BLOCK" *featuring two Santa Fe office buildings, was brought up-to-date by some German lithographer by simply adding two automobiles, paste-ups, to the original negative.*

Atchison, Topeka & Santa Fé Railroad Co.

PAY ROLL of 2nd V.P. & G.M. office

A. A. Robinson, February, 1892

No.	NAMES	OCCUPATION			AMOUNT	Check No
1	Curtis Chas. H.	Asst	24	25	211.05	
2	Lewis Benjamin J.	Office Asst		Mo.	190.00	
3	Wells Joseph E.	Secretary		"	135.00	
4	Nowers John W.	Clerk		"	125.00	
5	Sibley Joseph R.	"		"	120.00	
6	Jansen Wm. B.	"		"	85.00	
7	Hixon Wm. J.	Stenographer		"	85.00	
8	Nicoll David J.	"		"	85.00	
9	Norton Tristram	"		"	75.00	
10	Merrick J. Frank	"		"	80.00	
11	Hoener Albert M.	Clerk		"	65.00	
12	Tasker Henry B.	"		"	55.00	
13	Ranson Chester L.	"		"	50.00	
14	Felts G. W.	"	15	75	38.80	
15	Lautz Henry	Office Boy		Mo.	20.00	
16						
17					**1419.85**	

Thanks to our friend, Charles "Bud" Gobel, we are able to reproduce the February 1892 payroll of General Manager A. A. Robinson's office force. It includes the very first monthly paycheck of a new office boy—all of $20.00 for 16-year old Henry Lautz who 54 years later retired as general manager of Santa Fe's Eastern Lines.

The Stores Department

JAMES D. WALLACE

THE SANTA FE Stores Department, the organization for which my Dad (Thomas W. Wallace) and Aunt Mary (Mary Wallace Sash) worked so many years, and I for two, was a complex entity, stretching out to a degree over the vast area embracing the Atchison, Topeka and Santa Fe Railway Company. Although the purchasing agent and his staff were headquartered in Chicago along with the top Santa Fe executives; the main operation centered upon Topeka, housed in a number of buildings in the Santa Fe yards from the Shops and Steel Shed on the east to the Water Service on the west. It even included the lumber yards beyond the Branner Street viaduct and the scrap yards near the eastern end of the yards.

The Coast Lines possessed a stores headquarters at San Bernardino, and each division point had a division storeroom but the great bulk of the general stores items passed through the Topeka Stores Department with only certain special and/or items used in bulk ordered directly to sub and division stores. If a Division Storekeeper wanted a tank car of fortnite—the high quality kerosene used in the trainman's signal lamp, long since battery-powered—or the station agent at Spencer, Kansas (next stop east of Tecumseh), needed a half gallon can of the highly pungent creosote base disinfectant (which has always been associated with restrooms in railway stations) he submitted a requisition to the General Storekeeper at Topeka. The requisition would then be sent to the various sections handling the material so requested, the amounts shipped noted, and then the requisition was returned to the office to be priced.

Aunt Mary spent nearly all her adult life working for the Stores Department, most of the time on the price desk pricing requisitions. Dad worked for it from 1922 until his death in 1963. In 1947 they moved from the yards and, with the rest of the department including Price Desk, found new quarters in the General Office building on Jackson Street.

Around the 1920's and through the '30s, the Purchasing Agent was M.J. Collins in Chicago. The Topeka organization was headed by H.E. Ray, General Storekeeper, and his second in command, William Riach, Chief Clerk. The General Foreman, in charge of the warehouse forces, was A.T. Phillips, and his assistant was R.D. Roundtree. The warehouse was divided into sections, each with a Stockman whose duties included keeping an adequate but not excessive supply of stores and filling requisitions and shipping out these stores as required.

On Monday, January 27, 1936, I completed my undergraduate education at the University of Kansas. I had no plans for a job and was not expecting the windfall which came my way. When Dad arrived home that night, he asked if I would be interested in going to work as a laborer on the extra gang at the Stores Department warehouse. This being the Great Depression, there was only one answer to the question. On Tuesday morning, January 28, at about 7:50, I reported to Dick Roundtree, Assistant General Foreman, and was assigned No. 7-X on the extra gang.

The extra gang was a somewhat unusual arrangement. Obviously shift jobs or assembly line jobs must be filled by someone if the work is to continue. Should the regular man be ill, someone else must be called in. The Stores Department carried a group of men who reported in each morning. If three men were ill or for some reason off duty, the first three men (1-X, 2-X, and 3-X) were put to work. Five men off, five to work; seven men off, seven men put to work, etc. The odd part of this as regards the Stores Department is that the men replacing those off were not sent to the sections wherein the men were off duty; instead, they were kept together, generally, in a gang under the supervision of Homer Allison.

As a matter of fact, the only real purpose in bringing the extra gang in was to have the manpower available to do the various odd jobs which had to be done but not necessarily on a set schedule. As jobs were added or men quit or were discharged, each man on the extra gang moved up. Thus, I moved from 7-X to 6-X to 5-X and finally to a permanent number.

My first job was the sacking of charcoal briquets, a dirty job, and eventually included the unloading, handling, and reloading of a variety of items such as batteries, pipe, drums of oil, etc. That first month of work was cold—February 5, for instance, was warm, up to 20°. We worked inside when inside work was available, which was seldom. When at the end of February it began to warm up, we took on the task of unloading car sides. These were sides for new metal box cars which were being assembled in the car sheds. They came in on roadable cars, we unloaded them, with the help of the cranes at the east side of the shops, and reloaded them on bad-order cars, not suitable for road use but adequate for the yard.

On March 9 I had a brief respite, working for a couple of days for Clyde Slawson in Section P. This was cleaner and more interesting than unloading car sides. On March 27 we took on an unusual job, stripping Pullmans. When Pullman cars developed running gear or other problems requiring shop attention, it was necessary that all bedding be stripped out, bundled and stored until such time as it was again required. This chore fell to the extra gang.

Our normal work schedule was five days; however, in mid-April I worked my first Saturday—a most welcome 20% increase in pay. The job involved ferreting out the near useless scrap from that which could be repaired or recycled—the Santa Fe proved to be great string or scrap savers. Each spring was a clean-up period during which tons of scrap were hauled to the marshaling area.

In early May I received a break by being transferred temporarily to Section E, the brass corner with all the beautifully machined fittings. Unfortunately this lasted but a month and back I went to the extra gang. Now I started cutting weeds—a monotonous job based on a very real fear of fire in the yards. One thing that helped make all this somewhat more bearable to me was an irascible, cantankerous, crusty, and utterly delightful curmudgeon named Bill Rees. He and I were almost exact opposites in many ways; Bill was in his 60s, I was 22; he was a Democrat and I a Republican. One might say we complemented each other—both intelligent and not interested like so many others in the gang as to when they could next get in a smoke (something permitted only at noon and even then restricted to a few areas and never in the warehousing areas including only where metal was stored). We were wont to argue interminably but still accomplished a lot; he was sort of a straw boss in the extra gang, and I often worked with him on two-man assignments.

About this time I had an opportunity to work for the Kansas City Power and Light Company. However, I hated the thought of living in Kansas City, and, anyway, I wanted to work for the Kansas Power and Light Company.* With this prospect declined, on June 16 I was given a permanent position in the scheme of things and time card No. 200. Two weeks later I was assigned to Section F, the Oil House, where I was to spend the next 18 months.

The Oil House, rich in the aroma of oil, was a single-storied concrete building with basement a little north and east of the main Storehouse. It was equipped with a concrete dock, car high, along the west side, which dock was separated from the north dock by two sets of rails. As one might expect, the section handled oil in its many forms and flavors, and its many uses: gasoline

---

*The author, James D. Wallace, did get a job with KP&L in 1939. As senior vice-president of KP&L, he retired after 40 years of service on Oct. 1, 1979.

straight and gasoline mixed with machine oil, fortnite (a high quality kerosene) for use in signal lamps, freight car oil, passenger car oil, linseed oil, and a myriad of greases for lubricating. We managed paints of all kinds, from half pint cans up to brown mineral for box car painting in drums holding 55 gallons and weighing, when filled with brown mineral, up to 1400 pounds. We kept bales of rags and waste, a thready cotton material and highly absorbent for shop use; we kept sulfuric acid, both dilute and concentrated, and hydrochloric acid in carboys. We also handled many types of special boiler treating compounds and special types of no-oxide paints.

Our mission at the Oil House seems to have been keeping the Santa Fe system lubricated and painted and the conductors' and brakemens' lamps lighted. We also kept the toilets smelling like creosote. Fortnite, gasoline, and car oil were received in tank cars, in 50 gallon drums, and in tin containers, cylindrical in shape and sheathed in thin sheets of wood. Most of the gasoline which we shipped out was mixed with lubricating oil for use in the two cycle engines which powered the small track cars; the mixing house was some distance from the Oil House and rather isolated from other operations.

Much oil was received in 55 gallon drums, including several types of engine oil, linseed oil for paint, and even heavy brown mineral or gray lead paint.

Our section supplied the splashes of color that brightened up the system; paint came in everything from half pints to 55-gallon drums. When I was younger all Santa Fe stations were painted a deep, dull red, like box cars, with a black trim. Somewhere down the line the Santa Fe livened up a bit and by 1937 stations were painted Colonial Yellow with Venetian Red roofs trimmed in dark or Trim Green.

Two things fired our duties and kept them from becoming too routine; first were the monthly requisitions. Every month each division storekeeper sent in a king-sized requisition for what he estimated as his monthly requirements of routinely used items. And therefrom came one of those peculiarities of modern business which I have never understood. It was presumed that the division storekeepers always overestimated their needs, and thus the powers-that-be considered it good form to reduce their requisitions by a certain percentage. Naturally, it proved no task for the division storekeeper to calculate the percentage, since he possessed a record of what he had asked and what he had received; so, in self-defense he merely increased the next month's requisition. From time to time certain subtleties were introduced by varying the percentages among the items from month to month—

(Continued on p. 162)

The Fire

Editor's Note: The following was written by Mark Dinkel,
Washburn university Student of Dr. William Wagnon, Jr.

MARK DINKEL

On JULY 26, 1889 the future of Santa Fe's offices in Topeka was suddenly darkened by smoke from a fire. At five o'clock in the morning, night watchman Jimmy Coughlin interrupted his normal rounds on the second floor to investigate a crackling sound resembling fire coming from overhead. Looking up a hydraulic elevator shaft, he saw that the woodwork at the top was aflame. Coughlin immediately turned in an alarm. The fire quickly spread north and west from the shaft area along the attic floor where many old files were stored.

Soon, a Topeka city hose truck and a Santa Fe hose truck, both horsedrawn, arrived on the scene to combat the blaze. Since there were no windows in the attic, firemen had to cut holes through the roof in order to fight the flames. Many Santa Fe office employees arrived at the building to help control damages.

At about 7:30 a.m. the fire appeared to be losing some of its intensity and was succumbing to the constant streams of water. However, a water main broke and the unhindered flames soon engulfed the fourth floor of the structure which was occupied by H. C. Clements, freight auditor, and his force. The hose was restored to working order only after a critical twenty minutes of time had elapsed. In that period the fire had spread so swiftly that all hope of saving the structure was temporarily abandoned. Still, the firemen fought skillfully and by eight o'clock the blaze was again under control. Then, water pressure suddenly diminished and once again the flow stopped. Another water main had burst on Harrison Street. The general officers, feeling their hope of preserving the building rapidly eroding once more, ordered everything in the structure moved out to avoid almost certain damage from both water and fire. Over 100 express wagons and transfer vehicles of all varieties were collected to carry away the office equipment extracted from the burning building by employees. Fifteen minutes after the second main had burst, pressure was restored and by nine o'clock the fire was controlled. At 11:00 a.m. the fire departments withdrew, leaving two hose streams directed on the building.

While repairs were being undertaken on the building, offices were moved to different locations spread throughout the city. This situation made many Santa Fe employees recall similar conditions existing in 1883 when the railroad's offices were distributed around Topeka prior to construction of the company's first general office building at Ninth and Jackson.

When the smoke had cleared, gerneral manager A. A. Robinson estimated that $20,000 worth of damages had been done to the structure and $10,000 worth of contents had been lost. Santa Fe took advantage of the disaster by rebuilding the fifth story to accommodate office space instead of storage space. A connecting wing extending eastward from the south end was erected in 1906-7 to help ease crowded conditions.

TOM KING

City Passenger Agents, Topeka, Kansas

GEORGE F. SHERMAN, JR.

THOMAS LAING KING was born May 8, 1875 in Topeka, Kansas. He attended local public schools and the Pennsylvania Military Academy, Chester, Penna. In 1890 he started his railroad career with the Rock Island as a Ticket Clerk. After 5 years he quit his railroad position to enter the grain business with his Father. In 1898 he went to work with the Santa Fe as Office Boy at the Depot Ticket Office under W. C. Garvey. His rise was rapid and he was appointed City Passenger Agent in 1899 which position he held until December 31, 1916. In connection with his work he became an Agent for domestic and foreign steamship lines. He married Imo Dell Blakstead on September 30, 1915 and they had two children, a daughter Barbara, born May 20, 1917 and a son Thomas L. King Jr., born Sepember 17, 1918 who now owns and operates the King Travel Service in Topeka. Effective January 1, 1917 he was promoted to Traveling Passenger Agent for the State of Kansas succeeding W. J. Curtis who was appointed General Agent at Salt Lake City, Utah. Because of the war many off-line offices were closed on May 1, 1918 which necessitated Mr. King returning to the Topeka Depot as City Passenger and Ticket Agent which position he held until his retirement June 1, 1938. He was a member of the Topeka Rotary Club, Topeka Chamber of Commerce, Topeka Country Club, Siloam Lodge No. 225, A.F.& A.M., Scottish Rite Bodies, Arab Shrine and the Episcopal Church. He died October 22, 1939.

WILLIAM J. RODGERS

WILLIAM J. RODGERS was born in St. Louis, Mo. June 16, 1902. He moved with his parents to Topeka in 1909 where he attended local schools and Strickler's Business College. He went to work for the Santa Fe in the Depot Ticket Office on June 15, 1917 as Telephone Operator. He held various positions until June 1, 1938 when he was appointed City Passenger and Ticket Agent succeeding Thomas L. King who retired. On November 1, 1941 he was appointed Division Passenger Agent at Topeka; February 1, 1947 Division Passenger Agent, Oklahoma City, Okla.; September 1, 1950 General Agent Passenger Department, Kansas City, Mo.; March 1, 1952 Passenger Traffic Manager, Gulf, Colorado & Santa Fe Ry., Galveston, Texas; April 1, 1964 Passenger Traffic Manager, Topeka; which position he held until his retirement November 1, 1967. He married Mildred N. Bennett October 10, 1922 and they had one son, William J. Rodgers, Jr., born August 13, 1923, and died October 14, 1977. He was a member of the Topeka Rotary Club, American Association of Passenger Traffic Officers, Chicago, Ill., Topeka Santa Fe Retired Employees Club. He died February 18, 1978.

FOREST E. WRIGHT

FOREST E. WRIGHT was born September 14, 1893 in Franklin, Nebraska. His parents John and Lucy Wright moved to Manhattan, Kansas and in 1903 moved to Topeka. He graduated from Topeka Elementary and High School and then attended Dougherty's Business College. He entered service with the Santa Fe in October 1911 as Office Boy in the General Passenger Office. Through the years he worked in several departments and returned to the Passenger Department as Stenographer to the General Passenger Agent. On November 1, 1941 he was promoted to City Passenger and Ticket Agent at the Topeka Depot succeeding W. J. Rodgers. He married Naomi Sheafer in 1928 and she died in 1938. They had one son James C. Wright, born April 1, 1938 who is now an Attorney in Topeka. In June 1939 he married Frances McCord. He was a member of Golden Rule Lodge No. 90 A.F. & A.M., Topeka, Scottish Rite Bodies, Arab Shrine, Shawnee Country Club, Topeka Traffic Club and Seabrook Congregational Church. He retired August 1, 1963 at which time his duties, except solicitation, were taken over by the Local Freight Agent. Solicitation was handled by the Passenger Department from the General Office Building. He died October 23, 1963.

Santa Fe and Four Generations

BY JOSEPH DALE KONRADE

IN THE COURSE of writing my family's autobiography for a class at Washburn University, I became more fully aware of how much the story of my family has been intertwined with the Santa Fe Railroad. To have several family members working at the Santa Fe is not so unusual for Topeka, but as a fourth generation Santa Fe employee, I found out in talking with my relatives that the railroad's operations heavily influenced the private lives of our family. That influence extended from daily scheduling to career opportunities.

My family's relationship with the Santa Fe began in the early 1880's when my great-grandfather, Edwin G. Dale, immigrated from England to Topeka where he began working as an engineer. He had married Sarah Islip in England and they had one son before moving to Topeka. As the family responsibilities increased with the birth of my grandfather, Charles H. Dale, great-grandfather Dale decided to transfer to Las Vegas, New Mexico where he could make more money as an engineer in a more hazardous work area. That move in 1887 proved to be hazardous indeed. My great-grandfather Dale was killed on July 17, 1888, while driving his locomotive pulling ten cars between Las Vegas and Sulzbacker Station. Heavy rains had caused a washout on the line causing the fatal accident.

Great-Grandmother Dale returned to Topeka with her children when my grandfather was four years old. The family settled in with relatives, but at the earliest opportunity grandpa Dale took a job with the Santa Fe as an office boy in the Topeka freight depot. He had several different office jobs, including a stint in Las Vegas for a few years.

Among his positions in Topeka was one in the freight depot as a night clerk. Quite frequently the tasks of the night clerk were completed early, but the clerks had to remain on the job in the event of an emergency. To pass the time my grandfather and his fellow clerks would call up the telephone operators from the station and chat with them. During one such visit my grandfather got acquainted with one girl who eventually became my grandmother.

Charles Dale married the former telephone operator, Catherine Birmingham, in Topeka in 1906. They lived at 1114 Quincy near the offices where my grandfather worked. After they began having children he attempted to become an engineer like his father and his brother. However, because he was only five feet two

Edwin G. Dale    *Charles H. Dale*

inches, he was unable to meet the physical requirements. Thwarted in his attempt to follow in his father's footsteps, he continued to work as a clerk in the Santa Fe offices retiring with 50 years of service to Santa Fe in 1949.

My grandfather Jacob Konrade on my father's side of the family also worked for Santa Fe. He came to Topeka in 1911 with his wife and daughter where many German-Russian immigrants from the same area in Russia had settled earlier. Word had gone back that work and good housing were available. He began work at the Topeka shops as a laborer, but was promoted to a boilermaker helper. Somewhat later he became a flue welder, which was very demanding but higher paying. Daily my grandfather had walked the railroad bridge connecting the shops with the Little Russia section of North Topeka where he lived in a close knit community of fellow Russian immigrants and Santa Fe employees.

With both of my grandfathers working for the same company it was not hard to see how their jobs affected the daily lives of both of the families. The Dale family ate all three meals to coincide

Woodrow Konrade   *Joseph D. Konrade*

with grandpa's working time. They ate breakfast before 7:30 so it would give the family time to get ready for school and work. Lunch was served at 12:10 each day which was just enough time for grandpa Dale to walk from the general offices at Ninth and Jackson to home. Supper was at 5:10 every night. Fixed times for all meals were as much a family tradition as reunions at Christmas. Meals were served on a time table set by the Santa Fe.

The Konrade family did not have its meals on as regular a basis, but their lives were affected by the working time table of Santa Fe. My aunt related a story to me about when she was growing up. When the whistle would blow in the afternoon it meant it was time to stop what they were doing and head home for supper. In the evening when the whistle would blow for the evening shift at the shops to begin their lunch hour it was time for the children to head for home and get ready for bed.

The old adage, like father like son, applies to both my father and mother. They both worked for Santa Fe in the same area as their fathers. My mother, Charlotte Dale began to work in the offices as soon as she graduated from high school during World War II. She had a number of clerical jobs until the birth of her first son in 1949. Until the advent of Affirmative Action the Santa Fe had a policy of hiring sons and daughters of employees. Both grandfathers relied on this to assure that each of my parents got work at Santa Fe.

My dad, John Konrade was working in Denver as a baker with his older brother when my grandfather wrote him and told him to come back to Topeka because Santa Fe was hiring. Although my dad returned and was hired as a coach carpenter apprentice, World War II interrupted his employment at the shops. He joined the navy in 1943 and was discharged in 1946. Because he had volunteered rather than being drafted, he was not assured of getting his old job back. However, after some effort he returned to his job, which he kept until he retired.

When my mother and father were married in 1948 they both were working at Santa Fe in the same areas and almost the same capacities as their fathers. My mother worked at Santa Fe only until my older brother was born. She told me that when she and my dad were both working, he encouraged her to save her salary to be able to buy something special when they began to have a family. Soon after my older brother was born, they made a down payment on a house at 1719 Buchanan and bought most of the furniture for it with the money that they had saved from her job. Today my mother still lives in that house and she still has some of that same furniture, although after seven children, it has had to be recovered and repainted.

There was only a span of a few months between the time that

(Continued on p. 169)

Isaiah Hale and His Santa Fe "Safety First" Automobile.

Santa Fe *"Safety First"* Taught by Phonograph

VERNON FRENCH

IN THESE days, the teacher of foreign languages is familiar with high fidelity recording devices as a means of aiding learning. He might be surprised, however, to learn that back in 1915, the Santa Fe railroad was using Spanish phonograph recordings to help its Mexican employees to learn important rules of safety. Compared to present-day standards, the recordings must have been rather primitive, but early experiments resulted in fewer injuries and accidental deaths among the workmen, who were supposed to have a certain fatalistic attitude toward life.

The Topeka *Daily Capital* of April 25, 1915, carried a long story about the Commissioner of Safety on the Santa Fe, Isaiah Hale, a Topekan, who was making preparations to go on a 20,000 mile trip during which he would visit Mexican workmen. He had a Cadillac automobile equipped with flanged wheels so that it could run on the railroad tracks. Knowing little Spanish, Hale traveled from division to division along the railroad, visiting gangs of trackmen and teaching them rules of safety by phonograph recordings. These rules had been translated "by an expert linguist into the purest Mexican," the article stated, then recorded by the Edison Phonograph Company for Hale's use.

The article went on: "It is a study to watch the expression on the faces of the Mexicans as they gather about and watch the box from which come words of safety advice, spoken in their mother tongue. First there is a look of incredulity, which quickly changes to rapt attention." To the serious business of safety, Hale added a sentimental musical touch to please his listener. Two well-known Spanish songs were played, *La Paloma*, and *La Golondrina*, and the latter was particularly appealing to the Mexicans, who asked to hear it again and again.

As he traveled from place to place, Hale picked up train orders so that he could meet any trains by taking a siding. "The inflated rubber tires under the flanged steel rim take up every bit of the jar, and passengers in the auto feel no vibration as they pass over a rail joint or a switch frog." With the possibility of going some 60 miles an hour, Hale limited himself to 35. The car would very likely not have held to the rails at a pace much faster than that!

Good Old Days

From Santa Fe Employes' Magazine, February, 1925
From Topeka Correspondent

Not long ago a truck belonging to one of the trucking companies plying between Kansas City and Topeka, backed up to the door of the Campbell Drug Co., Topeka, with a box of freight from Kansas City. Mr. Campbell told them he would accept the box but they were to bring no more to him, as much of his business came from Santa Fe employees, and he wanted his freight shipped by Santa Fe.

A few days later a truck backed up to his door with a large consignment from Kansas City, and Mr. Campbell told them to take it back to Kansas City, and then ordered the shipper to send all future shipments by Santa Fe as ordered.

★ ★ ★

March, 1925

Rescheduling Train No. 21 to 12:30 PM allows many employees who have 12:00 to 1:00 noon hour to lunch at Fred Harvey's. A vote of thanks to general manager McKinney. But we do wish he would cut the price of a cut of pie from 15¢ back to 10¢.

THE SANTA FE
Sporting Scene

DOUGLASS WALLACE

WHEN one of the first excursions on the young Santa Fe RR left Topeka for Wakarusa in May, 1869, a *Daily Commonwealth* reporter was there who noted that "several of the sporting gentry were along and took advantage of the occasion to indulge in a little fishing and shooting." Undoubtedly, train crews and other road workers indulged in the same when time spared (or didn't); regardless, sports activity proved a relief from the often dull, hard routine. As this new rail venture grew up with the American West, so did it grow up with the uniquely American sport of baseball. For some, the Santa Fe and baseball became synonymous, their lives revolving around both.

Whenever Santa Fe families gathered, a ball game ensued. Indeed, for picnics like those of the Stores Department, the game often served as star attraction at such places as Ripley, Garfield, or even the Boys Industrial School parks. Nevertheless, other sports were played, too. For example, Ripley park in 1926 hosted the A.T. & S.F. system's third annual picnic, a gathering of nearly 30,000. The Santa Fe people, according to the July 28 *State Journal*, engaged all afternoon in boxing, wrestling, and baseball as well as more exotic activities like nail driving. More popular for some, though, was women's diving at the pool "in which," stated the paper, "some of the most beautiful maidens of the Santa Fe system will participate [sic]. The crush around the diving tower was enormous, but no fatalities were reported."

Sports enthusiasm in the Santa Fe, however, required no special occasion. By the late 1800s more and more accounts are noted of Santa Fe employees playing with other members of the community. Along with the rest of the nation, the Golden Age of Sport at the railway coincided with the decade of the '20s and '30s. A quick glance of the monthly *Santa Fe Magazine* confirms this athletic interest, particularly the numerous accounts of league play by teams from the G.O.B. (General Office Building) and the Shops.

Leagues were formed for other endeavors than baseball. The February, 1931, *Santa Fe Magazine* reported on the status of the second half of season for the G.O.B. Basketball League. The Freight Traffic team led the field of eight with a perfect record of six wins and no losses. The Freight Auditor, General Managers, Car Accountants, Ticket Auditors, Telegraph, Treasurers, and Claim Department followed in order, the last three with 1 and 5 records. An elimination tournament succeeded the regular season play for G.O.B. champion. The Shops had a league, too, though as the May, 1932, edition explained, sometimes circumstances beyond their control caused game postponements. For that year the Stores Department and the Upholsterers "shared" the honors.

The General Offices' Recreation Club oversaw many of these activities, promoting such diverse events as ping-pong and indoor golf. The former consisted, in 1936, of seven teams of about five players each, all intra-club play. The February, 1931, *Santa Fe Magazine* announced establishment of a golf "range" in the G.O. basement approximately 16 feet long "where the golf fans now can keep themselves in trim... without having to brave inclement weather." Smoking on the premises, however, invoked loss of club membership.

Serious golf, of course, took place outdoors. In a match November 24, 1935, John Woodley of the General Storekeepers office, with a 74, defeated Bill Collins at the White Lakes course; for the effort he took home a turkey. A year and a half before, July, 1934, the employees' magazine advocated a "challenge of the sexes" match between Woodley and Miss Edna Crowl, "the champion woman golfer of the stores department." To say the least, she quickly gained the services of a caddy.

Regardless, baseball was king. Indeed, there evolved almost a feudal air about the sport—levels of play from the strictly informal, spur-of-the-moment contest at a picnic, to the organized intra-departmental game, and then to the semi-pro city league play with other Topeka teams (often other railroads). An example or two of the first in July, 1930, the Shop Supervisors held a picnic at Murphey's Grove in Tecumseh. The Locomotive Foreman and Car Foremen played two games with the latter winning both, 29 to 22 and 13 to 8. While exerting themselves, they and the spectators consumed 17 cases of beer, 20 cases of pop, and 20 gallons of ice cream. The following July, the Stores Department threw a stag picnic at Gage Park with three ball games. Clarence (Punk) Simpson managed one team, while golfer John Woodley proved, in the opinion of the *Santa Fe Magazine* (September), "the best with the stick."

Those who wanted to play ball usually found a team somewhere in the Santa Fe complex in Topeka. The G.O.'s Recreation Club in 1931 sponsored the G.O.B. League, and it featured all the trappings of a professional setup—a president, secretary-

(Continued on p. 142)

137

From Santa Fe Apprentice 1927 Year Book, "The Iron Horse."

TOPEKA FOOTBALL TEAM

E. L. PETTERSON

The Topeka Football had a successful season. They finished the season in second place by winning five of the seven games on their schedule.

The two games dropped were both lost to the A. J. H. Club at Newton.

From Santa Fe Apprentice 1927 Year Book, "The Iron Horse."

TOPEKA BASEBALL TEAM

Much credit for the success of the Topeka team is due to the coaching of C. E. "Punk" Simpson of the Store Department.

The following are the scores of the games that were scheduled:

Topeka 0, Newton 20; Topeka 24, Wellington 0; Topeka 24, Clovis 7; Topeka 0, Newton 6; Topeka 12, Cleburne 0; Topeka 13, Wellington 7; Topeka 1, Cleburne 0, (Forfeit).

BASEBALL LORE

The 22d of September, 1896, is well remembered in Topeka as the occasion of one of the most thrilling contests ever conducted on a baseball diamond. A team of prominent Santa Fe men was selected to play a team composed of prominent business men, for the benefit of a well known charity.

The personnel of the Santa Fe team is shown in the accompanying picture. The teams paraded the streets of the city, the Santa Fe men carrying a banner reading, "Feed no peanuts to the substitutes; they have just been fed." Upon reaching the ball grounds the teams were welcomed by a large concourse of fans.

C. M. Foulks, deceased, umpired the game, with the assistance of a large Colts forty-four. The Santa Fe team lined up with W. J. Black in the box, and, while the knuckle curve was not known in those days, he had everything else in the catalogue.

Try as the entire infield might, not a ball thrown succeeded in passing over W. B. Jansen, who covered first base. E. L. Copeland pulled off some sensational stunts in the way of hitting. Al Rankin did some wonderful sidestepping in the sun garden, and F. E. Nipps contributed to the error column because of his inability to successfully stoop over. J. J. Kinney discovered a clew near second base and followed it clear to the fence, where he lost it. Tom Boyd and Harry Tasker played heavy parts in the hitting line. C. W. Kouns and O. J. Wood successfully managed the team from the bench.

After the final inning had been played and the committee on accounting had traversed the error column, the umpire awarded the game to the Santa Fe team by a score of 14 to 8.

The most remarkable coincidence in connection with the Santa Fe team in question is that practically every member has risen to an official position of importance. Al Rankin is now train inspector, C. W. Kouns assistant to the second vice-president, O. J. Wood assistant solicitor for Kansas, W. B. Jansen fourth vice-president, W. J. Black passenger traffic manager, and E. L. Copeland secretary and treasurer.

NEARLY CAUSED A COLLISION

Retired Roadmaster: "That's the worst put together switch I ever saw."

The Merry Widow: "Sir, I want you to understand that that is my own hair—no switch about it!"

JANSEN'S SOUTHPAWS
Rear row, left to right—Messrs. F. E. Nipps, J. J. Kinney, H. A. Dunn, Al Rankin, C. W. Kouns and O. J. Wood.
Middle row—Messrs. Tom Boyd, W. E. Jansen and W. J. Black.
Front row—Messrs. F. L. Copeland, D. S. Fero, H. B. Tasker and W. Scott.

WEAR'S GLASS ARMS
Rear row, left to right—Messrs. Lewis, Holliday, Lord, Lingafelt, ———, Curry, Stilwell and Strong.
Front row—Messrs. Pounds, Stansfield, Wear, Crane, Robert Pierce and Captain Pierce.

(Continued from p. 137)

treasurer an executive committee, and team managers and captains. For the 60 games total to be played, the group divided that year into the following six teams: Operating Department, Telegraph Department, Auditor of Disbursements, Car Accountants, and two teams from the Freight Auditors office—"A" and "B." Freight Auditor "A" won the first half of the season, 9 wins and 1 loss, while the Car Accountants nosed them out in the second half. Despite such thorough organization, some teams had difficulties in recruiting players; so, as time went on some men and teams dropped out with new ones to take their place. Ball diamonds could be found all over Topeka, but the Shop teams possessed one in their backyard immediately northeast of the boiler shops. Wedged between the old Steel Shed and Chandler street, a board fence enclosed this Santa Fe park.

At the highest stage stood semi-pro ball, something to which many a lad aspired. The Santa Fe as well as other Topeka institutions fielded teams in the 1910s, '20s, and '30s. Here the A.T. & S.F. met its rail competition, the U.P. and Rock Island (Rock Island players had several diamonds to chose from including one west of the yards and north of the Ward farm, now the Ward-Meade House). Players at this level were good and versatile such as Clarence (Punk) Simpson, a Stores Department clerk who could pitch, hit, and manage. Hitting over .300 in 1930, he and others on the Shop Crafts team fought for the city lead with a standing in mid July at 7 and 0, thus besting Rock Island at 6 and 3, Topeka Santa Fe 4 and 3, Union Pacific 2 and 5, Peoria Life 2 and 6, and North Topeka Merchants 1 and 4.

Softball originated with indoor baseball and something very much like it was promoted here prior to the First World War. For a time Santa Fe employees played all three sports, indoor, outdoor, and softball. The Freight Auditors, 9th floor, won the championship Men's Indoor in 1930, closing out the first half of the season 9 and 2 with a play-off victory over the 8th floor team, 16 to 11. The obvious advantage of the game with its large ball and small bat was that it could be played in inclement weather during the winter. A G.O.B. club that same year (1930) traveled to Kansas City on December 27 to battle a Kansas City Athletic Club team. The Santa Fe Boys defeated the Missouri opposition 17 to 9 collecting 26 hits to Kansas City's 22.

Softball, or indoor baseball played outdoors, offered a number of advantages over the real thing, including time and size of the field. This new sport received some support back east, especially around Minneapolis, but the Stores Department and Motive Power employees quickly gave it a home. A group of Motive Power Building workers in April, 1916, bought an indoor ball and bat and then experimented with it at a nearby vacant lot, now site of the present Motive Power Building. A noon hour vocation, by using indoor equipment and more or less applying outdoor rules, they began play.

This soon attracted others in the Shops and the Apprentice School who immediately took up the hybrid sport. For the remainder of that decade and on into the early 1920s, the Shop players altered and tested rules and equipment; the bases at one point a scant 33 to 35 feet apart (due, of course, to size of field) before they were moved the still short (by modern standards) distance of 36 feet apart. The Upholstery Shop worked on ball improvements, and in 1920 a representative from A.G. Spaulding Sporting Goods Co. came to Topeka to help with these developments. Thus, by the 1920s a distinct softball league had formed in the Shops only to be dissolved in a few years.

Nevertheless, a seed had been sown so that in 1926 a Santa Fe Shopcrafts team entered the newly formed Parkdale City League at Chandler Field. Other Santa Fe teams joined or, on a smaller scale, organized intra-company leagues like the General Office's in 1934. From the start the sport aroused interest in the Santa Fe; according to a brief history of the game found in the "Santa Fe Night, Garfield Park" program, July 24, 1938, as many as 500 fans crowded the stands for the noon hour games in the Shops. The beauty of the sport may be seen—and applauded by management—that a full nine inning game could be played in 34 minutes, as was the case for one exhibition in May, 1922, which also saw five double plays and, by the Motive Power team, two triple plays.

As in the 1920s, for some years in the 1930s no Santa Fe team entered League play, but in mid-decade a Santa Fe Shopcrafts team slowly rose to prominence. In 1937 they fought their way to the top, city champs with a trophy to prove it. Unknown to all, at the same time the pinnacle of the "Golden Age of Sport" had passed. Still, the Santa Fe people thought of themselves and their community as the "birthplace of Soft Ball." An overstatement* to be sure, nevertheless, the Motive Power men in 1916—L. E. Smith, Harvey Landon, Ivan Gregory, P. I. Isaacson, A. Kay, John Isaacson, H. H. Lanning, D. P. Beaudry, George Anderson, M. A. Hefner, Elmer Meyers, Frank Dawn, Julius Oberer, and George Boon—had reason to acknowledge their contribution to sport and sport in the Santa Fe.

From ping pong to bowling to golf to volley ball to basket-

---

*Most authorities agree that softball was invented in 1895 by Lewis Rober, a member of the Minneapolis, MN, fire department. By 1900 a city softball league had been formed in Minneapolis.

(Continued on p. 178)

NOW IN ITS 85TH YEAR

Santa Fe's Topeka Time Service

WILLIAM O. WAGNON, JR.

Railroading brought the demands for accurate time keeping into the lives of Americans in profound ways. As tracks conquered distance and connected cities together, trains and trainmen needed standard times and schedules in order to dovetail passenger and freight exchanges safely. The Santa Fe responded vigorously and imaginatively by establishing its Time Service Department at Topeka in 1893. It eventually grew to have a central office with a staff of twenty-two, connected to over 200 local jewelers—watch inspectors—who were scattered all along the Santa Fe system from Chicago to San Francisco, Los Angeles and Galveston. Trainmen, enginemen and yardmen depended on this corps of workers for accurate time keeping.

Prior to the 1890s timekeeping on railroads was rather informal. Only passenger trains attempted to keep a schedule while others ran mostly "by smoke," meaning that switching depended on sight observations. However, in 1891 a serious accident on the Lake Shore Railroad occurred because key watches on two colliding trains *differed by four minutes.* Fearing reoccurences, railroad officials across the nation began devising more accurate methods for timekeeping. Santa Fe President Edward P. Ripley turned to Topeka jeweler, Henry S. Montgomery, to develop such a system.

Montgomery had moved his family from Lincoln, Nebraska, to Topeka in 1888 and opened a jewelry store at 400 East 5th. He subsequently became a local watch inspector for the Santa Fe, and railroadmen brought their watches to him for cleaning and repair. His reputation among Santa Fe employees caught Ripley's attention and in 1894 Montgomery was designated General Watch and Clock Inspector for the Santa Fe. Montgomery proved to be more than an experienced watchmaker. He was also a skilled administrator who created and managed a system for accurate timekeeping all along the Santa Fe's tracks.

The General Inspector's connection to the Railroad was that of an inside contractor. The railroad paid him a monthly salary out of which he hired his own staff. He received office space, at times located at 900 Jackson and at 5th and Quincy, travel

H. S. MONTGOMERY

passes and whatever supplies were needed to keep the railroad's timepieces functioning accurately. By 1898 Montgomery employed ten persons in his office, including watch and clockmakers, repairmen, stenographers and clerks. His Time Service Department was responsible for the accuracy of the watches certain employees were required to have.

Montgomery continued using local jewelers, numbering some 50 by 1898, in towns where train crews changed shifts. These watch inspectors would rate each watch at stated intervals for accuracy, do any necessary repair work and report the maintenance record to the Topeka office. In addition to keeping records on thousands of watches, the department also maintained the clocks and timing mechanisms used by the railroad.

Control of the railroad clocks became the important linkage on a day-to-day basis between the Time Service Department and train operators. The General Inspector devised a method which placed a mercurial pendulum clock, usually made by Seth Thomas, at each division point. Conductors, enginemen and engine foremen were required to check the accuracy of their watches daily against the Standard clocks. The accuracy of each watch was reported to Topeka, and persistent variations resulted in having inaccuracies corrected.

To assure that the Standard clocks were correct, Montgomery received daily time signals from Western Union's Master clock in

St. Louis. In an elaborate daily ritual these signals were dispatched over wires to verify the time settings of division point Standard clocks. People in all walks of life throughout the Santa Fe territory looked to the railroad for the time, and Topeka controlled that time.

Over the years this system expanded and Montgomery's responsibilities grew. To protect against interruptions of the daily signals from Western Union, the General Inspector acquired a master clock in 1908. This precision clock, made by Seth Thomas and operated with a gravity escapement, could be relied on for short-term independence from Western Union.

Montgomery also worked to improve the ability of trainmen to tell accurate time from their pocket watches. By 1908 he had designed a watch dial including bold, upright hour numbers as well as clearly marked, upright numerals for each minute. After patenting the dial, he created a company to license its use by watchmakers for railroad quality watches. The Montgomery Dial proved very popular among watch carriers and was widely used by the nation's railroaders.

By 1918 the General Watch Inspector was receiving $2900 per month to run the department. However, with the end of World War I the Time Service Department had become so important to the Santa Fe that Montgomery's status as an inside contractor was terminated and he and his staff became employees of the railroad. In 1920 their offices were permanently located in the office building at 9th and Jackson.

Henry Montgomery retired in 1924 and he and his wife moved to Los Angeles where he managed his dial company until he died in 1927. His son Ralph D. became the General Inspector. The younger Montgomery began the watchmaker's trade in 1892 under his father and had also trained at the Parson's Horological School in Peoria, Illinois. He, too, had been associated with the Time Service Department serving in various capacities, the most recent as Assistant General Inspector.

The department expanded its scope in 1927 as the number of Santa Fe employees required to carry reliable watches more than doubled. The new General Inspector enlarged the reporting system so that he received quarterly reports on the rating of individual watches, and also sent out reminders to each employee when his watch needed recertification. By 1939 when Ralph Montgomery died, the Time Service Department was keeping track of over 100,000 watches and issuing 25,000 time service cards each year.

To replace Montgomery the Santa Fe management recruited from the ranks of the local watch inspectors. Chanute jeweler

A. J. STROBEL *checks a hand-held time piece with one of the few Seth Thomas Mercury Compensating Pendulum Regulators still owned—and prized—by the Santa Fe System.*

Arthur J. Strobel became the General Inspector in April 1940. Strobel, a native of York, Nebraska, had acquired his trade working for various watchmakers in Nebraska, Kansas City and Lawrence, before opening his own business in Chanute in 1929. Working as a local watch inspector for the next decade, he acquired a far-flung reputation among railroad men for excellent watch repair. That reputation reached the highest levels of Santa Fe management in Chicago, so that when the railroad needed a

General Watch and Clock Inspector, Strobel was chosen. Although lacking administrative training, Strobel nonetheless moved to Topeka and set about mastering the organization. He traveled the system extensively, assessing the needs of the railroad for accurate time keeping.

After 1941, America's mobilization for World War II put new pressures on railroading and time keeping. The draft produced rapid employee turnover and made keeping up with their watches more difficult. Watch manufacturers stopped making watches and parts and converted to bomb-fuse production. Strobel traveled to Washington and got a priority for railroad watches and parts from the War Production Board. He also expanded the repair staff in Topeka and instituted a system whereby railroadmen could send their watches to the Topeka department if their local watch inspector could not get parts. He even contacted retired railroad employees and encouraged them to sell their watches to active employees to compensate for the scarcity of new watches.

Under these pressures the Time Service Department grew to its largest size and scope. The General Inspector had two assistants. Twelve watchmakers and repairmen struggled to service the flood of watches mailed into Topeka. A chief clerk kept five clerical assistants busy with the mounting paperwork.

Strobel trained his staff rigorously, asserting that anyone could get a watch to run, but making it keep accurate time took special skill. Indeed, the Time Service Department became a school for skilled workers, and men trained in the Santa Fe office fanned out from Topeka after the war, taking their improved methods with them. Many of them became local watch inspectors. At the war's end the activities of the Department began to change. New watches and parts were available again, together with emerging technology for watch repair. Strobel turned to streamlining the Time Service Department.

One postwar Strobel innovation was the greater use of traveling watch inspectors and clock repairmen. He equipped his inspectors with the latest devices which cut the time to determine a watch's accuracy from three days to three minutes. These inspectors would meet with groups of men at designated times in their workplaces and speedily determine the accuracy of their watches. Also traveling repairmen serviced the 6,000 clocks spread across the Santa Fe's 13,000 miles of track. Clock repairmen rode cabooses and exchanged cleaned depot clocks for those in need of service, cleaning them between stops and cutting down on the number having to be sent to Topeka for service.

Not only did these changes enable the Time Service Department to use fewer personnel with the same level of accuracy, but Strobel's office contributed to improving railroad timekeeping technology. In 1957 when a train out of Los Angeles wrecked while attemping a curve at too great a speed, division superintendents asked Strobel to develop a better method for measuring train speed. Strobel and his watchmakers developed and patented a light weight accurate speed indicator that became widely used on all railroads as well as on horse and automobile race tracks. By the 1960's Strobel and his six assistants, together with some 250 local watch inspectors, looked after the time needs of the Santa Fe. Improvements in the quality of wrist watches led to several being certified in 1962 by the General Inspector as railroad quality. Within sixteen months some 1500 had been rated and were in service on the Santa Fe. In addition the record keeping system developed by Ralph Montgomery became unnecessary and was discontinued. By the time Strobel retired in 1972, the Time Service Department employed only five persons. Strobel was replaced by Robert W. Wells.

Wells had been the Assistant General Inspector in charge of the San Bernardino office, which closed when he transferred to Topeka. Under his leadership the Time Department made further concessions to changing technology. In 1975 it began receiving electronic telephone communications to replace the old Standard Time hookup with Western Union. Two Years later Wells retired back to California and his chief clerk, R. Neil Crow, who had been a Santa Fe employee since 1953, became the General Watch and Clock Inspector.

Today Crow and two watchmakers supervise the entire Santa Fe system, testing and certifying railroad quality watches, repairing and maintaining the clocks and timing mechanisms used by the railroad, and negotiating contracts with about 250 local watch inspectors. Telephone communications now link division points with moving trains and electronic switching enables trains to run without relying on the accuracy of individual watches. However, Montgomery's legacy, the Time Service Department, continues to play a vital, though reduced, role in the smooth running of the Santa Fe Railroad.

From Santa Fe Employees Magazine, July, 1911

This limerick was printed in the *Topeka Capital:*

If you travel in safety today
You must ride on the Santa Fe,
The Montgomery Dial,
An invention worth while,
Is used on the "Safety Way."

> *On the very first trip of a Santa Fe passenger train—an excursion to Wakarusa, the end of the line—there were speeches galore by local dignitaries, all in praise of Col. Holliday and his associates. last but far from least was the Colonel's oration, part of which was reported in the local press.*
>
> *"Fellow citizens! Imagine, if you please, my outstretched right hand as in Chicago; my left in St. Louis. Eventually the railroad we contemplate will reach these cities and, crossing at Topeka, the intersection, we will extend to both the City of Mexico and San Francisco."*
>
> *The Colonel's imaginative theory was just too much for one of the guests, Major Tom Anderson, then agent for the Kansas Pacific.*
>
> *"Oh, Lord, please give us a rest! This is too much!"*
>
> *It was only a few years later that Major Anderson joined the Santa Fe family, and became one of Topeka's greatest boosters.*

THOMAS J. ANDERSON—An Arch Booster
by Glenn D. Bradley

From Santa Fe Magazine, July 1914

TOM ANDERSON never shoveled any dirt along the right of way. He appears never to have carried a railroad surveyor's chain; nor did he ever squint through a Santa Fe transit.

No, Tom was but a mighty booster. His whole life was spent booming and boosting. And while Tom was thus engaged his friends boomed him, for he managed to acquire about all the offices and titles that a man could get in Kansas. He staggered under the weight of his titles and emoluments. He enjoyed the rare distinction of being a Kansas pioneer. He was a military hero, a G. A. R. patriarch, a prop in the Masonic order, a politician of unusual skill, always a shining pillar of his town, a maker of Kansas history and a prime mover of things in general. Also he was one of the original Santa Fe boosters, and he was the man who made Topeka famous.

Tom's career as a railroadman was but a prolonged incident in a life of furious activity. Besides the achievements already hinted at, Anderson divides honors with the Russian Grand Duke Alexis in putting Topeka upon the map. He also rivals Colonel Holliday in having sported the finest set of side whiskers ever seen in Santa Fe service.

Anderson came into existence in Atwater, Portage County, Ohio, on May 29, 1839. He sprang from Scotch-Irish descent, the sturdy, tireless stock that has given us most of our illustrious pioneers. The Anderson family were well fitted by nature for pioneering. The biographers assure us that Tom was only one of eight brothers, each of whom was over six feet tall. Also there were four sturdy sisters. To us of these degenerate times raising a family of twelve stalwart children is a safe bid for notoriety. But not so with old Martin Anderson, Tom's father. Back in the forties having a big family was no uncommon thing. Besides, as the youngsters matured, life in a humdrum Ohio community grew stale for this vigorous clan. So to satisfy the Scotch-Irish love of excitement the family, in 1857, moved to Kansas, where there was excitement a-plenty, and settled at Grasshopper Falls.

They had adversity along with the excitement. The father at first ran a sawmill and the mother boarded the hands. The country was then rich only in drouths and malaria. It was strenuous pioneering, for times were desperate. Sorghum and corn bread were the staple diet. Then came the great drouth of 1860, when no rain fell the entire season. Speaking of that year Tom Anderson afterward said: "We had fifty-four acres of corn and did not raise enough to fill a mule's ear. We had some stock hogs and sold them to a St. Joseph dealer at one and one-half cents a pound. They were so thin that it took two hogs to balance the scales."

Also there were political troubles. The Andersons on reaching Kansas had promptly lined up with the free-state party. It was not long before the father was wounded, following a row with proslavery men. But the old gentleman soon recovered and was made a member first of the territorial council and then of the first state legislature.

It was in the midst of these scenes that Tom's booster spirit began to assert itself. Such spirits always had thrived in Kansas and especially in the Kansas of that period. So it may not seem strange that the Anderson family record now becomes obscured by the dust which Tom raised in the promotion of public welfare and in the acquisition of honors. And he now stands forth as the real hero of the Anderson family.

Soon after settling at Grasshopper Falls a church and a school had been erected. The church seems to have prospered but the district felt too poor to hire a teacher, badly as one was needed. Now Tom had received considerable schooling, together with a short course in civil engineering, back in Ohio. He therefore proceeded to make good use of his training. First he pitched in and taught a term of school to help his community out. Then, in the fall of 1858, he was elected surveyor of Calhoun county, which then comprised Jefferson and Jackson counties and a portion of Shawnee. This was a good step toward public recognition. Then came the Civil War, and Anderson's future was at once assured. Henceforth his name was seldom to be written without a "major," a "captain," an "Hon." or some other dignified title being prefixed.

Anderson of course enlisted, and he was mustered into service on August 2, 1861, as a private in Company A, Fifth Regiment of Kansas Volunteers. After the battle of Dry Wood, Mo., which occurred the next month, he was promoted to be a lieutenant and was assigned to the staff of General James H. Lane, then in charge of a Kansas brigade. He served with Lane until the following spring, when he was transferred to the command of General R. B. Mitchell, with whom he saw considerable service.

In February, 1863, President Lincoln appointed Mr. Anderson a captain and assistant adjutant-general of the United States volunteers. In this capacity he served Generals Blunt, McNeil and Thayer, respectively, who commanded the Second Division of the Seventh Army Corps, the so-called Army of the Frontier. This division was composed mostly of Kansas troops and nearly all of them came to know Anderson personally. This wide acquaintance contributed much to his success in public life in after years.

Prior to his last-mentioned promotion Mr. Anderson had been active in organizing the Fourteenth Kansas Cavalry and the Second Kansas Colored Infantry. It is not surprising that in that same year, 1863, he took the rank of major, which title has been most frequently connected with his name ever since.

In March, 1865, Anderson was brevetted a colonel, but he resigned within a few weeks at the request of Governor Crawford to become adjutant-general of Kansas. The following year he gave up this office and was appointed agent for the Kansas Pacific Railroad at Topeka. This job he held until March 1, 1873, when he was made general freight and passenger agent of the Kansas Midland, which position he retained two years.

Meanwhile he had been active in numerous secondary capacities. In the spring of 1864 he had paused long enough in the round of official duties to get married. From 1865 to 1869 he was busy systematizing war records and adjusting raid claims. He was a delegate to the first national G. A. R. convention at Indianapolis, in 1866, and a charter member of Lincoln G. A. R. Post No. 1 of Topeka.

Early in 1872, when the Grand Duke Alexis visited Topeka, then a raw country town, Anderson was marshal of the day. It seems that no hacks of the "low-necked" variety were then to be had in the Kansas capital and that to get up a good street celebration carriages had to be borrowed from Kansas City. So the carriages were secured, and when the duke arrived at the Kansas Pacific (now Union Pacific) station he was escorted with grand ceremony to the old Fifth Avenue Hotel. At the head of the procession, along with his royal highness, the governor, State Representative Cyrus Holliday and other dignitaries, rode Tom Anderson, the boosting railroad agent. And for forty years Tom was destined to head Topeka processions.

When the Santa Fe purchased the Kansas Midland in 1875 Anderson was made general passenger agent of the Santa Fe. In 1878 he was appointed Santa Fe agent for Kansas, Colorado and New Mexico. This larger position he resigned in 1881 to become postmaster in Topeka. He had been mayor of the city in 1875-1876, and he had managed to slip in a term or two as a member of the legislature between 1877 and 1881. In 1880 he was a delegate to the Republican national convention, where he voted thirty-six times for General Grant. In 1883 he was G. A. R. department commander for Kansas, and that year he boomed just a few less than ten thousand new members into the Grand Army.

All this may sound energetic enough, but it does not measure the full round of Tom's activities. He had helped organize the National Woman's Relief Corps and he had found time to serve in the old Capital Militia Guards. In 1883-1884 he was brigadier and major-general of the Kansas National Guard.

He then seems to have itched to get back into railroad work once more, so about 1887 he became general agent for the Rock Island, with headquarters in Topeka. In 1892 he was made assistant general passenger agent for the Rock Island lines west of the Missouri River. He remained in Rock Island service until December, 1897, when he withdrew to become secretary of the Topeka Commercial Club, a position peculiarly suited to a booster spirit. He had just disposed of another political "preference," having been delegate-at-large to the Republican national convention of 1896.

Before passing from his railroad career we ought to relate a Tom Anderson railroad yarn which went the rounds years ago. In the early days of the Santa Fe, when Anderson was general passenger agent, he was traveling over the lines with a big official from the East. The B. O. complained loudly that traffic was light, to which Anderson retorted that the Santa Fe engines were too light for heavy trains, and that there were not enough engines for more trains. Just a few days before, Tom explained, a passenger train had made a lunch stop at Emporia. The rear coach stood on a street crossing. While the passengers

TOM ANDERSON'S WHISKERS
He sported one of the finest sets of side whiskers ever seen in Kansas. This portrait was taken while he was in Santa Fe service.

were eating a farmer tied his mule team to this car while he did some shopping in a neighboring store. It soon was time to start the train. The bell rang, the conductor shouted "All aboard!" and the drive wheels began to revolve. Since the train did not move the engineer threw open the throttle and gave her plenty of sand. The drivers spun and the sparks flew, but they were apparently stalled. Things were getting mysterious when a depot lounger suggested untying the mules at the rear end. This was done and the train moved off in good shape.

After taking up the secretaryship of the commercial club in 1898 Anderson could not resist another flyer into politics. He was boomed for the United

States senate that year but this boom never got under way. In 1899, however, he was elected to the state senate and served one term, as a diversion from his boosting activities.

Mr. Anderson was secretary of the commercial club from 1898 to 1908. During these ten years he boosted the membership from 37 to 265.

We already have mentioned how he helped the grand duke put Topeka upon the map. He also helped keep Topeka on the map. At one time during his secretaryship there was grave danger of moving the big Santa Fe shops to some other city. Space forbids going into the details of that affair, but it was of course Tom Anderson who started a movement whereby the commercial club raised money, bought for the company part of the property where the shops now stand and saved them for Topeka. Afterward the business men who thus contributed were reimbursed by the city.

Anderson was again prominent as secretary of the relief organization during the big flood of 1903. He boosted hard in getting the Topeka auditorium built, and he boomed a lot of good pavement onto the streets of that city. And in still other ways did this intrepid booster clinch notoriety for his home town. He had a good voice and was fond of music. Since he never allowed a scrap of his talents to go to waste he started a musical club of male singers 'way back in 1868. For eight years this club contented itself singing at socials, revival meetings and home "benefits." Then, in 1876, came the Modoc Indian outbreak in the far West and the consequent transfer of a number of Modoc prisoners to the neighboring federal penitentiary at Leavenworth. Anderson saw his chance and launched a boom for the "Modoc" Musical Club. Within a decade this organization had sung in almost every big city in the country, and Topeka was known throughout the nation as the home of the Modoc Club. Tom Anderson did it.

He also was famous in freemasonry. He organized the Topeka chapter and the Topeka commandery and filled many prominent offices in that order. He was for some time head of the Knights Templar for the Ninth District, comprising Missouri, Kansas and Colorado.

After dropping the commercial club work in 1907, Mr. Anderson lived in practical retirement, dabbling a little in the insurance business.

In 1909 his seventieth birthday was honored by a celebration that gladdened the old man's spirit. Fully fifteen hundred guests, including the Modocs, the Topeka Choral Society, the Knights Templar, Marshall's Band, the K. and L. of S. Band and the Lincoln Post drum corps turned out. Topeka is still talking about it. The major's cards, which were distributed among his friends on this occasion, bore the following inscription: "Thomas J. Anderson, Topeka, Seventieth Birthday, May 29, 1909. Fifty-two years in Kansas. Forty-four years in Topeka. And never owned a hammer."

Death overtook Tom Anderson at his Topeka home on January 31, 1912. He was survived by a second wife and two children, the first Mrs. Anderson having died in 1886. His career will be a source of inspiration for generations to come. He was a rare type of man, the kind that can serve as well as lead; the kind of man not selfishly devoted to the narrow performance of salaried duties, but who has the public welfare at heart. He was a man who rooted continuously for his town. He was an arch booster. We can pay him no worthier tribute than this: "Fifty-five years in Kansas. Forty-four years in Topeka. And he never owned a hammer."

Topeka Herald, Mar. 22, 1905

NEW AUTO CAR.

Santa Fe Tries One on the City Railway.

The man-about-town, who under ordinary circumstances appears to be too busy to stop to look at unusual sights, forgot himself yesterday, and lined up along the sidewalks with all others to gawk at the latest novelty in the transportation line.

The new gasoline motor inspection car which was recently purchased by the Santa Fe and was being given a test on the tracks of the Topeka Railway company.

The inspection car was a novelty and it attracted more attention than the first automobile ever seen in Topeka.

by an expert chauffeur from the factory.

The new car is rated at seven-horse power, but it develops a much greater power. It is said that the car will develop a speed of from 40 to 50 miles an hour, which is considerably faster than it will ever be used for inspection purposes.

The test run made with the car over the street railway tracks proved exceptionally satisfactory. The car is specifically designed for use on railway tracks which do not have the sharp curves of a street railway track. However, the car took the curves of the street railway lines with great ease.

The inspection car is built very much like a regular automobile car except that steel wheels with flanges like railway car wheels are used instead of the rubber tires, and the front axle is stationary instead of being built for sharp turns under the

The Automobile Motor Car.

The Santa Fe railroad has been conducting experiments with the new style automobile inspection cars and the indications are that they will be adopted and supplied to all division superintendents on the system.

The car which was seen in Topeka yesterday was purchased for Dan Cain, general superintendent at La Junta, and was shipped to him today. The motor car is manufactured by the Oldsmobile company, and it was purchased by the Santa Fe of the Railway Appliance company of Chicago, through B. T. Lewis, who was formerly with the Santa Fe in Topeka but who is now connected with the Railway Appliance company.

The car has been in storage in Topeka for several weeks and it was given its first test last week. On last Saturday, General Manager H. U. Mudge, and General Superintendent J. E. Hurley made a trip in the car to Lake View. The car was controlled

control of a lever like an automobile. The car is susceptible of excellent control and may be brought to a standstill in a very short space.

The car was run over the Santa Fe tracks to Fifth street and moved over to the street railway tracks. A trip was made to Washburn college and another trip was made to Vinewood Park.

A speed test could not be secured on the Washburn line as well as on the Vinewood line for the reason that the car was not supplied with a whistle to warn people at street crossings and for the additional reason that it had to wait for street cars running on schedule time. The trip to Washburn emphasized one point which stood out distinctively. It was that the new steel rails of the Street Railway company have been put down with great care and that they are lined up so well that there was hardly a perceptable jar noticeable in running over the tracks.

The inspection car above has a counterpart in the Track Geometry Inspection car described on the following page.

Santa Fe Photo

Track Geometry Inspection Car

GOMER JONES

The Santa Fe Railway new Track Geometry Car is designed to measure 10 different track characteristics while being moved along the railroad at speeds up to 80 MPH. Discrepancies found by the Car are called to the attention of track maintenance forces for correction. The Car is reported to be the most sophisticated track inspection car developed by a railroad. A visual record graphically displays the magnitude and location of any unacceptable condition.

The Car is also being equipped with an on-board computer to supplement the analog traces with information in printed form to be used in studies to forecast and plan track maintenance.

Track characteristics measured include surface and alignment of both rails, twist, gauge, superelevation along lateral and vertical acceleration, key bench marks distance and speed. A recently developed electrostatic recorder constantly displays the measurements on an analog strip chart with a visual record of the magnitude and location of any unacceptable deviations.;

The car is the result of a joint design effort between the Santa Fe and Rail Tech-Modern Machine and Tool of Newport News, Virginia.

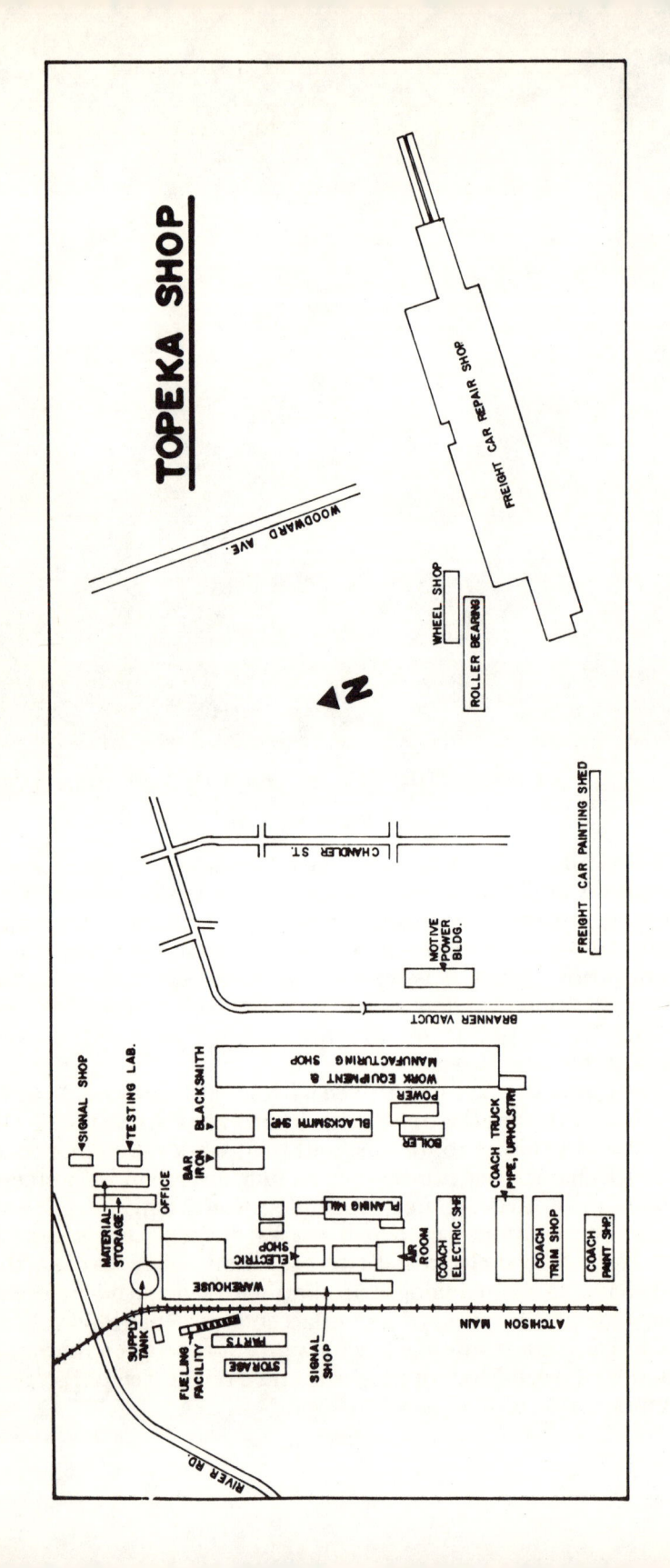

TOPEKA SHOP

THE SANTA FE SHOPS TODAY
(Diagram on opposite page)

(Santa Fe Photo)

Topeka Shops Today

GOMER JONES

The Topeka Shop attained its greatest size around the turn of the century, covering nearly 120 acres when the Santa Fe erected the Machine and Boiler shop which measured 152 feet by 850 feet followed by the 900 foot long car repair building when finished in 1910.

The Santa Fe Industries has grown from the 2 stall Roundhouse of the early 1870s with 125 miles of track to a major industry contributing to the diversified economy of Topeka. With the manufacture of rolling stock and the Santa Fe Research and Development Center, millions of dollars worth of products are turned out in a year, from the Super-Shock Control Box Cars and Super-Shock Multi-level Auto-veyor Cars along with the hundreds of component car parts for use over the system.

Shop orders include the manufacture of switches and frog parts furnished to the Newton Rail Mill for use and distribution over the system.

The Freight Car Shop builds 5 new cars a day in addition to the repair of freight cars. In 1977, 3657 cars were given heavy repairs and 3278 were given light repairs.

The 1.5 million dollar Wheel Shop is the center of production for 150 ton wheel assemblies per day that are shipped on specially built wheel cars over the system. 40,000 pairs of wheels are furnished annually.

The Loss and Damage on the Railroads had increased through the years to over $114,000,000 in 1958 along with loss of good will frequently associated with damage claims.

The Santa Fe has used and investigated through the years all different types of draft gears made available to railroads and it became apparent that the freight cars would have to have more cushioning capacity.

The Santa Fe has built or equipped over 44,000 Freight Cars with Shock Control since building the first car in 1958 at Topeka. Hydraulic cushioning appeared to be best, following problems with breakage of the bolsters, and distortion of the underframes during the past years on the freight cars purchased.

The hydraulic device is a double acting high pressure cylinder and piston contained within an outer housing which acts as a low pressure for the hydraulic fluid. It is so arranged that the movement of the car body on the sliding center sill causes the piston to move creating pressure within the cylinder of the hydraulic device which is automatically controlled to give the desired retarding effect, after which the car body and hydraulic device are automatically recentered by the return springs.

Assembly area at Santa Fe's Topeka shops where car sides are attached to the completed underframes of solid bottom, 100-ton gondolas. After this stage is completed, the cars move on through the production line to the paint shed where the primary coat of paint is applied. Afterward, cars are moved back into the car shop where decking is installed. Photo, Santa Fe Railway.

SANTA FE FREIGHT DIESEL No. 100—*The first diesel-electric locomotive built for Santa Fe for regular freight service. On Feb. 10, 1941, when this General Motors diesel-electric was returning to Kansas City after a demonstration run to Topeka (for benefit of shippers) Harold E. Naill made this photo from the Tecumseh overpass.*

A Child of Topeka... *(Continued from p. 5)*

and assigns held and firmly bound unto the said City of Topeka in the penal sum of Two hundred thousand Dollars lawful money of the United States to be paid to the said City of Topeka to which payment well and

The $200,000 penalty clause, from the original bond contract, apparently in Holliday's own hand writing.

dred others in urging Henry Bartling to become a candidate. Bartling, a former Indian Agent for the Department of the Interior, was then employed in the Land Department of the Santa Fe Railroad. Bartling graciously consented, through the local press, to such use of his name, and he was elected for one two-year term to the office in the election of 1873. Thereafter, by authority of a majority of those voting at a special election preceding which Holliday was the principal affirmative spokesman, the city of Topeka issued $100,000 in general obligation bonds for the assistance of the Atchison, Topeka and Santa Fe Railroad.

On September 22, 1874 a formal contract was executed on the part of the city of Topeka by Henry Bartling as mayor, and on the part of the Atchison, Topeka and Santa Fe Railroad Company by Thomas Nickerson as president, whereby in consideration of the receipt of the donated bonds the railroad company agreed "to forever hereafter permanently maintain and keep its said general offices, principal machine, car and repair shops at the said city of Topeka ... and as a further indemnity and guaranty to the said city of Topeka for the faithful performance of the above agreement on the part of the said railroad company it doth hereby acknowledge itself, its successors and assigns held and firmly bound unto the said city of Topeka in the penal sum of two hundred thousand dollars lawful money of the United States to be paid to the said city of Topeka..." Thus, it would seem that Holliday, in avoidance of too outward an appearance of possible double-dealing, had sacrificed the mayor's office to an agreeable successor and had convinced Santa Fe management that a bird of $100,000 in hand was worth a penalty of $200,000 in the bush. He not only secured the initial location of these valuable facilities in his city but he also secured for Topeka the permanence of their location. A careful study of the original document makes it rather convincing that the contract is in the handwriting and composition style of Cyrus K. Holliday, and that it was prepared by him for the quite willing execution of the two signatories.

While meetings of the Santa Fe board of directors ordinarily were held in Boston or New York, the annual meeting of the stockholders invariably were held at the general offices of the company in Topeka. Traditionally, Cyrus K. Holliday, in formal attire complete with silk hat, would meet the "directors' special" at the Santa Fe station and he would lead the small procession of distinguished visitors on foot throughout the downtown streets to the red brick general office building at Ninth and Jackson Streets.

When the Santa Fe finally had come into its own as a giant in the transcontinental railroad industry, occasionally there were some who asserted that they, or others, were entitled to part, or all, of the credit for its founding. These claims were promptly and indignantly refuted by Holliday, who had retained in his safe the documentary evidence of his solitary inspiration and personal achievement. When, in Holliday's twilight years, such a claim of distinction surfaced again following the death of some individual, Luther C. Challis who had progressed from the small banker of Atchison to a successful Wall Street financier, came to the support of his old friend by asserting publicly that of his personal knowledge Cyrus K. Holliday of Topeka was the true "father of the Santa Fe."

Until he died on March 29, 1900, there never was any attempt on the part of Cyrus K. Holliday to conceal his indivisible pride in the dream come true—"our town"—and the materialized vision of a great railroad that for so long was visible to his eyes alone. Without the one it is doubtful that there might have been the other.

Steam Heat For Santa Fe Cars

From North Topeka Mail, *Feb. 6, 1891*

The old reliable Santa Fe Route has a new system of steam heating on the plug train between Topeka and Kansas City, which is one of the great inventions of the age. Steam is communicated directly from the engine to the coaches and it is claimed that even temperature is maintained. The invention is by a Topeka man. It is controlled by Topeka parties and the train thus equipped was made in the Topeka shops.

(Continued from p. 125)

the idea being to catch the division storekeeper napping. Of course, he played the same game in his requisitioning.

As a real shocker, on occasion, we sent the division storekeeper exactly what he had requisitioned. This we thought very erudite and it was certainly unnerving to the storekeeper. His only possible retaliation, after several months of jitters, was to omit sending a monthly requistion. This really raised hell as we couldn't be sure whether he had deliberately omitted it or if it had been lost in the paper shuffle. It was all part of what Kim would have called The Great Game.

The second change from routine was the supply cars. These were actually store houses on wheels which made the rounds of the entire system. They dropped off minor items of supplies at points too small and remote to be supplied otherwise. Supply cars dealt in a myriad of small things; it was fun to help replenish their stock.

In the course of delivering materials to various locations—the shops, the boiler shops, the car sheds, the lumber yards, etc.—I got around the yards quite a lot. At that time the Santa Fe shops was one of the largest locomotive repair shops in the world and looked it. There was a bustle entirely lacking today in this age of slinking and stinking deisels. The yards jammed with locomotives—true, many of them were the old Santa Fe type decapod waiting to be scrapped—but many were there to be repaired. The south end of the shop would have its big doors open in spring and summer and one could see the giant steam locomotives lined up in various stages of repair and re-assembly.

In several areas of the shop oxy-acetylene torches could be seen cutting side rods out of inches thick steel forgings. In the blacksmith shop the giant steam hammers were always busy during the day forging shapes out of steel ingots; the scream of suddenly released steam and the dull thud of the striking hammers could be heard all over the yards.

At the north end of the boiler shop was situated a tube rattler, one of the noisiest creations of all mankind. A cylinder of some length, it rotated several revolutions per minute by an electric motor. Half filled with boiler flues or tubes (the steam locomotives were equipped with fire tubes instead of water tubes), the lid was clamped on and the motor started. The purpose was to jar loose the ferric oxide scale from the tube surface, and jar it loose it did with a rattling noise heard half way across Oakland.

Alas, all this activity is gone; true the shops are active but at smaller and quieter tasks. The glory has departed forever.

While I worked in the oil House, the Santa Fe bought the famous "Blue Goose," No. 3460, a streamlined Hudson Class steam locomotive (Baldwin built, of course) for large and fast passenger service. I remember seeing and admiring her on the locomotive scales at the east side of the lower shops just west of the Branner Street viaduct. They purchased her along with five sisters of conventional appearance; one of these, No. 3463, now rests on a siding at the Kansas Free Fair Grounds along Topeka Blvd.—last of a magnificent, glorious breed.

Regarding the scales, I also remember one day when the Union Pacific brought over one of their big jobs; one of the 9000 class, I believe, with six pairs of drivers, to be weighed. We marveled at its size and the low moan of its whistle. The Union Pacific used a low pitched moaning whistle, pleasant to the ear but much different from the medium pitched and delightfully shrill whistle of the Santa Fe. There was no mistaking which was which; I loved them both but favored the Santa Fe's. That too is gone from the shops. Has progress brought us anything better with the disappearance of the clanging bell, the thumping of the great side rods, and the shrilling sounds of a locomotive far, far away in the night?

We had regular watchmen who made complete rounds of the main warehouse building and the Oil House between the hours of 4:00 P.M. and 8:00 A.M. each day. Each Sunday one of the laborers was selected on a rotating basis to watch during those hours. If you assume we were paid at an overtime rate you have assumed wrong; we received our regular hourly rate and were eager for the extra $3.44 we would make. I well remember watching the Oil House on June 13, 1937, and became quite an expert on lubrication, spending part of the day in Leonard's office reading the Santa Fe's lubrication charts while eating my lunch of cold fried liver sandwiches.

That fall we noticed a slacking off with more and more of our doubling off on jobs. Then in December things finally bounced wide open. Some of the higher rated crane operator and supply car jobs were abolished, at least temporarily. On the Santa Fe system this meant bumping on a grandiose scale. On the 17th a supply car man bumped me out of the Oil House and back to the extra gang. Early the next spring more changes occurred as I was first shunted to cutting up old car frames for scrap and then to the lumber yard—work next to the bottom of the totem pole. That seemed so pointless and dreary that I think I was even a little relieved when I was laid off on Tuesday, April 26, 1938.

(Continued from p. 85)

Copeland Hotel for a brief meeting with dignitaries before moving to the Governor's mansion for dinner with Gov. W. J. Bailey. The atmosphere there in the beginning was unexpectedly romantic, since the electric light fuse blew at the last minute and the guests assembled in candle light.

Then it was back to the streets and the crowd on the way to the auditorium for the main address.

Arriving late, the party was met with a blare of trumpets "cutting Lt. Gov. James A. Troutman's three-minute speech squarely in two." The President again "rained words" on the "rapt faces, upturned to the generous man." His message, punctuated with frequent "Amens" and "Hallelujahs" from a zealous front-bencher, was a glowing tribute to fidelity, manliness, heroism, character, initiative, loyalty, boldness, obedience, piety, generosity, mutual sharing, hard work, and wisdom—all characteristics he found in the railroad men there present. Railroading as a profession, he observed in a voice now cracking from over-use, was one "in which man has to show the qualities of courage, hardihood, of willingness to face danger, of cultivating the power of instantaneous decisions under difficulties—the very qualities which go to make up the virile side of a man's character." (Applause!) Railroads contributed to the "material well-being" of the nation whose "wisdom grew with wealth." (Applause!) The speech ended praising the YMCA members for their "manliness which makes a man able to do his own share of the world's work with that fine and lofty love of one's fellow men ... for the common good of mankind in general. I congratulate you." (Prolonged cheers and applause!)

The crowd was again waiting as the procession moved back to the train which would carry the Presidential party to a number of major Kansas stops and even more 15-minute pauses at nearly every crossroad station, including an address in German at Victoria in Ellis County and a larger rest period at Sharon Springs.

It had been a glorious day and even the President seemed pleased. The crowd had had its show, including a dramatic incident when a man persisted in attempting to climb on the President's carriage. The press, totally captivated, editorialized, "The President noticed the man and might have taken a hand if the fellow had become obstreperous." No one was more happy than the professional pickpockets who were undoubtedly ardent Roosevelt followers that year. The police reported ten cases, all unsolved.

Behind the bombast and showmanship, however, the President was playing a subtle and quite serious game for high political stakes. The press had noted that the seventeen guests to the Governor's dinner were "political ice cutters of a high degree" and expressed considerable surprise that Cyrus Leland was not among them and that William Allen White's invitation had been specifically called for by the President. Both maneuvers were part of the President's Midwest strategy. Leland was a Hanna man. He had rendered service to Hanna as one of a combination of little-known state leaders who had wrested power from the old bosses in 1896 and 1900. Roosevelt chose to ignore the counsel of his old friend, William Allen White, who had urged him not to turn Leland out of his post as Commissioner of Pensions for the Misouri Valley. When he did oust Leland, members of the GAR, in White's words, "came out like a swarm of bees, buzzing their anger." Roosevelt felt justified in his actions since Hanna thus had been directly challenged and rendered powerless in patronage awards in Kansas. Although he might feel more politically secure with Leland out of office, Roosevelt knew that White's own feelings must be assuaged. The dinner was to serve as the setting for that purpose. At the moment the strategy appeared to be necessary and masterful but was to prove in the end totally unneccessary. Hanna, the cause of much of Roosevelt's anxiety, unexpectedly died before the election was held and with his rising popularity Roosevelt carried the day, 336 electoral votes to his opponent's 140.

Still, Topeka had had its day in the nation's limelight and the YMCA's cornerstone was solidly in place. For the twelve hours he had been in the city, it had been, indeed, the best show in town.

MARATHON ENTERTAINMENT

Matinee at R.R.Y.M.C.A.
27 Acts—Count 'Em—27!

WHAT may have established an all-time record for continuous performances at any local institution, was given at Topeka's Railroad Y.M.C.A., during the afternoon of January 1, 1917. We are indebted to one of the entertainers, Mrs. John C. Warner, Verona, N. J. (Florence Fair, Washburn College, BA '19), for the printed program given during the afternoon only, on New Year's Day.

Piano solo, Miss Hazel Shaw; reading, Mrs. Joseph P. Hicks;

(Continued on p. 177)

(Continued from p. 98)

roundhouse, regularly made up trains and delivered cars to customer loading and unloading tracks. By the mid-fifties they had been replaced entirely by diesels.

One of the more unusual classes of diesel switch engines on the Santa Fe was the little 44-ton General Electric, of which several regularly worked in Topeka. The 44-ton weight was significant because operating rules allowed switch engines of that size or smaller to work with an engineer only. All other engines, prior to the 1960s, had to operate with both an engineer and a fireman whether they were steam or diesel. The 44-ton units were dubbed "one-man switchers" by the railroaders.

One of the odd jobs that the steam engines from the Topeka roundhouse occasionally were called on to perform was that of "pusher" up the hill that runs on the Santa Fe main line southbound from 10th street to Pauline. This is one of the more challenging grades in eastern Kansas. Diesels, with their superior traction, seldom fail to move a train up that long climb. But an exceptionally heavy train occasionally left a steam engine help lessly spinning its wheels halfway up the hill. Therefore, during the steam era, a switch engine sometimes would push against the rear of a train from 10th street south for a few blocks, to generate enough speed to allow the main engine to reach Pauline successfully[6].

Diesel locomotives require much less servicing than the steam engines, so the completion of the dieselization process doomed the Santa Fe roundhouse in Topeka. In 1951 the five north stalls on the remaining portion were converted to storage space for store department materials. The machinery and tools used to work on steam engines were disposed of in 1954[7].

The end finally came for the roundhouse when a wrecking contractor purchased it for $100 in December of 1964. By February of 1965 it was gone, its space soon to be occupied by a company parking lot. The stone from the old roundhouse was loaded into railroad cars and deposited as riprap at various points along the Santa Fe line. The steel was cut up and sold as scrap. Over 4,000 feet of railroad track, 200,000 board feet of lumber, and 9,000 feet of steam heating vents were removed from the structure. The floor of the old roundhouse, made of high-quality Coffeyville paving bricks, was purchased for use in one of the clubrooms of the downtown Ramada Inn.[8]

This author, as a small child, occasionally visited the interior of the Santa Fe's Topeka roundhouse, walked on those bricks, and peered up in wonder at the huge steam engines. That was during the final years of steam power on the Santa Fe. The demolition of the roundhouse, the second and last in Topeka's Santa Fe history, symbolized the end of an era, the time when the railroads and their steam engines dominated the American scene.

(Continued from p. 68)

In the summer of 1954, President Eisenhower set forth "a grand plan" to build the most ambitious engineering project in modern history, the Interstate Highway System. The Federal Highway Act was passed in July, 1956. The Kansas Turnpike was completed between Wellington, Kansas and Kansas City, Missouri, in October, 1956, and it paralleled the Santa Fe Railway. Local inter-city traffic, under 300 miles, began moving by private automobiles. With the resulting loss of passenger revenues it became necessary to go to the various state corporation commissions to secure authority to discontinue local passenger trains.

On October 7, 1967, the federal government took all the mail off the railroads and started moving it on the air lines. With the resulting loss of revenues it was necessary to go to the Interstate Commerce Commission for permission to discontinue through passenger trains.

On April 30, 1971, Santa Fe discontinued all passenger trains—after 102 years of serving the traveling public.

The next day, May 1, 1971, the National Railroad Passenger Corporation (known as Amtrak) took over the operation and operated only two trains in each direction over Santa Fe tracks and only one train each way passed through Topeka.

SANTA FE PASSENGER TRAINS WHICH SERVED TOPEKA, 1869—1971

Compiled by George F. Sherman, Jr.

All Santa Fe Passenger trains which served Topeka May 1, 1869 - May 1, 1971

1-2 and 3-4	1869-N.A.	North Topeka - Burlingame
Pueblo Mail	1876-N.A.	Kansas City and Atchison - Pueblo
Atchison and Kansas City Mail & Express		Pueblo - Atchison and Kansas City
Emigrant		Kansas City and Atchison - Pueblo
California Express	1881-N.A.	Kansas City - Deming - Los Angeles
Atlantic Express		Los Angeles - Deming - Kansas City
Nickerson Accommodation	1883-N.A.	Kansas City - Nickerson
New York Express		Newton - Kansas City
Pacific Express		Atchison - Pueblo - Raton
Colorado Utah Express		Atchison - Pueblo - Raton
Wichita Express	1884-N.A.	Kansas City - Wichita
Santa Fe "Plug"	1884-1897	Kansas City - Topeka
	1897-1912	Kansas City - Osage City
	1912-1931	Kansas City - Emporia
California Express	1886-1887	Kansas City and Atchison - El Paso - Mojave
	1887-1888	Kansas City and Atchison - Los Angeles
Vestibule Express	1888-N.A.	Chicago - Denver - El Paso - Mojave
California Mexico Exp	1888-N.A.	Kansas City and Atchison - El Paso - Los Angeles
Denver and Utah Exp	1886-1887	Kansas City - Pueblo
	1888-1889	Kansas City - Denver
	1889-N.A.	Chicago - Denver
Denver Fast Express	1888-N.A.	Kansas City - Denver
Denver Express	1889-N.A.	Chicago - Denver
Vestibule Express	1889-N.A.	Chicago - Denver - Los Angeles - Mojave
	1890-1905	Chicago - Los Angeles - San Diego - San Francisco
Atlantic Express	1886-1887	Mojave - El Paso - Atchison and Kansas City
Texas and Oklahoma	1887-N.A.	Kansas City - Galveston

Name	Dates	Route
Express		
Colorado Express	1887-N.A.	Atchison - Wichita - Pueblo
Eastern Express		Pueblo - Wichita - Atchison
Colorado Express	1888-N.A.	Chicago - Denver
Chicago Express		Denver - Chicago
Denver Fast Express		Kansas City - Denver
Kansas Express		Kansas City - Caldwell
Arkansas City Express	1889-N.A.	Kansas City - Arkansas City
Denver Limited	1890-N.A.	Chicago - Denver
Missouri River Express	1890-1893	Los Angeles - Kansas City
	1890-N.A.	Denver Kansas City
Limited Vestibule		Chicago - Mulvane
108-107 and 106-105	1891-1932	Topeka - St. Joseph
58-57	1932-1954	Topeka - St. Joseph
56-55	1954-1958	Topeka - Atchison
The California Ltd	1892-1896	Chicago - Los Angeles
		Discontinued service May to November -1896
	1896-1900	Semi-Weekly and Tri-Weekly Service Nov. to June Service discontinued June to November
	1900-1901	Tri-Weekly Service from November to June, and Semi-Weekly Service June to November
	1901-1905	Daily Service November to June and Tri-Weekly Service June to November
	1905-1954	Daily Service - Chicago - Los Angeles
Columbian Limited	1893-N.A.	Los Angeles - Chicago
Chicago Vestibule Exp		Galveston - Chicago
		Denver - Chicago
Colorado Flyer	1902-1933	Kansas City - Denver
Missouri River Flyer	1902-1904	Denver - Kansas City
Fast Mail	1902-1907	Kansas City - Purcell
California Fast Mail	1904-1916	Chicago - Los Angeles - San Francisco
Los Angeles Express	1905-1916	Chicago - Los Angeles
Texas Fast Mail	1905-1915	Chicago - Galveston
Kansas City and Chicago Express	1906-1910	Galveston - Kansas City
Texas Express	1906-1916	Kansas City - Galveston
New State Express	1906-N.A.	Kansas City - Purcell
Mexico Express	1906-1909	Chicago - El Paso
	1909-1910	Kansas City - El Paso
Chicago Fast Mail	1910-1915	Denver - Kansas City
		Galveston - Kansas City
Texas Flyer	1910-1927	Chicago - Galveston
Tourist Flyer	1911-1916	Los Angeles - Chicago
Texas Mail	1915-1916	Chicago - Galveston
Chicago Flyer	1915-1917	Galveston - Kansas City
	1915-1931	Denver - Kansas City
The Navajo	1915-1922	Chicago - Los Angeles - San Francisco
	1922-1939	Chicago - Phoenix - Los Angeles - San Francisco
The Scout	1916-1925	Chicago - Denver - Los Angeles
	1925-1949	Chicago - Los Angeles
The Ranger	1916-1933	Kansas City - Galveston
	1933-1948	Chicago - Galveston
Chicago Express	1918-1920	Chicago - Galveston
	1920-1927	Kansas City - Galveston
	1920-1929	Galveston - Chicago
West Texas Express	1920-1921	Chicago - Clovis
	1921-1927	Chicago - Amarillo
Fast Fifteen	1932-1937	Kansas City - Galveston
The Grand Canyon Ltd	1929-1937	Chicago - Los Angeles
	1938-1948	Chicago - Los Angeles
	1929-1947	Chicago - Ash Fork - Phoenix
The Grand Canyon 23-24	1949-1951	Chicago - Los Angeles (First Section via Topeka)
123-124	1949-1951	Chicago - Los Angeles
23-24	1951-1958	Chicago - Los Angeles (Via Ottawa Junction)
123-124	195101963	Chicago - Los Angeles
23-24	1963-1971	Chicago - Los Angeles
The Kansas Cityan	1938-1939	Chicago - Wichita
	1939-1957	Chicago - Oklahoma City
	1957-1960	Kansas City - Oklahoma City
	1960-1968	Kansas City - Fort Worth - Dallas
The Chicagoan	1938-1960	Oklahoma City - Chicago
	1960-1968	Dallas - Fort Worth - Chicago
Centennial State	1940-1949	Kansas City - Denver
		Denver - Kansas City
Texas Chief	1948-1965	Chicago - Galveston
		Galveston - Chicago
	1965-1971	Chicago - Houston
		Houston - Chicago
San Francisco Chief	1954-1971	Chicago - San Francisco
		San Francisco - Chicago

N.A.   Not available

FOUR GENERATIONS... *(Continued from p. 24)*

ticular fields, have graduated from the schools. Graduates really acquire two trades, as all are qualified draftsmen."

Pratt, who currently is in charge of apprentice training, said the "general concepts" remain much the same as when Thomas started it. He emphasized, however, that "the school work is always being up-dated to include the many technological changes that are taking place. Other departments assist the training department in order for the apprentices to receive the most up-to-date information.

"Special classes (correspondent or classroom) are conducted for the mechanics or supervision in order for them to up-date their skills on newer equipment and practices."

Pratt said several factors determine the number of apprentices in training. He said Santa Fe forecasts required labor needs "to be sure there will be a mechanic's job for the apprentice at the completion of his apprenticeship."

The number in training varies from 400 to 750, "about one-fifth being located at Topeka." Some 200 apprentices graduate to full-fledged mechanics each year, he said.

Only the past May, something new and different was added: Theresa Officer became the first woman to graduate from the apprentice school and have her status jump from apprentice to journeyman machinist. She earned her journeyman's rating, like so many hundreds of men before her, in the Santa Fe's Topeka shops.

APPRENTICE SYSTEM... *(Continued from p. 133)*

my dad retired as a coach carpenter and I began to work as a sheet-metal worker at the Topeka shops for Santa Fe. As a young boy I was indoctrinated to the Santa Fe way of life by way of my father and grandfathers. Grandpa Dale would take me to the Topeka yards where he had began his career as a clerk. As a clerk he knew most of the engineers; as a result we were able to go up in the cabs of the locomotives, which for me was one of the greatest thrills that I have ever had.

The other thing I remember that I enjoyed and feel that it always made me feel like I really wanted to work for the Santa Fe was when my mother took my Boy Scout troop on a tour of the shops. I was so amazed with all of the different things that were going on with the cars. It was great to see the final product rolling out of the shops and down the tracks.

What happened at Santa Fe affected the way I was raised, where I lived and what I did. With Santa Fe having such a profound effect on my life it is little wonder that I wanted to work there and carry on the family tradition of working for the railroad.

(Continued from p. 17)

a hundred miles down the road from Topeka, seemed to be going bankrupt. This lunch room was situated in the Clifton Hotel, a two-story frame building put up in 1876 by local citizens. Morse had made arrangements for the operation of the lunch room with Ben Putnam, who was also one of the owners of the hotel. After reviewing the situation Fred Harvey took over the operation. On January 1, 1878 he signed a contract with the Santa Fe, one of the terms of which was that the Santa Fe would stop its through mainline passenger trains for two meals per day at the Florence dining station.

Travelers noticed the change in cuisine very quickly. A visitor from Kingman, having dined there, wrote February 23 in his newspaper: "The railroad eating place at Florence—the proprietor has no cards and we do not know his name—but he set a square meal all the same. Everybody takes breakfast and supper there." The hotel had been entirely refurnished with solid walnut pieces; fine china and Irish linen were provided for the dining room. Within a year the building had to be enlarged. "For the past several months traveler after traveler had to be taken to other hotels, just for lack of sleeping accommodations." Originally fifty feet in length, the hotel building was extended seventy feet at one end, more than doubling its space.

This growth in business was ascribed to William H. Phillips, a manager Harvey had hired sometime in 1878 after trying others. A British sportsman, who came to spend several days hunting grouse around Florence, noted the "beaming, rubicund, jolly British face" of Phillips and wrote about him in the March 1879 issue of *Field and Garden,* London, England.

> The management of the refreshment rooms along the Atchison, Topeka and Santa Fe last year was shocking, but they are now in charge of Mr. W. H. Phillips, an Englishman, formerly of the Cardiff Arms, Cardiff, next of the well-known Centennial Globe Hotel, where he fed 500,000 people at one pound per day each during the Philadelphia Exhibition and last of the world famed Tremont of Chicago. The fish and game breakfast, dinners and suppers given by Mr. Phillips at this season of the year along this line . . . are each one marvels of luxury and neatness. . . .

Certainly it was clear to all that W. H. Phillips and Fred Harvey incidentally (though he was seldom mentioned) had made a great success of the Clifton Hotel at Florence. The local newspaper did not fail to report on the local balls, when "mine host" Phillips served more than a hundred guests, the tables groaning with sumptuous fare.

Phillips catered for others in other places, for one, the dinner and dance given by the Commercial Travelers Association at

St. Joseph, Missouri. But of all the dinners, the most noted was the inaugural dinner of the British Association of Kansas, held December 25, 1879, at the Clifton Hotel in Florence. Thirty-six members attended, seven from Omaha, six from Denver, Jordan Lee of the Sante Fe and G. F. Jones, *State Journal* newsman, from Topeka. All three Topeka newspapers reported the event at great length. No mention was made of Fred Harvey but at the end of the menu—which was printed in full by two of the newspapers—were the credits: Fred Harvey, Proprietor and W. H. Phillips, Manager.

FIRST ANNUAL DINNER
of the
BRITISH ASSOCIATION OF KANSAS,
holden at the
Clifton Hotel, Florence, Kas., Dec. 25, '80

BILL OF FARE.
Little neck clams on shell.

SOUP.
Game, oysters in cream.

FISH.
Baked red snappers in Port wine. Potatoe croquettes.

BOILED.
Leg of mutton caper sauce, boiled potatoes, string beans.

ROASTS.
Goose stuffed apple sauce garnished with faggots, baron of beef o d Engli-h style, roast moulded potatoes, green peas, sugar corn.

ENTRIES.
Roast fillet of beef, larded mushroon sauce gardner- style. quail on toast with sa t pork, small patties of oysters.

COLD ORNAMENTAL DISHES.
Potted Hare Yorkshire sty.e, boned turkey hunter'- style young pig in natural form. goose and quail in p mage, pyramid of lobster in shell, ham decorated in jelly, chicken -alad plain dressing.

GAME.
Roast saddle of antelope with currant jelly. Stewed tomatoes, mashed potatoes.

PASTRY AND CAKES.
English plum pu ding brandy sauce, ornamental fruit cakes, pyramiu of Maccarons, pyramid of jelly cake, fancy cakes.
Tea, coffee.

TOASTS OF THE EVENING.
The Queen. The President of the U. S. Our friends at home. The British Legation of Denver. The Ladies.

FRED. HARVEY,   W. H. PHILLIPS,
    Proprietor.   Manager.

Joan T. George, Topeka, whose 64 years in the Harvey organization began as a waitress and ended as a manager, demonstrates the "come-and-get-it" gong, now property of the Kansas State Historical Society.

Meanwhile the Santa Fe was growing mightily. By mid-year 1879 the rails reached Las Vegas, New Mexico; by February 9, 1880 they arrived at Lamy, New Mexico just six miles from the old town of Santa Fe. As soon as they were built at these two places the eating houses were taken over by Fred Harvey. The Santa Fe railroad recognized the growing reputation of the Fred Harvey management and featured him as early as 1881 in timetables.

The pattern was now set. As the railroad built into new territory, the new eating houses would automatically come under Harvey's supervision. Others, mostly in Kansas, established under other managements, would more gradually be turned over to him. In 1882 Fred Harvey resigned from the Burlington and devoted his entire attention to his business with the Santa Fe. By 1883 Harvey controlled seventeen eating places on the main lines of the Santa Fe railroad. Of these, seven were in Kansas, including those already mentioned with others at Newton, Hutchinson, Wellington and Arkansas City. There was one at LaJunta, Colorado and nine in New Mexico for by that time the Santa Fe had built well into New Mexico. When he died in 1901 Fred Harvey operated the food service in 45 eating houses and 20 dining cars. His successors carried on the business almost unchanged under the Fred Harvey name.

Through the first years little was heard of the Topeka lunch room due to its restricted space. But probably more passenger trains were serviced at that station than any of the other early houses under the Harvey supervision. And it was there that Fred

Harvey tried out many of the rules and rituals that would for many years attend the feeding of the travelers on the Santa Fe trains. At first as has been said, only male help was used in the Topeka lunch room, perhaps until November 1881 when the new brick station was finished with dining facilities on the second floor. In 1904 an addition on the first floor provided a lunch room seating 45 and a dining room seating 110 diners.

Harvey could provide all the concomitants of fine dining—the excellent food, pleasant surroundings and quick, skilled service, but he could not provide more than thirty minutes for the diners to enjoy these pleasures. Hence the ritual devised to make the service fast and smooth yet avoid any suggestion of haste or hurry. An hour before the train's arrival, the brakeman went through the cars asking passengers if they planned to eat at the next dining stop. His report was wired ahead. The engineer's whistle five minutes before the train arrived at the station alerted the waitresses to get the first course on the table.

There are still men and women in Topeka who remember the scene at the depot when the train came in. A white-aproned waiter, beating a brass gong with a wooden mallet, brought the passengers quickly to the dining room door. (That same gong, beaten a hundred years ago in Topeka, is still preserved in the Kansas State Historical Museum.) The first course was on the table and as soon as the diner was seated, the waitress went down the table asking, "Tea, iced tea, coffee or milk," and at the same time positioning the coffee cup at each place accordingly, so that the girl coming behind to pour the drinks knew just what to pour. The service in the dining room was table d'hote with two choices for the main course. The plates already served in the kitchen with meat and vegetables, were quickly placed on the tables.

At least once during the half hour, the manager circulated through the dining room announcing, "Passengers have plenty of time. Ample notice will be given before the departure of the train." If a freight train started up outside and some diner got up to dash to the door, the manager was there to intervene and reassure. Generally the passengers got through eating in plenty of time—as they had been told they would. But if one or two lingered until they were about to delay the train, the brakeman appeared in the dining room and stood looking at them with his watch in his hand. Only as a last desperate resort did the conductor come in and yell "All Aboard!" Nobody got left. The diners went back to their trains feeling quite unhurried and well satisfied.

When occasionally an individual headed for the dining room in his shirt sleeves, he never made it. The manager intercepted him, and after a few words the diner either accepted a black alpaca coat, which the manager furnished, or went to the lunch room. Usually the coat was accepted with good grace. Fred Harvey believed the atmosphere of his dining rooms demanded a certain dignity of dress and demeanor. The lunch counter was more permissive.

In the Fred Harvey system, the lunch rooms were open twenty-four hours a day; the dining rooms only when trains were scheduled to stop for a meal or when a dinner or banquet was being catered for a local group. There is little evidence now remaining of Topeka's use of the dining room at the Santa Fe, though families remember what a treat it was to go there for Sunday dinner. In the early 1900's the lunch room was the fashionable place for the young people to go for refreshment after a dance.

Women were in scarce supply in the early days of Kansas and the West generally. Fred Harvey could not find enough girls locally to staff his eating houses and he began recruiting waitresses, advertising in the eastern and mid-west newspapers, "Women of good character, attractive and intelligent, 18-30 years." As a result Harvey has been credited with civilizing the west and providing it with wives. Novels and movies have elaborated on this theme, romanticizing the Harvey Girl. While there is much truth in this thesis there is also some fantasy. No doubt the young ladies were a softening, refining influence on the westerners and they did marry the ranchers, cowboys and town promoters, but mostly they married the men they worked with, Harvey and Santa Fe employees.

There are still some Harvey girls about to tell us of their working days in the Harvey system. One, Joan Thompson George, lives in Topeka and reminisces about the old days. She was a Milwaukee girl and answered an ad in a Chicago newspaper. She was hired after an interview and sent on a Santa Fe pass out to Hutchinson, Kansas for training. As a waitress she earned $25 a week, room and board and tips—a better wage at that time than was paid most Kansas school teachers. Within a year she married John Thompson, a baker in the Harvey system. On her wedding day she had to get up at five o'clock to help service a World War I troop train.

It was not easy to work for Fred Harvey. The hours were bad and irregular. Whenever the train came in, late or on time, it had to be serviced. While Harvey paid good wages to all his employees, he demanded a high standard of performance. And this standard, just as the quality of his food, was maintained by frequent, unexpected and rigorous inspections. A Harvey girl was clean and neat. She was always on time, she never chewed gum, never put her pencil behind her ear or talked with other girls in the dining room. She thanked her guests for their patronage, never argued or talked back for the customer was always right.

Joan Thompson lost her husband, and with her daughter went back ten years later to again work in the Harvey system. She worked in many of the towns along the Santa Fe lines, her daughter living with her in the Harvey hotels or in the dormitories built near-by. She became a manager and in that capacity was sent as a relief manager to Topeka in 1932, during the period when Alf Landon was running for the Presidency and when the Harvey House was busy with the many political meetings and dinners. At that time the Topeka Harvey House employed eighteen to twenty waitresses, the majority of them girls who lived with their families in the city. The others had rooms on the second floor of the Santa Fe station directly over the lunch and dining rooms. An apartment for the manager was also located there.

As competition between railroads had grown fiercer and time was of the essence, more and more dining cars were put on the Santa Fe trains with the Fred Harvey system operating the food service. There was no longer time to stop the trains for meals. Then Americans began traveling more and more in their own automobiles and passenger travel declined on all railroads. The Harvey system spread out in other directions.* In Topeka the old Harvey rooms needed refurbishment and air-conditioning, an investment not warranted by the local patronage. Joan still a Fred Harvey manager, though now married to W. E. George, a Santa Fe electrical foreman, was sent to Topeka to terminate the business in this city. The twelve remaining employees were transferred elsewhere. Mrs. George gathered up the linens, dishes and other equipment for storage and in January 1940, after 64 years of service, the Topeka Harvey House was closed.

*Along highways.

(Topeka Capital, Dec. 11, 1895)

A MAN WITH NERVE

Col. Sam Radges the Only Topeka Man to Bid at the Auction.

Col. Sam Radges prides himself on the fact that he is the only man in Topeka who had the nerve to bid at the sale of the Santa Fe yesterday.

When Judge Johnson called for bids, Sam spoke up promptly:

"Fifty millions."

He did not say whether he meant dollars or doughnuts or grains of corn.

Edward King bid $60,000,000, and the road was knocked down to him.

Mr. King knew of Sam's intentions beforehand. Col. Radges met Judge Johnson on the street yesterday morning and announced to him that he was prepared to put in a bid for the property. Mr. King happened to be with Judge Johnson at the time and after being introduced to Col. Radges, said he was glad he was going to have some competition here—he was afraid he would have things all his own way.

"Well," said the colonel, "you won't. I have a message from Jay Gould authorizing me to bid fifty millions."

"Is that so?" said the man from Wall street. "Well, coming from Jay, that ought to be hot stuff."

After the sale was over Colonel Radges said he would have raised Mr. King's bid, but he considered fifty millions all the road was worth. It is a second hand road, anyway, he said, and the ties are all rusty.

Gleed and Reorganization . . . (Continued from p. 54)

$60,000,000. On December 12 the charter of the Atchison, Topeka and Santa Fe *Railway* Company was filed, and the new company took possession of the property on January 1, 1896.

The last major decisions made by the reorganization committee involved selection of the officials and board of directors of the new company. The *Railroad Gazette* noted that there were "a number of important interests asking representation on the new Board," but Gleed and Cheney both were retained as directors, and they thereby had their names included on the new Santa Fe charter as incorporators of the company. Kansas statutes required that at least two Kansans serve as directors of any corporation chartered in the state. Gleed's unusually active service in presenting the viewpoint of western shippers, passengers, and employees to other members of the Santa Fe board from 1894 to 1920 suggests that this was a wise law.

Throughout the remainder of his life, Gleed enjoyed the reputation of having played an important role in the reorganization of the Santa Fe in 1894 and 1895, although it was not clear to most people just what his contribution had been. Many sources exaggerated his role and suggested that he was primarily responsible for devising the complex plan used in reorganizing the bankrupt railroad. Gleed himself never claimed to have been the author of the plan, and on one occasion he remarked that the scheme which finally proved acceptable to the diverse interests involved resulted from the work of many different individuals.

In 1895 a Topeka attorney, Howell Jones, praised Gleed as the key negotiator in obtaining the compromises necessary for reorganization of the railroad:

> I, as well as others, have recognized the great ability, sagacity and skill you have shown in the reorganization of the Santa Fe. The work was fittingly and well performed by you, and, in my judgment, could not have been done by anyone else. You are the only one who could go unchallenged and be welcomed in all the hostile camps. You are the only one who could take up the points of difference and argue them with the various parties representing conflicting interests. After you had ascertained the points of agreement among the contending parties, you were the only one who could go to the other and represent how far they agreed. I am in a position to know what great services you performed, and I hope that the meritorious work performed by you will not go unrewarded.

There may be some validity in Jones' comments; but it should be noted that at times, such as in the struggle with the Protective Committee, Gleed was more of a combatant than a compromiser.

In later years Gleed became involved in the telephone business, in banking, in mining, and in numerous other business activities. His participation in the Santa Fe reorganization brought him contacts with important financiers in New York, Boston, and St. Louis; and he was widely regarded as a man who could obtain financial backing for western business ventures from his wealthy friends in the East.

Matinee at R.R.Y.M.C.A.... (Continued from p. 165)

vocal solo, Miss Marjorie Cole; cornet solo, Miss Ethel May; reading, Miss Esther Freeman; selections by a male quartette; instrumental duet, Misses Ethel and Eva May; whistling solo, Miss Florence Fair; reading, Miss Elsie Saville; vocal solo, Miss Isla Romig; Dutch dance, Miss Florence Mower and Miss Julia Keller; songs, parodies, etc., Scoville Davidson; reading, Miss Thelma Day; violin solo, Miss Mary Hall; farce, "Brain Contortionists," Dorothy and Ross Crichton; sherpardess dance, Miss Florence Mower; vocal solo with harp accompaniment, Miss Mary Sanck; reading, Mrs. A. A. Graham; instrumental trio, Misses Eva, Ethel and Ruth May; vocal solo, John Brown; reading, Miss Clara Belle Banta; vocal duet, W. E. Hall and W. E. May; vocal trio, Misses Lillian and Ellen Malmstrom and Mrs. P. Armunderig; reading, Miss Alice Ellenberger; reading, Miss Mabel Malstrom; vocal solo, John Shaw; club swinging, Raymond Reeser.

So much for the matinee. The Modoc Club (male chorus) presented the evening program.

(Continued from p. 42)

Dozens of letters came from local Reading Room managers, praising her and the company and asking for their return. From Clovis: "The best program that has ever been here." From Needles: "She has been the talk of the town ever since." From Slayton, Texas: "The company captured the admiration and attention of an audience of 1200. Everybody asking when they are coming back." She was called the "vest pocket comedienne, charming, peppy and lovable."

Miss Elmore sang, danced, did impersonations with costume changes and ventriloquism, with her two "children," Sambo and Susie, or sometimes Gus and Susie. Publicity for an appearance at Needles, Feb. 14, 1930, said, "The mention of Lucile Elmore and the printing of the above program is sufficient guarantee to Santa Fe audiences of a great entertainment. She has been over the Santa Fe before with great success and comes to us again with an entirely new company. She is without doubt one of the cleverest impersonators of today and her take-off of Ted Lewis, famous band leader, the 'Mechanical Doll' and her 'Preacher Number' are as good as any vaudeville show."

In 1939 the entertainment circuit was practically eliminated. It had done what it was intended to do and had even exceeded the expectations of President Ripley and the Santa Fe. Other entertainment was coming to the western towns—motion pictures, radio, commercial recreation, school and church entertainments, country clubs, sports. The Santa Fe touring entertainers had played leading roles in the maturing of the West and set a standard of entertainment for the people. A concert a week was more entertainment than most small towns anywhere in the nation was enjoying. Over nearly 40 years the "noblest and sweetest" movement had done its work.

Santa Fe Sporting Scene... *(Continued from p. 143)*

ball to football; these were just some of the activities sponsored for Santa Fe employees in Topeka. However and appropriately enough, baseball was still king. In a young and growing America, life for many centered upon the ball diamond. And in their dreams at night came the distant sound of a train whistle leading to some exotic adventure in a far away land. The Santa Fe led to adventure in the great Southwest, and it, too, for a time was a king.

(Continued from p. 111)

By October of the same year the results of the July walk-out were known. The *Journal* headlined, "Strike Is History," and the article read, "The Santa Fe shop strike is finished, so far as the railroad is concerned. The former shop employees who went out on strike on July 1 may return as new employees when there are vacancies for them."

In April, 1925, the *Capital* did a feature article on John Purcell, an asistant to the vice-president, who had been the first superintendent of the Topeka Shops. Purcell had risen through the ranks from machinist apprentice. In that same issue of the paper was another Santa Fe story with a headline reading, "Shop Payroll Is Biggest Item in Topeka's Income." The reporter went into great detail about the size of the shops and the Santa Fe in general: "The Santa Fe shops, at Topeka, largest on the system ... are an integral part of the Santa Fe's existence in Topeka." He continued, "During 1921 there were employed in the shops an average of 2,600 men, and the monthly payroll averaged $280,802 for the same period—making a payroll of $3,363,624 for the year." Topeka citizens had every right to be proud of their railroad.

The depression years rolled across the Santa Fe as bad as anywhere else in the country. As the '30's crawled by everyone began to wonder when would it end. By 1937, in the depth of bleak times, the Santa Fe went to a five-day work week and finally, in 1938, had several months of three-day work weeks. Therefore, the headline, "Santa Fe Back to 5-Day Week As Business Up," was hailed with great hope. The *Journal* reported, "The announcement that a return to five days a week will be effective July 1 was heralded with pleasure in Topeka today." So the second half of 1938 was definitely going to be better.

War clouds loomed in 1939, even if no one wanted to admit the possibility. That year Santa Fe announced a major $21,000,000 development program. The headline called out, "Huge Santa Fe Program Ready," with a sub headline reading, "Railroad's $21,000,000 Plans Include Reconstruction of 900 Box Cars in Topeka." Also included in the proposal was completion of double-track from Chicago to Los Angeles. President E. J. Engel was quoted, "The program includes purchases of 91,000 tons of rail and fastenings, 2,800 new freight cars, rebuilding 2,500 box, auto and refrigerator cars in our shops, a largely accelerated locomotive and car repair program:... This is our contribution to insure continuance of adequate railroad transportation in the United States for the presently increased rail traffic or any increased business now in prospect." The railroad was planning for what was ahead.

"Santa Fe Shops to Full Speed on Defense Demands," read

a headline of April 11, 1941. War had come and the railroad was doing its part. The article continued: "National defense demands and national defense precautions have reached the vast Santa Fe railroad shops here now—and a new box car is rolling out into service every hour." The author went on to describe in detail the precautions being taken at the Topeka shops.

In 1943 the news was "Santa Fe Adds 605 Here; Pay Up $97,000 for Year." Because of war conditions and added business this increase was necessary. In Topeka the railroad employed 4,515 workers. President E. J. Engel pointed out in the article, "The first three months of 1943 have been one of the most active periods in the history of the Santa Fe shops in Topeka. In that time 32 locomotives, 58 passenger cars and 1,140 freight cars have been repaired here."

"Women Workers Knock at Santa Fe Shop Gates," was the headline in March of 1944. The article opened: "One of the few remaining fortresses held exclusively by the men, the Santa Fe shops in Topeka are tallying higher draft casualties, and the din and sweat boys hear rumors of a threatened invasion by women laborers." The article continued, acknowledging the fact that women labor was quite the accepted thing nationwide but not so on the Santa Fe. The concluding paragraph wrapped it up nicely: "The general office building itself now has a woman elevator operator. That's not unusual even in the lowest depression of peace time, except for the Santa Fe. They've always been men before."

As WWII wound down in July of 1945, readers of the *Capital* were learning about the Santa Fe's Chinese visitors in an article headlined, "Nine Technicians from China Here Studying Repair Methods of Santa Fe Railway Shops." Ray Morgan, author of the article, went on to describe the men; their education and family life and reason for the trip. He quoted one, "We want to learn about your government institutions, your industries, and other aspects of your life so that we can use them to advantage among our own people when we return to China." The men were scheduled to stay for nine months, spending most of their time in the Santa Fe mechanical repair and maintenance shops.

"SF Shops Shutdown Will Affect 2,500," was the headline for May 11, 1950. Because of a strike by the firemen, which had halted a great deal of railroad traffic, the Santa Fe was closing the Topeka shops. Eventually the offices and other areas of the line would be affected. Five days later the headlines were in a happier vein, "Santa Fe's First Trains Returned to Service Early." A settlement had been reached and all employees would be returning to work as their services were required. Another ordeal had ended.

In 1968, as the Santa Fe made ready to celebrate its 100th anniversary, the papers were full of stories relating the history of the company. One article headlined "SF Shops Are Largest," gave an historical overview of the shops and listed interesting events chronologically. It was noted at the conclusion of the story that as a result of the '66 tornado the Topeka shops were being enlarged and modernized, and when completed the main building would be twice as long as before. Progress was continuing on the Santa Fe.

Following the history of the Santa Fe shops through headlines has been an interesting proposition. Through good times, through strike and depression, through war and modernization, there was never a time in the life of the A.T. & S.F. when the railroad was not newsworthy.

Holliday Park . . . *(Continued from p. 7)*

Beyond these facts, historians may only speculate about just how the city believed it possessed the deed to the park.

One theory which has been offered involves a mixup which may have occurred when Mrs. Holliday deeded to the city a similar property in the same area.

Records do show that Mrs. Holliday did transfer by quit claim a smaller triangular piece of land a short distance from Holliday Park with the express proviso that it be used for a public park.

That tract lies along the north side of Huntoon between Taylor and Polk, part of which is now a vacant lot immediately south of a residence at 1234 Taylor. It is possible that the transfer also included nearby land that is now a circular flower garden.

Since Col. and Mrs. Holliday had vast real estate holdings in the city—some 300 parcels in all—it is conceivable that Mrs. Holliday did intend to give the city a tract now known as Holliday Park, but inadvertently deeded the other property by mistake.

From the Commonwealth, March 15, 1876

An immense immigration is going down the Santa Fe railroad. We notice many land hunters around the land department of that railroad.

(Ed: The Santa Fe Land Department was then located in an office building on the northwest corner of 6th and Kansas Avenue.)

★ ★ ★

The Kansas Pacific has a fine new ticket case at the postoffice, and the Santa Fe at Rowley's drug store. They are both fine pieces of work, and are a general convenience to our citizens to be able to procure tickets to any part of the United States without going to the depots.

(Continued from p. 81)

the Santa Fe took place in Shawnee county on the presumption that jurors would be prejudiced in the Santa Fe's favor. Possibly there was some merit in this attitude as illustrated by the case of George Strayer who sued the Santa Fe in Shawnee county in 1885, seeking $10,000.00 damages for a shattered jaw bone that would prevent him from ever again working as a switchman. He recovered only $300.00.

We have a record of brilliant, ingenious lawyers who represented their client well through the days of bankruptcy and reorganization in 1895, the coming of federal regulation in 1879, and of Kansas regulation in 1905 as supplemented in 1911. As this is being written, the word is "de-regulation." Should the entire era—spawned in the days of A. A. Hurd and Judge Smith—come to an end, the best that their present day successors can hope for is that they will leave a record worthy of being recorded by a new George Holmes.

CYRUS K. HOLLIDAY *(in top hat) is about to board a special train carrying delegates on an excursion to Ft. Leavenworth, sponsored by the Brotherhood of Locomotive Firemen, July 29, 1885. The locomotive, built in 1881, was named for the first president of the company, Cyrus K. Holliday.*

The Topeka Daily Capital.

VOL. XIX. TWELVE PAGES. TOPEKA, KAN., WEDNESDAY, SEPTEMBER 29, 1897. FIVE CENTS. NO. 233.

TO-DAY THE SANTA FE OWNS THE CITY.

What the Road Has Accomplished==History of the System==Topeka Shops and General Offices.

The Santa Fe railroad is Topeka's pride and boast. There are other railroads in Topeka and each plays a very important part in the upbuilding of the city and the development of its resources; but the Santa Fe was born contemporaneous with the city's prosperity. The baptismal font of the one became the cradle of the other.

Topeka takes pride in the Santa Fe because the Santa Fe takes pride in Topeka. This fact is amply proven by today's big celebration. The Santa Fe could not arrange a celebration of like proportions at any other point on all its lines, were it so disposed. Topeka is the nucleus of its power and here are to be found the mainsprings of its phenomenal success. The concession was mutual, for on the other hand the Santa Fe brings to Topeka an army of workingmen and millions of dollars of taxable property.

The ramifications of this great system extend to the finger tips of the globe. Its shining steel rails are laid on mountain 1,313 miles of track. The number of locomotives owned in 1872 was 38; at present the number is 1,066. In 1872 it had 1,622 cars; now it owns 20,944.

TRAIL OF THE SANTA FE.

The History of the Route Enshrouded in Romance.

"In the half forgotten era,
With the archive of old,
Seeking cities that were told
To be paved with solid gold,
In the kingdom of Quivera—

"Came the restless Colorado
To the open Kansas plain;
With his knights from sunny Spain,
In an effort that, though vain,
Thrilled with boldness and bravado."

—*Ironquill.*

The main line of the Santa Fe system through Kansas follows very nearly the line of the famous Santa Fe trail.

The history of this old trail teems with romance. It has been celebrated in song and story. The deeds of border heroism which have been enacted at points along this historic pathway are as dear to the boys and girls of the state.

The old trail now is dim but the memory of it is fresh in the mind of every old settler. Not all of the deeds in its history have been heroic, and the shame pose of driving the French out of Louisiana territory. But their enterprise had a most disastrous ending as they encountered bands of hostile Indians and met the very fate they had reserved for others.

This body of Spaniards in passing through Kansas must have followed very nearly the present line of the Santa Fe railroad, and this statement is amply borne out by historical facts.

THE RAILWAY HOSPITAL.

Something About This Very Important Institution.

Not the least of the Santa Fe's many institutions in Topeka is the big railroad hospital on East Sixth street.

This building was opened to the public in June, 1896. It is a very handsome superintendents and foremen in charge of the locomotive and car shops:

John Player, superintendent of machinery.

George A. Hancock, assistant superintendent of machinery.

George W. Smith, division master mechanic.

John Hodge, master car builder.
Malcolm Manson, general foreman.
John Harley, foreman paint shop.
Joseph Davies, foreman cabinet shop.
John Isaacson, foreman planing mill.
Charles Swanson and Frank James, foremen car repair.
Frank J. Gunther, general foreman locomotive shops.
Archie M. Baird, foreman boiler shop.
John French, foreman blacksmith shop.
Wm. B. Price, foreman machine shop.
Wm. S. Lawliss, foreman water service.
Louis Deutscher, foreman tin shop. complete its equipment. The department has in operation a complete system of electrical alarm boxes.

THE WATERWORKS SYSTEM.

Entire Capacity of Pumping Plant Is 2,000,000 Gallons Daily.

The waterworks in connection with the shops are equipped with boilers having a total capacity of 360 horse power. The plant possesses two single acting Knowles pumps and one Duplex Compound Deane pump.

The entire capacity of the pumping plant is nearly 2,000,000 gallons per day of 24 hours, or 1,200 gallons per minute. The daily duty of the Deane Compound pump is 1,000,000 gallons of water every 24 hours. The pump house is an isolated building of stone. The water is taken from two large wells sunk to the gravel and fed from the Kaw river through this gravel stratum.

CAPACITY OF THE SHOPS.

1,450 Cars of Every Description Are Made Every Month.

A word is necessary as to the capacity of the Topeka shops.

On an average eighteen engines are re counts and accounts intimately connected with them, and the weekly and monthly reports of ticket agents, baggage agents, etc. —

OFFICE OF SECRETARY AND TREASURER.

Opposite the office of the auditor of passenger receipts are located the offices of the secretary and treasurer, Edward Wilder.

It is the secretary's duty to keep a record of all the proceedings of the main line and of the numerous subordinate corporations. In this office is filed all contracts, agreements, leases, bonds and mortgages representing every phase of the business of the great system, from the grading of its roadbed to the traffic arrangements with connecting lines. The records of the main corporation are voluminous, covering a period of thirty-seven years, and being contained in a number of bulky volumes of nearly 400 pages each.

The record books are all indexed by the same method, so that it is an easy matter to find the record of any vote or proceeding taken by any corporation at any time in its history. All original agreements of every nature are kept in the secretary's office and from these copies are furnished to all other departments interested.

COMPLETE ROSTER OF SANTA FE EMPLOYEES IN TOPEKA

On Sept. 29, 1897, the Topeka Daily Capital in a special edition promoting Santa Fe Day at Topeka's Fall Festival, published for the first and only time, we believe, a complete roster of every Santa Fe employee in Topeka. Perhaps you'll find the name of your grandparent, or great grandparent, in the list.

THE TOPEKA DAILY CAPITAL:
WEDNESDAY, SEPTEMBER 29, 1897.

ROLL OF OFFICE EMPLOYES.

List of All Those Employed in the General Offices.

GENERAL SUPERINTENDENT.
H. U. Mudge.

A. S. Rankin,
J. J. Mower,
Mattie Payne,
David B. Sibley,
E. L. Pierce,
Elmo B. Whitmore,
Earl V. Case,
Thos. Warren.

ASST. SUPERINTENDENT.
Avery Turner.

A. E. Sweet,
Frank W. Booth.

GEN'L WATCH AND CLOCK INSPECTOR.

H. S. Montgomery, F. E. Pirtle.

AUDITOR OF PASSENGER RECEIPTS.
C. M. Atwood.

Jno. F. Mitchell,
Josie L. Sexton,
S. C. Nesbaum,
Alva Gentry,
Harold Robinson,
Geo. E. Bell,
Chas. A. Gardner,
Wm. H. Bowlby,
Pearl W. Bruce,
W. W. Harris,
A. P. Fulcher,
Schuyler Nichols,
W. L. Faulkiner,
E. H. Bachelder,
J. H. Good,
Jno. Fasker,
Kitty Ragland,
W. W. Bollard,
W. C. Laucks,
D. E. Wetherbee,
O. E. Parmelee,
Wm. Elder,
L. C. Bronson,
H. W. Bomgardner,
G. B. Huron,
H. V. Albaugh,
D. F. Wickman,
W. R. Frederick,
Chas. M. Rigdon,
Wm. Davis,
W. R. Smith,
Earl R. Stiles,
Zella M. Zook,
E. C. Clark,
G. L. Mason,
Eva M. Ingersoll,
A. P. G. Anderson,
R. V. Magoffin,
J. R. Irwin,
O. Stiles,
R. G. Bradford,
H. C. Seabrook,
L. E. Wilson,
S. C. Wood,
E. G. Smith,
R. K. Snell,
H. B. Weiler,
W. H. Springer,
T. S. Stover,
T. B. Hiskey,
J. L. Shepherd,
Mason White,
S. L. Herriott,
T. B. Boyd.

SUPERINTENDENT CAR SERVICE.
C. W. Kouns.

J. M. Torrence,
J. W. Dugan,
J. H. Brinsmaid,
S. W. Wilder,
F. M. Tuckerman,
D. A. Hayes,
J. D. Brusil,
Zena M. Freeman,
Sadie M. Stickney,
Bert Himmel,
Alice Holdridge,
C. E. Mattingley,
M. C. Rice,
Claude Dew,
J. D. French,
J. J. Schneider,
W. O. Shreves,
Mary M. Shipler,
Robert Black,
Ora Hubbard,
Mary E. Smith,
Jessica W. Smith,
Carrie C. Fauble,
Victoria Scott,
Lelia M. Green,
Myrta M. Eversole,
Nettie S. Harris,
Maude E. Luce,
Mrs. W. J. Lea,
Miss Frank M. Scott,
Sadia R. Signor,
Minnie Oliver,
Mary E. Strohm,
C. Grace Akin,
F. L. Sturgis,
W. B. Whitson,
A. L. Hudson,
J. B. Brinsmaid,
S. C. Garrard.

GENERAL FREIGHT OFFICE.
F. C. Gay.

B. F. Williams,
W. N. Akers,
G. P. Beck,
Stewart Boyd,
Fannie L. Black,
A. Brewer,
R. E. Bunner,
Jennie Cantwell,
Rolla Cunningham,
G. W. Curtis,
F. D. Gahagan,
G. H. Hamilton,
Wilbur Hogeboom,
E. F. Hollies,
G. R. Houghtelin,
H. S. Irwin,
J. R. Koontz,
L. L. Karn,
H. Macferran,
B. F. E. Merrick,
W. J. Morrow,
J. E. Mulhall,
W. G. Pyles,
Wm. Rickenbacker,
T. S. Roberts,
W. F. Ryus,
A. G. Sheer,
G. E. Shelden,
Daisy M. Smith,
Herbert Smith,
C. D. Speer,
S. Stoddard,
F. C. Stauffenberg,
D. W. Thomas,
J. Q. Thomas,
Jas. P. Wahle,
G. D. Walp,
J. D. Waters,
H. A. Weaver,
Annie E. Whitelock,
Grace M. Whittlesey,
H. J. Whittlesey.

BAGGAGE DEPARTMENT.
P. Walsh.

A. C. Sowle,
A. C. Walsh,
G. L. Slusher,
Anna C. Bahn.

GENERAL MANAGER.
J. J. Frey.

B. T. Lewis,
J. W. Nowers,
J. M. McCarthy,
J. R. Sibley,
D. T. Nicoll,
H. B. Lantz,
Hal Jansen,
E. W. Cartlidge,
J. E. Hawes.

AUDITOR FREIGHT RECEIPTS.
C. S. Sutton.

W. J. Healy,
Bessie Van Amburgh,
Annie D. Witt,
H. Scott,
Wm. Trautmann,
T. D. Alden,
F. L. Bond,
G. H. Bowhay,
Jas. Conglin,
C. B. Durham,
E. Gaylord,
J. N. Haddick,
W. E. King,
F. E. McLauchlan,
J. R. Ness,
J. W. Smith,
J. Quine,
A. Spangberg,
E. H. Shumway,
C. C. Henshaw,
F. S. Brown,
F. C. Boorman,
B. A. Buzich,
H. C. Cook,
F. L. Cooper,
Geo. Coleman,
C. C. Crosky,
W. E. Davis,
W. F. Houston,
J. S. Jones,
A. Larson,
F. N. Kessler,
A. C. McKitrick,
Omar Olney,
W. B. McLaughlin,
E. Parson,
H. C. Pribble,
O. V. Pyles,
S. G. Ekstrom,
C. W. Sowle,
A. Torrence,
C. M. Winebright,
A. Black,
P. Coughlin,
E. C. Fowler,
H. Lyddon,
Mary B. Morrison,
Mayme R. White,
J. D. Mason,
R. Palmquist,
F. C. Stein,
J. K. Thompson,
Leni L. Yohey,
C. Brenning,
E. H. Shepherd,
H. Bell,
W. C. Haswell,
J. B. Kline,
W. C. Kellar,
F. E. McFarland,
C. C. Moore,
C. J. Rolfe,
F. B. Wilcox,
H. Hartwell,
J. H. Davis,
J. T. Riggs,
L. C. Wilson,
C. C. Huston,
W. W. Decker,
C. H. Lerrigo,
T. Y. Hoeton,
G. E. Woolverton,
G. W. Hunt,
Norman Jury,
F. H. Bevelle,
G. J. Smart,
G. W. Scott,
T. W. Kendall,
A. A. Hayes,
R. W. Rigdon,
E. B. Dietrich,
H. E. Disbrow,
Jos. Johnson,
C. N. Nelson,
G. G. Wheat,
A. A. Black,
Theo. Rickenbacher,
B. A. W. Olsson,
O. H. Spencer,
E. J. Warner,
E. M. Denning,
Fred Gilyeat,
A. J. Maxwell,
Mabel H. Hayes,
Alice A. Pyles.

SPECIAL.

H. E. Overholt,
F. Loheman,
J. B. Worden,
J. B. Richardson.
Minnie S. Bacheler,
R. W. Short,
Ellis Smith.

LAW DEPARTMENT.
A. A. Hurd.

Walter Littlefield,
Owen J. Wood,
Geo. N. Holmes.
Alfred A. Scott,
J. B. McKee.

STATIONER.
F. A. Wilson.

Ed McDonald,
H. O. Coughlin,
Norris Stevenson,
John B. Hall.

GENERAL PASSENGER DEPARTMENT
W. J. Black.

E. J. Shakeshaft,
Richard Shakeshaft,
W. U. Cust,
N. A. Black,
L. B. Smith,
G. E. Martindale,
T. J. Martindale,
E. Davis,
J. P. Hoffman,
Annie L. Knox,
W. U. Newby,
Louis Wingart,
W. E. Thrapp,
R. J. Connell,
F. S. Savage,
J. N. Stewart,
H. E. Crow,
F. Burch,
H. N. Donaldson,
E. Newlin,
Myrtle Fordyce,
Janet P. Morrison,
Maud Tegart,
L. N. Snyder,
S. G. Junmerman,
H. A. King.

184

(Continued on p. 187)

R. J. PARKER.
Superintendent of Middle Division.

C. T. McLELLAN.
Superintendent of Eastern Division.

AVERY TURNER.
Assistant General Superintendent.

H. U. MUDGE.
General Superintendent.

J. L. BARNES.
Superintendent of S. Kansas Division.

F. T. DOLAN.
Superintendent of Southern Division.

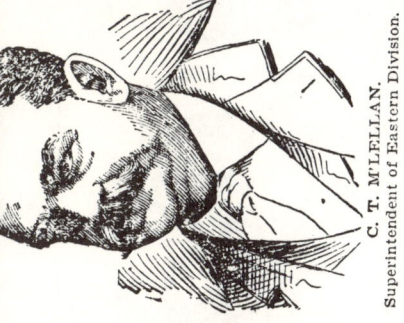

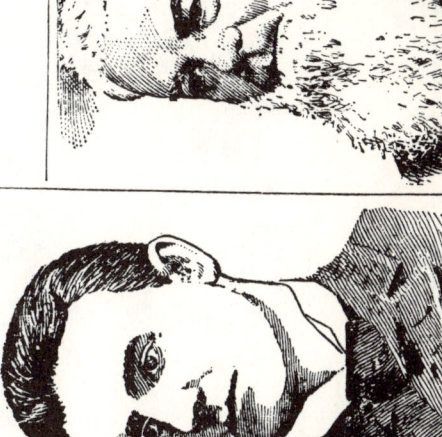

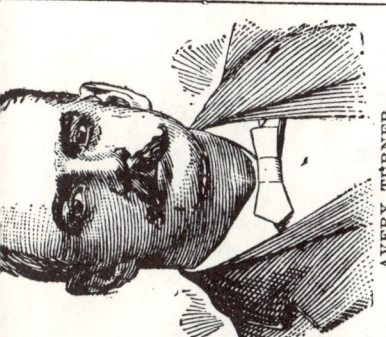

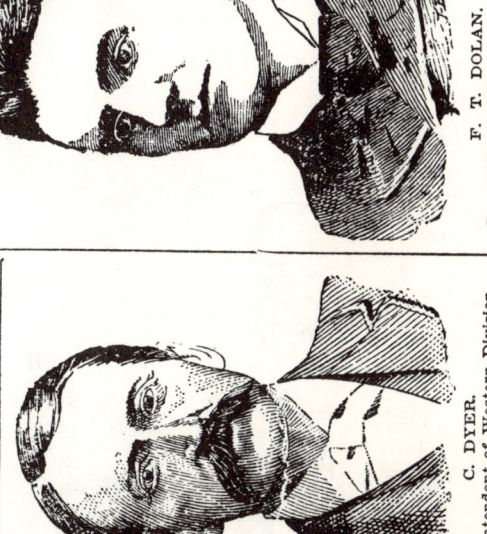

C. DYER.
Superintendent of Western Division.

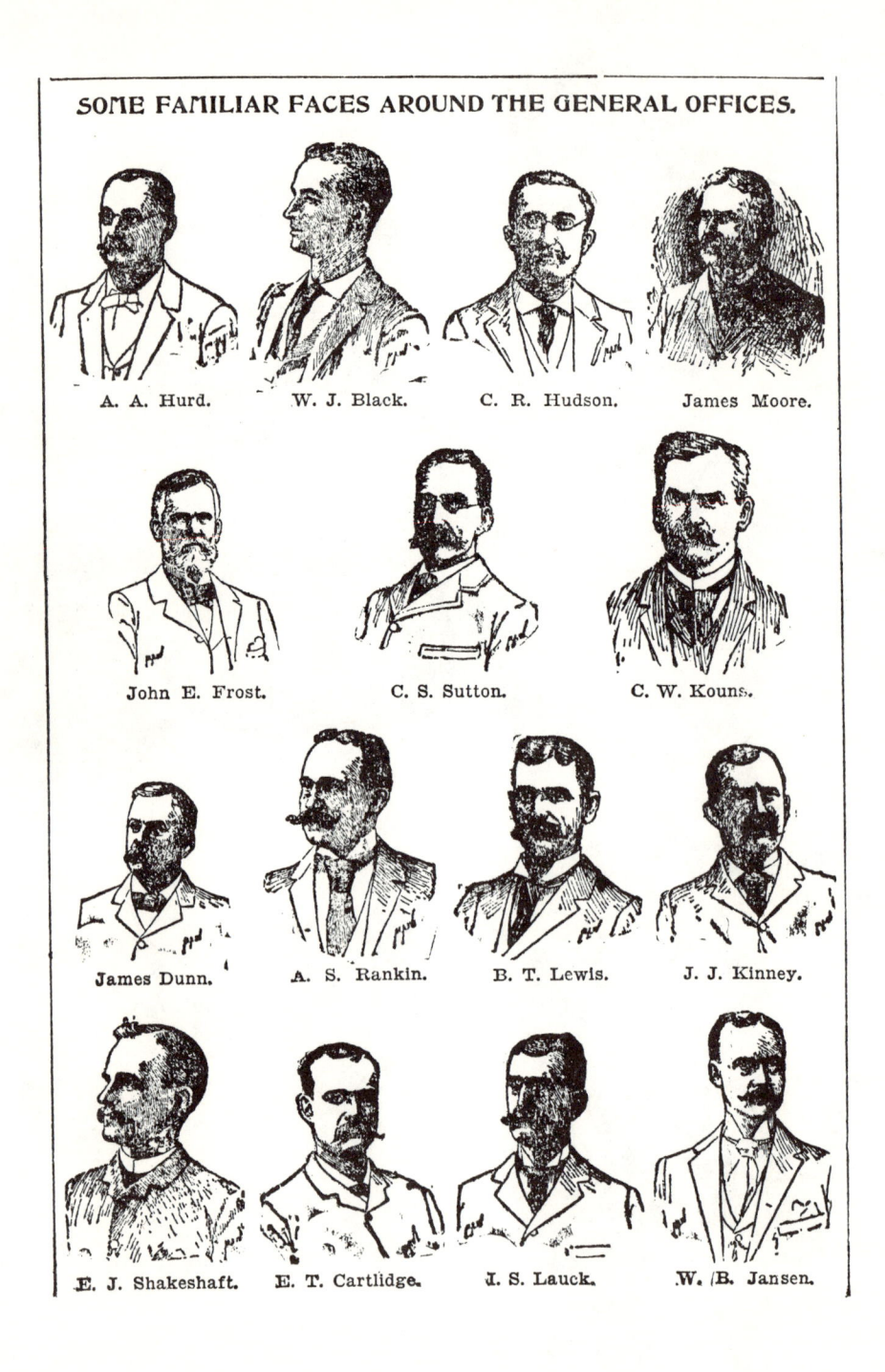

SOME FAMILIAR FACES AROUND THE GENERAL OFFICES.

A. A. Hurd.   W. J. Black.   C. R. Hudson.   James Moore.

John E. Frost.   C. S. Sutton.   C. W. Kouns.

James Dunn.   A. S. Rankin.   B. T. Lewis.   J. J. Kinney.

E. J. Shakeshaft.   E. T. Cartlidge.   J. S. Lauck.   W. B. Jansen.

CLAIM DEPARTMENT.
C. W. Ryus.

H. J. Franklin, R. F. Gridley,
C. L. Cline, E. H. Hemus,
H. A. Chamberlain, P. W. Zimmerman,
W. M. Smith, Mary M. Mass,
Harry Wayler, Jose G. Chavez,
J. C. Foulks, R. J. Lyddane,

LAND DEPARTMENT.
John E. Frost.

W. D. Gossett, A. Boyle,
E. J. Cartlidge, W. M. Glasscock,

TREASURY DEPARTMENT,
E. Wilder.

Jas. Moore, A. O. Wellman,
W. C. F. Reichenbach, T. R. Hyatt,
C. J. Bell, J. D. Walker,
Clara Ebright, D. R. Evans,
Carrie Merrick, F. L. Waggoner,
E. L. Copeland, D. S. Shook,
A. D. Gray, S. F. Davison,
Ed McBride, Ethel Watson,
W. G. Johnston, Harry Jameson,
N. T. Reickenbach, G. W. Smith,
M. R. Lee, Theo. McKibben,
Bruce Aird, Blanch Bozarth,
J. F. Scott, Annabel King,
Cora Loux, Lillie W. Stevenson,
G. W. Porter, Anna Dunn,
C. E. Hawley, Emily Mancey.
J. H. Norton,

ACCOUNTING OFFICE,
I. S. Lauck.

J. W. White, J. A. Hass,
W. M. Gibson, J. H. Simmons,
H. E. Tasker, J. R. Ferris
H. E. Hubbell, H. W. Davis,
D. L. Clark, J. H. Bonhan,
G. A. Ege, M. M. Monaghan,
W. B. Foley, W. H. Stuart,
G. B. Gallon, Merle C. King,
F. C. McMillan, H. D. Davis,
C. Smith, H. C. Short,
C. F. Cavert, E. L. Mooney,
Benn Akers. L. E. Damon,
R. R. Simcock, A. L. Conrad,
H. H. Arthur, A. S. Jennings,
J. W. Roberts, J. E. Hutt.
Geo. E. Hayden, L. J. McQuade,

LAW DEPT., TAX DIVISION.
E. T. Cartlidge.

R. K. Jamison, O. W. Dalton.
W. L. Crenshaw,

SPEC'L SERVICE DEPT.
J. J. Kinney.

R. E. Taylor, G. C. Montgomery,
Josephine Van Amburgh, D. N. Burge,
W. F. Watson,
Mayme E. Taylor, Thos. Gorman,
E. B. Weigle, J. T. Botkin,
F. Harris, J. A. Matthews,

JANITOR.
J. M. Hayes,

G. B. Kirk, D. Hyde,
Jno. Hayes, Sam'l Shuck,
A. Beronius, Chas. French,
Jas. Coughlin, J. H. Morris,
Isaac McElroy, Jno. Thompson,
W. B. Wright, Frank Thompson,
W. H. Anderson, J. H. McCloskey,
Jas. Bigger, E. Grier,
Jno. Wessley, L. Woddell,
E. Drain, S. Higgins,
B. F. Thompson, W. H. Washington.
R. Slaughter,

TELEGRAPH DEPARTMENT.
C. G. Sholes.

L. M. Jones, L. A. Laurent,
M. R. Ackley, H. H. Arthur,
L. B. Dailey, T. B. Finley,
Etta Stauffenberg, H. T. Flint,
T. J. Ragland, L. M. Baird,
R. L. Stotler, H. E. Bray,
L. C. Badgley, O. H. Olsson,
W. S. Alvord, Jno. Carrier,
G. W. Mitchell, F. A. Lyddan,
Daniel Callahan,

CHIEF ENGINEER.
James Dun.

C. D. Purden, J. A. Dailey,
W. J. Smyser, C. M. Roquette,
C. B. Kilmer, W. J. Whitson, jr.
A. F. Robinson, H. E. White,
Wm. Archer, P. Dailey,
V. Spangberg, Lewis Fletcher.

ROLL OF SHOP MEN.

List by Departments of Those on the Topeka Rolls.

SUPERINTENDENT OF MACHINERY—
Office.

Dan E. Cain, C. J. Swanson,
Thos. Mason, J. C. Prescott,
E. Mueller, F. H. Atkinson,
E. C. Beynon, E. Fowler,
B. T. Payne, Chas. H. Jett,
R. H. Barber, John W. Morgan,
D. E. Fitzgerald, C. E. Naylor,
W. L. Shilling, W. J. Riley,
Frank Cain, W. H. Bush,
F. H. Niles, R. M. Armstrong,
H. C. Robertson, A. H. McDonald,
C. D. Welsh, W. Wadleigh,
H. Shull, P. Laird,

SUPERINTENDENT MACHINERY—
Machine Shops.

G. W. Smith, Chas. Desch,
F. J. Gunther, Casper Dechant,
M. P. Gregory, R. Schaefer,
C. J. Fleisch. J. Oberer,
F. H. Syler, F. Beeler,
W. C. Squires, E. P. Dyer,
W. A. Powers, J. Dwyer,
G. E. Stolpe, J. Ohlbrendt,
A. Walker, J. Sheetz,
F. H. Benton, P. Schneider,
J. Volkert, H. Vice,
J. Benke, R. H. McClure.

WATER SERVICE DEPARTMENT,
G. W. Smith.

W. S. Lawless, A. Malmstrom,
J. O'Brien, P. Oberhousen,
W. J. Coats, Wm. Beeson,
J. Hill, C. Carlson,
J. Kieninger, A. B. Croskey,
A. Lawless. A. J. Dodge,
C. H. Reid, W. Hahn,
F. Killer, W. Schmittendorf,
V. Parkinson, Henry Burel,
H. Youngblom, Wm. Boyes,
J. W. King, Owen Callahan,
F. McKown, Wm. Cavender,
J. Aigner, P. Cart,
J. Armstrong, J. J. Frays,
J. G. Cofran, R. N. Furze,
G. H. Anderson, Wm. Runq,
E. Stephens, Luke Rockford,
W. T. Sexton, E. Tuetnow,
W. E. Snyder, H. H. Tillotson,
J. K. White, J. T. Thomas,
J. H. Wood, W. H. Bowman,
A. S. Coyne, H. Buhlmayer,
W. R. Mercer, Wm. Bauer,
Geo. Rollins, J. Bledsoll,
Oscar Meyer, G. Brentnall,
C. S. Smith, B. F. Cloud,
G. H. Atkinson, Israel De,
S. Bauer, J. Dubeck,
H. J. Cleary, J. Enler,
H. Checksfield, E. Fletcher,
A. A. Hope, G. N. Griggs,
C. J. Devlin. A. Hartwick,
A. A. Flannelly,

BLACKSMITH DEPARTMENT.
G. W. Smith.

J. French,
T. W. Israll,
A. Allis,
C. Bennett,
S. D. Bedwell,
F. A. Clements,
C. Fairbanks,
Geo. Fraser,
H. A. Fiske,
W. Hazen,
A. Hardie,
C. A. Holmgren,
C. Kaiser,
F. Kettler,
J. F. Kelley,
A. Kundson,
G. Inganthorn,
O. Larson,
J. R. Manpin,
D. R. Manpin,
J. M. Morgan,
I. O. Miller,

Wm. H. Sheehan,
R. F. Tasker,
J. J. White,
W. A. Anderson,
W. T. Allison,
J. E. Brown,
R. T. Burgess,
A. Byone,
J. J. Byone,
J. J. Boyne,
J. S. Burdge,
Chas. Bostrom,
Thos. Clohessy,
F. Clawsey,
W. Crawford,
A. B. Coyne,
D. C. Crotchett,
R. Dillon,
C. B. Dodge,
T. H. Devlin,
M. Etzel,
A. E. Erickson,

A. Patterson,
R. Stevenson,
J. D. Thompson,
J. D. Alexander,
Chas. Bewall,
G. Ballotte,
W. A. King,
J. R. Morgan,
P. J. McNamara,
Jno. McMahon,
P. Oderman,
J. Russell,
J. W. Romerman,
M. Stevens,
A. D. Watts,
G. S. Grout,
C. W. Johnson,
Henry O'Brien,
Jno. Jacobs,
J. W. Jurrens,
Wm. Jamieson,
A. A. King,
Edward King,
S. E. Kelley,
M. Kipples,
C. Kaiser, jr.,
A. Lamprecht,
C. Lundquist,
P. Moffitt,
J. C. Monroe,
W. J. Musick,
J. E. Miller,
R. Mohler,
Jno. P. McCambridge
J. B. Mullen,
Jas. Onion,
C. Peterson,
C. Renarde,
A. Raab,
W. B. Ramsey,
Chris Rupp,
M. Sawyer,
R. W. Service,

J. C. Fletcher,
John Foy,
J. Fentiman,
F. Gibler,
H. G. Gregg,
Jno. Grubbs,
E. C. Garner,
O. S. Geisert,
R. Garham,
T. F. Henry,
C. J. Hinchman,
P. Heery,
W. F. H. Heise,
G. W. Hobson,
Jno. Hoffner,
Thos. Johnson,
H. Shute,
Edward Doyle,
A. Doyle,
Frank Tucker,
W. H. Payne,
E. Pcleyn,
Eric Norline,
T. W. Cole,
Wm. Fritz,
A. Johnson,
J. P. Williams,
A. Bergert,
H. Hanson,
W. H. Kientz,
J. H. Paul,
J. G. N. Firth,
J. Degant,
T. White,
Hugh Devlin,
W. H. Fargo,
W. H. Hanser,
O. S. A. Morris,
F. C. Onion,
Jno. Thomas,
P. Swanson,
H. A. Snyder,
Geo. Domme,

F. Sams,
P. Schanfeld,
J. F. Skaggs,
Geo. Spahn,
Paul Sorenson,
C. R. Smith,
H. Schmidt,
R. W. Stockwell,
W. F. St. Mary,
W. F. Stevenson,
P. Todd,
H. L. Tubbs,
W. E. Williams,
J. E. Wilson,
G. W. Betts,

U. M. Pettit,
G. Bolanger,
H. C. Cooper,
Seth Day,
O. Lawrence,
J. H. Lacock,
W. E. Pettit,
F. Reeves,
L. Reeves,
C. H. Richardson,
C. F. Stone,
G. W. Shay,
Jno. Vetter,
Jas. Walters,

MACHINE DEPARTMENT.

J. B. Price,
C. Anderson,
H. Bergman,
Wm. Barnes,
F. C. Boltz,
J. F. Boyle,
E. J. Broberg,
Jas. Clark,

C. L. F. Marin,
Wm. G. Smith,
J. P. Donahue,
F. Davis,
O. Espelin,
D. W. Fleming,
J. W. Gardiher, jr.
Wm. H. Green,

W. H. Conry,
C. A. Conroe,
T. D. Cook,
E. D. Coon,
J. L. Chatham,
Thos. M. Coughlin,
J. C. Dwyer,
Geo. Gillies,
J. Gunther,
Grant Gill,
A. A. Graham,
J. E. Godfrey,
C. W. Hunt,
C. H. Hart,
W. L. Jury,
J. J. Kinsella,
C. M. Kemplin,
Wm. Lauterback,
H. E. Miller,
F. McKeirnan,
S. McKibben,
W. Mueller,
J. A. Nicholas,
Jno. Nichols,
C. F. Peck,
E. M. Roberts,
M. J. Gunther,

Thos. P. Hannigan,
F. Harris,
I. F. Henry,
W. G. Imbler,
H. T. Miller,
Carl Marin,
L. O. Paddock,
H. Parfitt,
C. E. Paddock,
W. R. Powell,
G. Follinger,
D. Saxton,
C. G. Stolpe,
W. H. Stewart,
R. C. Taft,
R. K. Wallace,
F. E. Wilcox,
C. Roth,
G. R. Shirk,
L. Schaefer,
H. J. Schnoor,
H. Schuler,
J. W. Guffey,
G. Hoag,
D. Hesson,
J. Oppitz,
T. O'Brien,
H. Scheibelbein,
A. Teske,
J. H. Coe,
J. G. Campbell,
E. E. Jenks,
J. P. Peach,
F. H. Austin,
J. Aigner, jr.,
A. Binder,
C. J. Birget,
E. Beer,
E. L. Brown,
G. Bruncklacher,
F. Blakemore,
F. J. Bush,
R. Craig,
J. M. Covert,
Wm. R. Carrie,
F. L. Carson,
H. U. Daub,
E. J. DeWitt,
F. J. Eccleston,
E. J. Espelin,
A. Ford,
L. Gabler,
I. L. Gerberick,
Wm. Heise,
H. F. Horton,
J. Kaiser,
W. E. Lyons,
D. McCall,
W. A. Mitchell,
T. Magill,
A. A. Olson,
P. Reynolds,
G. Spahn,
E. R. Saunders,
J. Schmidt,
B. J. Tumelty,

Wm. Stewart,
W. F. Sauerland,
Henry Schwalm,
J. Shannon,
F. Sandmeyer,
H. K. Sharp,
J. Seiber,
J. W. Taylor,
R. P. Taylor,
A. F. Tuer,
E. Whipple,
E. L. Wood,
A. J. Adams,
J. F. Armstrong,
F. A. Beyer,
C. H. Boltz,
R. Boyd,
H. Bair,
G. D. Bartel,
J. Brown,
H. Benke,
O. Becker,
C. A. Coult,
L. F. Conklin,
N. E. Cafferty,
A. Checksfield,
Eric E. Walgren,

Wilson Butler,
S. A. Bradfield,
P. A. Bruner,
Jos. Beyer,
F. Bovey,
L. Clark,
Jas. De Bar,
C. Eichar,
F. G. Erickson,
J. L. Hammond,
J. P. Johnson,
M. G. Goehring
A. H. Knauer,
O. King,
F. Marks,
W. Opperman,
J. Paddock,
E. Thomas,
Jno. Wunder,
J. Schlegel,
N. N. Confer,
J. Spaan,
C. Engstrom,
Geo. Faber,
E. E. Gorham,
J. R. Harrington,
W. B. Hoeck,
R. Jones,
E. E. Kelly,
E. J. McMullen,
E. F. Munier,
W. S. Mitchell,
W. Nelson,
L. Pietske,
J. W. Records,
C. Shaeffer,
J. Schlegel,
J. J. Spendlove,
D. Thomas,
C. F. Wheeler,
E. J. White,
Jos. Cramer,
G. Finch,
Chas. Killiam,
J. B. Price, jr.,
J. J. Coggins,
G. H. Dreyer,
N. S. Dwelley,
C. W. Eccleston,
J. F. Espelin,
J. H. Frizell,
R. Furguson,
D. Gillies,
Jno. Henshaw,
C. E. Hopkins,
S. Joslin,
J. H. Long,
Jno. Maher,
E. A. Miller,
G. E. Monaghan,
B. J. Phelps,
W. M. Snyder,
J. M. Snyder,
E. Sheetz,
E. J. Short,
F. E. Thompson,

Machine Dept. (Cont.)

J. D. Wallace,
G. W. Wilder,
Chas. Cremer,
J. Dwyer,
Chas. Kistler,
Jas. Miller,
G. W. Cooper,
P. H. Donovan,
H. DeCamp,
P. J. Donohue,
L. Emme,
Peter Bower,
E. Calkins,
E. H. Davis,
Robt. Fuller,
J. O. Gustine,
Fred Irion,
G. E. Kathary,
H. D. Miller,
C. C. Reardon,
F. H. Shaffer,
P. Seig,
E. L. Smith,
S. Wendleim,
A. Snyder,
A. C. Hayes,
P. E. Higgins,
M. Mulvahill,
W. H. Bigham,
Fred Jansen,
A. Sheetz,
N. Spahn,
F. A. Woodruff,
Fred Semon,
M. Binder,
Jos. Bender,
P. Domme,
G. Degent,
C. Grosch,
Jno. Heim,
J. Ikes,
J. P. Kestner,
Jno. Leonard,
Geo. Spahn,
A. Specht,
Jno. Steel,
Robt. Weir,
David Heinzel,
S. H. Wright,
G. Baird,
J. R. Cowdry,
A. Furze,
J. A. McMullen,
Byron C. Player,
H. K. Stewart,
P. Limenberger,
C. Schultz,
A. Desch,
Wm. Hess,
Jno. Spahn,
A. Semon,
J. Lewis,
Wm. Tasker,
J. H. Cooper,
M. Connell,
Jno. Eichar,
M. Freibott,
J. E. Hughes,
J. D. Jones,
A. M. Lozier,
R. M. Nightengale,
L. W. Snyder,
Chas. Schram,
A. Schwert,
H. C. Wheeler,
W. T. Wooters,
Samuel Short,
A. Baum,
Geo. Kaberlin,
Seth Reub,
C. Holzmeister,
J. L. Beardsley,
Geo. Cooper,
Jno. Domme,
Gust Espelin,
G. L. Gandy,
Emil Heber,
C. Kushera,
Jas. Mullin,
Thos. Norwood,
Jno. Espelin,
F. H. Roebuck,
Wm. Hayes,
Geo. Lippert,
J. E. Wallace,

R. L. Lott,
T. J. Mulvahill,
A. E. Maze,
C. Schramm,
A. Stone,
A. H. Schooeter,
J. H. Thomas,
H. J. Thomas,
G. Thompson,
E. Wynkoop,
Lee Altman,
G. Batz,
C. F. Buell,
F. Brindle,
James Brennan,
G. W. Baird,
B. F. Burke,
G. E. Clark,
W. L. Crawford,
J. Clawsey,
J. Cooper,
W. Clawsey,
W. Cox,
E. Crawford,
J. Degant,
Jesse Dixon,
L. Fultz,
J. C. Ford,
H. Ferris,
J. M. Givens,
N. Griley,
Geo. S. Hill,
W. S. Sheldon,
J. Shockey,
G. W. Shultz,
A. Saylor,
W. B. Woody,
I. O. White,
A. Coyle,
W. Hoppe,
A. A. Licht,
F. O'Brien,
W. E. Nash,
Andrew Rupp,
T. J. Brennen,
F. Sanderson,
L. Alsdorf,
G. Rison,
H. B. White,
L. L. Frantz,
F. Baumor,
W. R. Crandall,
C. Larson,
A. McNair,
D. Page,
J. Q. Maze,
F. Owen,
A. Royer,
M. Collins,
H. Johnson,
N. P. Johnson,
T. P. Shields,
C. Kipperly,
J. W. McNown,

TIN SHOP.

L. Duetscher,
C. Duetscher,
E. Elsner,
A. P. Peterson,
H. Ruppel,
R. Trebbe,
J. Bauer,
F. H. Bartlett,
P. J. Barnett,
F. V. Benson,
Harry Voegtle,
G. Warren,
C. Younggreen,
J. F. R. Heinisch,
B. Dreger,
J. Deischer,
C. T. Goulding,
F. Johnson,
E. J. Kerwick,
E. S. Richner,
J. Rupple,
J. Ulmer,
F. Roehrig,
F. W. Becker,
A. Meyers,
R. F. Stellhorn,
J. Walker,
F. Vogel,

PATTERN DEPARTMENT.

S. R. Miller,
Geo. T. Bond,
C. W. Dehn,
J. H. Ellenberger,
W. N. Rhodes,
T. A. Ridings,
D. Warren,
C. D. Cronenberg,
Wm. G. Greer,
W. H. Glenn,
A. S. Loux,
J. M. Chase

BOILER DEPARTMENT.

Archie M. Baird,
A. C. Seiler,
D. Ammell,
C. J. Allen,
Jno. Broser,
G. W. Brosamer,
E. Betts,
G. W. Crawford,
Benj. Dustin,
Jas. Dedurin,
H. C. Dustin,
Edward Dustin,
J. A. Dustin,
Jas. Grant,
Geo. Henry,
Frank Henry,
Wm. Kettler,
Jno. Lawrie,
W. A. Maze,
Jos. McKeon,
Bert Nichols,
Wm. Purcell,
Thos. Purcell,
W. A. Reddy,
H. Senne,
Jno. Stebbins,
Elmer Schlegel,
E. Stitt,
J. B. Schaefer,
J. W. Betts,
J. Cooper,
C. F. A. Strickrott,
E. F. Crumm,
W. Dwyer,
J. Devlin,
J. J. Treibott,
W. Grant,
J. Humbert,
W. L. Kieninger,
L. L. Hustus,
G. H. Hulbert,
F. W. Humbert,
W. H. Hougtelin,
C. E. Johnson,
J. A. Jones,
Thos. Kennedy,
Geo. Kipperly,
F. G. Kingsley,
J. Kern,
W. Lewis,
A. P. Lindell,
J. Lesser,
C. E. Maze,
R. Maze,
J. T. Maze,
J. E. Maze,
M. W. Minnick,
S. T. Mellinger,
H. McGivern,
P. Malchor,
C. C. Maze,
A. Nelson,
Chas. Ottman,
Chas. Ost,
I. W. Pasley,
E. H. Price,
J. E. Robinson,
R. S. Robinson,
G. W. Rhodes,
G. Ragsdale,
B. E. Shields,
C. R. Shaw,
A. W. Southerland,
Chas. Southerland,
F. B. Sawyer,
N. Sickeneger,
F. O. Southerland,
E. W. Smith,

ROUND HOUSE.

H. Player,
F. E. Edwards,
D. M. Shannon,
W. L. Bush,
W. Deveney,
C. Guthrie,
S. F. Brady,
S. Ash,
J. Ash,
G. W. Galletley,
W. E. Lewis,
E. McGinnis,
W. H. Best,
F. L. Coles,
N. McGowen,
F. W. Bartel,
J. Kindall,
W. F. Stitt,
F. G. Connell,
E. J. Mechan,
S. Smith,
L. M. Hartley,
B. Lewis,
E. J. Lungstrum,
J. Balke,
J. H. Phillips,
H. O'Brien,
P. Lamb,
J. Renshaw,
E. J. Gorham,

CAR SHOPS.

J. Hodge,
J. J. Wehe,
M. Manson,
F. Bradfield,
M. Thymian,
H. Ford,
S. R. Taylor,
J. Braun,
F. W. Piper,
J. Davies,
J. Buchschacher,
C. H. Dreyer,
C. Kottman,
J. Lindblad,
S. E. Moeser,
J. Swanson,
J. A. Wehe,
J. Fulford,
A. Johnson,
P. J. Johnson,
J. M. Keener,
W. A. Lewis,
E. F. Lockwood,
J. F. Michell,
J. Mueller,
C. D. McCauley,
J. L. Norton,
C. G. Overton,
N. Palmlund,
F. Phillips,
S. H. Peck,
S. H. Price,
P. W. Riach,
E. Redings,
J. C. Stevick,
G. F. Schultz,
F. Wahl,
H. Wunsch,

Car Shop (Cont.)

H. F. Stiles,
R. C. Bond,
J. W. Berett,
W. T. Frangen,
J. Goode,
C. D. Hudson,
C. Clinger,
F. Dickinson,
H. Dreyer,
G. N. Lake,
H. Martin,
O. McMahon,
E. Nash,
J. Plath,
J. W. Swartz,
R. V. Wells,
J. Sleter,
H. H. Cookerley,
W. S. McCallan,
J. A. Crouch,
J. Diehl,
T. W. Dixon,
A. Erickson,
J. Eshbach,
W. Gibbs,
W. H. Hayes,
G. Hutton,
G. W. Holden,
A. Johnson,
B. F. Kinsey,
J. E. Mooney,
J. M. Murrell,
D. S. Myers,
D. S. Marks,
W. Nuzum,
A. D. Odger,
C. H. Rhodes,
F. Smith,
J. Southerland,
J. J. Wilson,

J. Wilson,
P. B. Miller,
F. McKinney,
C. A. Peterson,
E. Roher,
H. H. Ruth,
J. S. Stevenson,
F. Weeks,
S. Detmore Wise,
P. Wright,
J. G. Wyman,
Olaf Ahlgren,
P. Anderson,
A. Burg,
G. Dumlen,
J. E. Brown,
J. Carlson,
R. Cunning,
G. B. Campbell,
O. Charlson,
J. M. Doyle,
B. Gilyeat,
C. R. Gardner,
D. M. Halloway,
E. Johnson,
F. Luddington,
J. P. Miller,
A. Newcomer,
J. Beeler,
J. B. Couture,
P. Diffenderfer,
G. Dahlman,
J. Havens,
J. H. Helwig,
D. S. Hill,
L. Herring,
G. Johnson,
W. H. Lambert,
W. H. Long,
A. L. Morris,
J. L. Massey,
H. J. Neiswinter,
C. Burghardt,
P. Burghardt,
O. Boyd,
J. Bauer,
J. Brinegar,
H. A. Brown,
G. Burghardt,

J. M. Child,
C. R. Harris,
A. A. Ridings,
A. Wahl,
G. Zeldier,
H. A. Barnes,
A. A. Dahlstrom,
O. Gash,
A. E. Hamilton,
V. Patneaude,
J. Wetterskog,
J. R. Freeman,
J. Hunt,
J. Inganthron,
T. C. Adams,
J. Anderson,
J. W. Baird,
T. M. Coulter,
L. Currier,
J. Isaacson,
J. E. Bressett,
E. A. Bressett,
N. A. Carson,
F. Carlson,
W. S. Copeland,
M. Carle,
C. J. Carlson,
A. Carlson,
C. A. Elinquist,
E. Erickson,
J. Frantz,
A. Fogalquist,
H. S. Grout,
Chas. P. Johnson,
F. P. Johnson,
Fred S. Jillson,
Thos. Loback,
A. May,
B. R. Waldron,
C. B. Parker,

J. P. Matson,
I. Heffner,
H. Hackley,
Chas. E. Karr,
F. Larson,
A. Nelson,
E. Karlando,
F. Olson,
J. Ruck,
J. Rohm,
H. Shultz,
J. W. Mergen,
A. Ahlstrom,
Thos. Birmingham,
J. S. Palmer,
J. W. Ruth,
J. S. Ray,
C. A. Rhodes,
M. Scott,
M. Vandenburg,
F. H. Vaughn,
W. J. Woodburn,
E. W. Withrow,
J. W. West,
C. Anderson,
W. T. Amos,
C. G. Ogilvoy,
J. W. Stuart,
J. S. Sheffield,
C. H. Sheffield,
W. H. Smith,
J. D. Sleeper,
C. F. Stacey,
M. R. Schultz,
P. L. Slusher,
Wm. O. Swanson,
H. D. Wood,
Z. Wood,
D. A. Wizer,
H. Splithoff,
M. D. Adams,
M. Burghardt,
C. Jacobs,
J. A. Johnson,
J. W. Johnson,
J. Kremz,
John Kisner,
A. Lambrecht,
B. Mischke.

J. Conrad,
J. M. Dix,
J. Diehl,
Peter Desh,
B. Edlin,
J. Frohmager,
J. Fogelstrom,
J. Geese,
J. C. Gregory,
R. Heath,
F. Henderson,
J. Hefner,
P. Hefner,
A. Ikes,
G. Spahn,
A. Suppes,
C. Suppes,
J. Stirkhl,
E. G. Stone,
P. Ulrich,
C. Swanson,
W. E. Applegate,
D. S. Allen,
C. P. Ackley,
G. Anderson,
H. R. Altman,
F. A. Allen,
H. Anderson,
Wm. Cardery,
A. Andlestedt,
G. Bradshaw,
N. V. Bernard,
Wm. Curry,
C. F. Cross,
E. A. Collum,
W. R. Dix,
J. H. Davidson,
E. Evans,
J. Fink,
A. N. Tender,
J. A. Fink,
D. B. Fink,
F. Gabler,
M. Growendyke,
J. W. Gormley,
T. Hows,
V. C. Hay,
W. L. Havens,
H. Hammingson,
S. C. Hope,
F. E. Hart,
N. A. Haggart,
J. Hoffman,
G. W. Hill,
J. W. Holliday,
W. C. Johnson,
N. Johnson,
W. B. Jones,
W. James,
R. Jones,
O. W. Johnson,
O. V. L. Jones,
L. Klebenstein,
A. Linden,
J. Liberg,
C. W. Lawson,
C. S. Leachman,
A. W. Murphy,
G. F. Martin,
D. Masterson,
G. H. Morns,
W. T. Morns,
J. Mildner,
J. W. Miller,
C. F. Miller,
D. M. Miller,
W. Morgan,
P. Merritt,
M. M. McBroom,
D. McIntosh,
P. A. Newburg,

M. Nowls,
M. F. Nighingale,
A. L. Olney,
E. Olson,
V. Olson,
C. E. Olnder,
A. W. Parsons,

J. B. McKinney,
J. Meldner,
A. Mider,
J. Mellinger,
J. Molcher,
C. Ottman,
A. J. Penwell,
E. Phanstead,
M. Rahn,
J. H. Runyen,
A. Schmidt,
I. Suppes,
J. Schmidt,
W. Skaggs,
F. J. Bragunier,
G. Bravo,
J. D. Bozarth,
J. G. Blumerstock,
S. Clary,
H. J. Caskey,
J. Clarke,
C. E. Cox,
A. Capley,
C. R. Constance,
T. W. Cattle,
D. N. Cornelius,
G. L. Coulter,
E. A. Chance,
J. Cochran,
A. Cullum,
E. Crouch,
J. E. Davis,
J. L. Drake,
F. H. Davidson,
G. Diggengen,
P. Dahlstrom,
J. Watterlund,
C. P. Warren,
A. W. Wennersten,
F. S. Watts,
J. Wood,
V. H. Waite,
J. O. Wilbourne,
J. R. White,
C. E. Wynne,
J. H. Williams,
W. H. Westerman,
W. E. White,
J. Warren,
A. Wood,
O. J. Wilson,
H. L. Wilson,
F. Zeidler,
H. Zinn,
A. Zart,
W. H. Zarker,
J. R. Franklin,
J. Havens,
C. Johnson,
E. Jones,
G. Gerberick,
E. Anderson,
F. Butler,
S. A. Bragunrier,
R. N. Chapman,
J. P. Erickson,
G. Fritton,
J. Hoult,
A. W. Hughes,
M. M. Lindemood,
G. W. Luddington,
J. E. Montgomery,
C. Nordstrom,
J. L. Nichols,
W. E. Peters,
C. Strecker,
W. F. Smith,
L. G. Short,
G. P. Tillson,
A. A. Vogel,
W. S. Wynne,

J. R. Williams,
W. F. Jones,
J. Burghart,
M. Child,
A. Wennergren,
N. B. Olson,
J. Franklin.

Car Shop (Cont.)

L. Paterson,
N. Paterson,
O. H. Pease,
C. J. Paterson,
J. Popp,
J. A. Pellett,
C. J. Paterson,
J. V. Robbins,
F. Rovein,
D. Roller,
G. W. L. Ray,
D. F. Robinson,
M. C. Reardon,
J. F. Robinson,
H. J. Ransdell,
G. Roe,
J. Rosen,
H. F. Stover,
L. Silvernail,
D. Stitt,
J. J. Seal,
J. D. Sherer,
J. B. Steel,
J. A. Smelser,
W. Smith,
J. A. Smelser,
J. C. Smelser,
W. Swain,
C. A. Sparks,
C. J. Swank,
W. G. Shaw,
J. M. Spraul,
J. A. Stiles,
P. Schoenfeld,
N. Swank,
F. L. Swanson,
J. A. Taggart,
C. E. Thorson,
L. A. Vick,
A. Vestor,
F. Cale,
D. B. Dawson,
H. Dahne,
A. Dahlen,
L. H. Daniels,
G. W. Druse,
S. J. Davies,
S. Dixon,
R. M. Dickey,
J. E. Engholm,
A. Egerstrom,
L. Eichar,
C. Eavendorf,
G. B. Frisbie,
D. C. Fleming,
S. Feldner,
C. T. Fleming,
M. Flusch,
J. J. Graber,
S. G. Gunnison,
F. Garland,
J. Gerberick,
J. Hefner,
G. Hornsby,
H. Hoffman,
L. Haney,
J. A. Hollingsworth,
C. Hilesberg,
B. F. Hibberd,
Wm. Hartman,
P. Hagan,
J. Huston,
A. R. Imbler,
Wm. Jefferies,
E. J. Johnson,
H. Jones,
N. Paterson,
J. R. Sims,
J. J. Sigrest,
C. Shultz,
R. E. Stiles,
R. Sparlock,
Thos. Smith,
C. Sawyer,
M. E. Steadman,
C. Steadman,
J. Sheldon,
P. J. Skogland,
N. W. Sloan,
J. Stadler,
F. Sawyer,
W. H. Slatten,
A. Skaggs,
John I. Short.

C. J. Cherry,
J. Dunn,
J. C. Greenfield,
J. F. Rater,
J. F. Crozier,
F. James,
A. G. Anderson,
C. F. Anderson,
A. Anderson,
J. Anderson,
E. F. Anderson,
J. Agel,
A. P. Anderson,
J. N. Blevins,
W. H. Bruffey,
Wm. Bartel,
H. C. Brown,
F. L. Bert,
A. R. Bowius,
P. Bower,
Peter Bagan,
C. G Carlson,
A. Crowder,
L. Collins,
H. L. Crawford,
C. Cunningham,
D. L. Carson,
E. N. Chapin,
A. Curry,
F. A. Carlson,
G. Christman,
C. A. Carlson,
E. W. Calkins,
B. B. Collins,
M. Croll,
A. R. Carlson,
G. Carnes,
A. T. Counter,
G. E. Cole,
J. T. Wall,
S. Johnson,
G. W. James,
A. Kelley,
E. A. Knapp,
J. Kincaid,
T. J. Lutz,
C. E. Lyons,
A. Lindgreen,
G. Larson,
D. B. Lanter,
T. J. Liggett,
G. Lagerburg,
J. Lang,
W. R. Lerow,
W. T. Love,
W. T. Maxwell,
J. T. May,
W. W. Norris,
E. Mischke,
A. Moore,
F. M. Monroe,
C. W. Norris,
G. J. McAuliffe,
W. W. McNeil,
A. Novell,
A. Nystrom,
A. Norman,
N. T. Nashlund,
A. J. Ottinger,
A. Olsen,
J. E. Payton,
I. W. Parker,
A. A. Penwell,
J. E. Pierson,
I. A. Panson,
E. Payton,
J. Swanson,
C. Stramberg,
A. Stridell,
C. W. Smith,
A. H. Torrens,
J. W. White,
B. W. Vail,
J. W. Van Buskirk,
B. W. Wilkerson,
S. S. Walkley,
J. Wash,
E. E. Wilson,
E. H. Wilson,
E. White,
J. Wall,
J. Wilmot,
U. L. Williams,

PAINT SHOP.

John Hartley,
G. Hall,
W. T. Birt,
J. A. Baratt,
E. Bailey,
J. Carlstrom,
E. A. Dreyer,
W. Doyle,
S. S. Earl,
W. S. Goss,
A. E. Hodge,
J. Hagan,
E. Hanson,
F. O. Johnson,
H. Johnson,
M. S. Kelly,
Wm. Lyon,
J. McNeal,
B. D. Milehan,
R. Mitchell,
R. Malick,
L. E. Mills,
C. R. Mack,
J. Nord,
G. W. Palmer,
W. Ramsbarger,
J. Stafford,
J. Scully,
L. Steinrauf,
F. L. Stevens,
W. Sheim,
F. A. Stoll,
C. H. Taylor,
S. P. Thompson,
B. F. Recob,
F. D. Russell,
G. R. Rethmeyer,
J. Harris,
B. Bauer,
H. L. Cooper,
E. W. Cooper,
E. Gustafson,
W. H. Hanson,
J. Kehler,
J. Lynn,
J. Mury,
L. Polson,
C. Peterson,
R. Sheffield,

F. Volker,
J. West,
R. Warring,
J. J. White, jr.,
J. J. White,
G. Youngman,
W. Zeigler,
F. M. Pribble,
A. Wizer,
A. Coller,
A. Duder,
W. Erdman,
R. Fritz,
A. Gliddon,
J. E. Galloway,
W. Hewitt,
K. Hanson,
P. Heck,
L. Johnson,
C. F. Johnson,
B. J. Kelley,
D. Lane,
G. M. Lippert,
E. Miller,
G. Mercier,
J. McGiveran,
P. Miller,
M. McAndrews,
T. Norton,
M. Schoenfield,
J. B. Sands,
J. W. Watts,
J. W. Gibbons,
R. J. Coultis,
D. Greenstreet,
J. Henzo,
N. Lauterback,
P. B. Ross,
J. Bauer,
F. Kammor,
J. Ludwig,
A. E. Smith,
A. Batty,
J. Semidt,
W. C. Jennings,
J. M. Larty,

CAR SHOPS AT DEPOT.

G. H. Elliott,
F. M. Pribble,
J. L Crook,
A. Davis,
J. F. Simmons,
H. E. Brownlee,
J. W. Carll,

J. M. Crumm,
H. G. Perkins,
A. S. Palmer,
J. A. Parkhurst,
S. W. Stewart,
J. A. Searing,
A. P. Skidmore,
B. D. Russum,
R. Wells,
J. D. Jones,
M. Slusher,
A. A. Adair,
J. A. Alexander,
B. E. Brown,
F. Conrad,
H. J. Deever,
G. Dutscher,
A. A. Elliott,
J. First,
W. Gibbens,
B. B. Holzle,

J. W. Hughes,
W. Johnson,
J. A. Lowe,
D. Morgan,
J. C. Marsh,
R. B. Newton,
J. Porter,

W. Porter,
J. B. Prickett,
E. F. Purdy,
F. G. Richie,
E. E. Sellman,
G. W. Symms,
J. T. Smith,
L. Vernois,
J. D. Wilson,
A. Courtney,
W. E. Cook,
F. Ehrhart,
J. W. Feldner,
E. J. Jones,
E. McPherson,
J. B. Gibbens,
W. T. Bassett,
F. Jones,
J. Wimmer,
E. C. Symms,

Photos, Florence J. Servi

Floats including a **Daily Capital** *truck carrying the Santa Fe Hobo Band, were all part of the Santa Fe picnic and parade Aug. 27, 1927.*

A few samples from the immense collection of railroad passes given to Henry Tisdale, general manager of the Southwestern (Overland) Stage Line that made connections with many trains in southern and western Kansas. (Kansas State Historical Society)

Santa Fe Magazine, May 1911

Photo by Gay Hamilton, Staff Photographer

GROUP OF OFFICIALS LOCATED AT TOPEKA, KAN.—1911

First row, left to right—J. R. Koontz, general freight agent; C. F. W. Felt, chief engineer; R. J. Parker, general superintendent; C. W. Kouns, general manager; E. L. Copeland, secretary and treasurer; H. W. Jacobs, assistant superintendent of motive power; J. M. Connell, general passenger agent.

Second row—John Purcell, superintendent of shops; M. H. Haig, mechanical engineer; P. Walsh, general baggage agent; W. R. Smith, solicitor for Kansas; J. D. M. Hamilton, claims attorney; J. H. McGott, mechanical superintendent; A. D. Gray, cashier; James Moore, paymaster.

1, J. W. Nowers, car accountant; 2, T. S. Stevens, signal engineer; 3, L. M. Jones, superintendent of telegraph; 4, J. F. Mitchell, ticket auditor; 5, E. H. Bunnell, auditor of disbursements; 6, A. A. Hayes, freight auditor; 7, R. G. Merrick, assistant general freight agent; 8, J. C. Burnett, assistant general freight agent; 9, E. J. Shakeshaft, assistant general passenger agent; 10, J. F. Jarrell, publicity agent; 11, H. S. Montgomery, general watch inspector; 12, E. T. Cartlidge, tax commissioner; 13, F. A. Wilson, stationer; 14, J. N. Irwin, assistant general baggage agent; 15, A. O. Wellman, assistant treasurer; 16, H. C. Pribble, freight claim auditor; 17, F. J. Houston, motive power accountant; 18, C. N. Swanson, superintendent of car shops; 19, E. H. Hernus, chief claim adjuster; 20, W. W. Strickland, assistant freight auditor; 21, H. Hobson, signal supervisor; 22, H. B. Lautz, assistant to the general manager; 23, J. M. Gavin, chief electrician; 24, S. C. Nichols, assistant ticket auditor; 25, W. F. Ryus, traveling live stock agent; 26, B. F. E. Marsh, division freight agent.

NOTABLE FOR THEIR CONTRIBUTIONS—*The late Walter Johnson, Motive Power Dept., inventor of an improved outrigger snow plow twenty years ago, but still standard equipment with derrick wreckers. Below, left, George "Bud" Goebel, retired station master, whose valuable collection of railroad antiquities will eventually be housed at the State Historical's new museum. Right, William E. Treadway, retired Santa Fe attorney, whose recently published book, "Cyrus K. Holliday—A Documentary Biography," is a valued contribution to the Santa Fe's history.*

OFFICERS AND TRUSTEES

SHAWNEE COUNTY
Historical Society
Topeka Kansas

P.O. Box 56, Topeka, Kansas 66601

President
William E. Treadway

Vice-President
James N. Nelson, M.D.

Recording Secretary
Dorothy Huggins

Treasurer
Sims V. Firestone, Jr.

Director of Publications
John W. Ripley

Secretary
Camilla Maichel

Associate Director
Robert W. Richmond

TRUSTEES

Terms Expiring December 5, 1979	Terms Expiring December 5, 1980	Terms Expiring December 5, 1981
Jett Carkhuff Elmer	Henry L. Hiebert	Donald A. Chubb
Grace Kreipe	Robert E. Jacoby II, M.D.	Roy W. Engler
Catharine W. Menninger	Chet Kelsey	Mrs. Roy Hatke
Nyle H. Miller	John K. Knoll	Mrs. Carolyn D. Jones
Mike Printz	Chester M. Lessenden, M.D.	David M. Neiswanger
Nancy Lykins Sherbert	George Mack, Jr.	Mrs. Arthur H. Saville, Jr.
Charles C. Todd	Jessie E. Nichol	Lee M. Stratton
William O. Wagnon	Nancy Perry	William E. Treadway
Jewell K. Watt	Donald K. Rude	Thomas R. Webb
Larry E. Wolgast	Carol Wilson	Mrs. C. Bruce Works

EXECUTIVE COMMITTEE—*Georgia Neese Gray, Mrs. Carolyn D. Jones, Chester M. Lessenden, M.D., Camilla Maichel, Catharine W. Menninger, James N. Nelson, M.D., William E. Treadway, William O. Wagnon, Thomas R. Webb.*